IRISH ILLEGALS

Recent Titles in
Contributions in Ethnic Studies

IRISH ILLEGALS

Transients Between Two Societies

Mary P. Corcoran

Foreword by Leonard W. Doob

Contributions in Ethnic Studies, Number 32

Greenwood Press
Westport, Connecticut • London

Library of Congress Cataloging-in-Publication Data

Corcoran, Mary P.
   Irish Illegals : transients between two societies / Mary P.
Corcoran.
      p.   cm.—(Contributions in ethnic studies, ISSN 0196-7088 ;
   no. 32)
   Includes bibliographical references and index.
   ISBN 0-313-28624-8 (alk. paper)
   1. Irish—New York (N.Y.)   2. Alien labor, Irish—New York (N.Y.)
3. Aliens, Illegal—New York (N.Y.)   I. Title.   II. Series.
JV6629.N7C67   1993
305.8'916207471—dc20   92-42671

British Library Cataloguing in Publication Data is available.

Library of Congress Catalog Card Number: 92-42671
ISBN: 0-313-28624-8
ISSN: 0196-7088

First published in 1993

Greenwood Press, 88 Post Road West, Westport, CT 06881
An imprint of Greenwood Publishing Group, Inc.

Printed in the United States of America

The paper used in this book complies with the
Permanent Paper Standard issued by the National
Information Standards Organization (Z39.48–1984).

10 9 8 7 6 5 4 3 2 1

For Beatrice, and in memory of Tom

Contents

Foreword

The field of ethnic studies focuses on the problems that arise when people with different cultures and goals come together and interact productively or unproductively. The modes of adjustment or conflict are various, but usually one group dominates or attempts to dominate the other. Eventually, some accommodation is reached: the process is likely to be long and, for the weaker group, painful. No one scholarly discipline monopolizes the research necessary to comprehend these intergroup relations. Consequently, the emerging analysis is inevitably of interest to historians, social scientists, psychologists, and psychiatrists.

This book is devoted to the very recent immigrants from Ireland to the United States as many of them settle, temporarily or more or less permanently, in two boroughs of New York City. "As an Irish person myself" with past experience as a waitress in a Manhattan restaurant and as a woman and hence "non-threatening," she was "perceived as an insider rather than an outsider," so that she could function as a participant observer in these Irish communities and could conduct in-depth interviews. Her advantages and her methods of collecting intimate data can be appreciated instantly: she brings us close to her informants whose views are quoted at length most naturally and appealingly. Also the author expresses herself in a similar straightforward manner as she reviews the general history of Irish emigration, relevant theories concerning Irish-Americans, and the legal restrictions these people are frequently able to circumvent. It is indeed delightful to gain both theoretical and practical insights unencumbered by the usual academic jargon and pontifications.

Their particular kinds of uniqueness make these Irish fascinating. Unlike most of their predecessors from Ireland, and unlike other ethnic groups who have come and continue to arrive here as "bread and butter immigrants," they do not leave home necessarily because they are unemployed: Britain more frequently has been the host of the unemployed Irish. Many Irish migrants to the United States are sojourners who wish to return to Eire or Northern Ireland. Not easily distinguishable from other Euro-American groups who have long been part of America's establishment, the Irish have suffered less completely from the discrimination the Afro-Americans and Hispanics have felt. The author depicts the bars or pubs in which the Irish congregate and which play a significant role in their lives as well as in preserving their ethnic identity.

By far the most salient feature of the "New Irish" is the tremendous number of them who remain in the United States illegally. Without the "green card" that allows them to settle down and lead "normal" lives in every respect—obtaining decent or more respectable jobs, paying taxes, participating fully in our society—they lead a somewhat furtive existence and only with great difficulty are they able to visit their homeland. Their inconspicuousness enables illegals, nevertheless, to carry on reasonably satisfactorily and perforce they have acquired their own set of values and beliefs. They have formed organizations enabling even more of them to be favored in achieving legal status.

Legally or not, the Irish are outstanding in the American labor movement, in American politics, and in sports. Surely we all can recall many persons with Irish names who are or have been prominent throughout the country. This volume provides background material concerning them and hence increases our understanding of past, present, and future changes.

Leonard W. Doob

Acknowledgments

The Wenner-Gren Foundation for Anthropological Research provided me with a research grant to conduct my field work. I gratefully acknowledge their support. I wish to thank the members of the new Irish community in New York City who gave so freely of their time and spoke so movingly of their experiences. Without their co-operation, this book would not have been possible. I owe a special thanks to my doctoral dissertation supervisor, Professor Herbert Gans, who helped to bring this work to fruition. Above all, I wish to acknowledge the love and support of my husband, Alex White, whose constancy extends above and beyond the call of duty.

Introduction

This study explores the lives and experiences of recent Irish immigrants in New York City. During the 1980s, many thousands of Irish people entered the United States seeking work. Although they came legally on tourist visas, they violated the terms of entry by overstaying their visas and by seeking work without permission. Thus, they embarked on deviant careers as illegal aliens or undocumented workers, located primarily in the informal labor market—in the construction industry, the restaurant and bar trade, and as child minders and companions in private homes.

The illegal Irish (or the "new Irish" as they call themselves) may be thought of as an invisible population. Unlike the Mexicans who swim the Rio Grande only to be apprehended by immigration officers on the American side of the border, the Irish enter the United States legally and encounter only sporadic difficulties from the immigration authorities. The Irish are not easily identifiable by their racial characteristics and, so far, have not come in sufficient numbers to warrant regulation by immigration officials. (For estimates of the number of Irish illegals see chapter 1.) Notwithstanding their invisibility, the new Irish face constraints in terms of employment opportunities, mobility, and security of tenure because of their illegal status. Their difficulties have been compounded by the passage of the Immigration Reform and Control Act (1986), which makes provision for imposing fines on employers who knowingly hire illegal aliens.

Given these constraints, how have these immigrants fared in New York City? What prompted the decision to emigrate? How have they coped with life in the city? What types of social and economic relations have they formed? How has their status as illegal aliens affected their lives? These are some of the questions that I attempt to answer in this book.

I am concerned, in particular, with the nature of the social and economic relations that the new immigrants form with the established Irish community on the one hand, and with American society on the other. This population is unique in the sense that as an English-speaking immigrant group it ought to have a much easier time moving out of ethnic enclaves and ghettos; however, it is also illegal and thus limited in how much assimilation can be carried out. This raises the question of how illegality affects the processes of assimilation and adjustment that are central to our understanding of ethnicity. This is a complex issue and to date little or no sociological research has been conducted on the social effects of illegality on ethnicity, although there is a growing body of literature on the illegal immigrant populations from the Caribbean and Latin America.

Irish illegals, who are well educated and English speaking, do not experience racial discrimination. They are also in a position to exploit contacts in the Irish ethnic enclaves, which to some extent privileges them in the informal economy. At the same time, their illegal status has important consequences for their economic and social relations within the Irish-American community and for the degree of commitment they can make to the host society. Lacking the documentation and legal status that would allow for some forward planning, most of these immigrants have come to see themselves as *sojourners*, and to view their stay in New York as a temporary and transient one.

To adequately contextualize the experiences of contemporary Irish immigrants, some attention must be paid at the outset to the historical, economic, and sociological dimensions of Irish emigration in the past. Such a review is contained in chapter 1. In particular, history of Irish immigration to the United States is examined, as well as current immigration trends. The experiences of earlier generations of Irish immigrants and their modern counterparts are appraised in light of contrasting sociological perspectives.

Data was gathered during a year-long field study conducted among illegal Irish immigrants in a predominantly Irish neighborhood in Queens, New York, from August 26, 1987, through August 10, 1988. Chapter 2 describes the methodology and research design. The data is analyzed thematically throughout the remaining chapters.

Chapter 3 examines the motivating factors that caused these young Irish people to embark on an uncertain journey to the United States. The evidence of this study suggests that emigration is related to, but not solely determined by, high rates of unemployment. Widespread disaffection with poorly paid, mundane jobs, which offer little prospect of promotion, is a prime motivating factor. Furthermore, some of these illegals were prompted to leave purely by a desire to explore new horizons. In terms of background conditions and personal motivations, the population of Irish illegals falls into three categories: (1) bread and butter immigrants, (2) disaffected adventurers, and (3) holiday-takers. A range of facilitants, which underlie this wave of emigration, are also explored. I discuss the options facing the Irish illegals and assess whether they will become settlers, continue as sojourners, or return home.

The theme of work is explored in chapter 4. The evidence suggests that while relatives (kinship networks) are generally helpful in providing short-term accommodation to the new immigrant, they are much less important in terms of securing jobs. Almost all immigrants rely on their own efforts primarily in gaining their initial foothold in the labor market. Ethnographic accounts of the three sectors in which the majority of Irish illegals are employed—construction, restaurant and bar trade, and private home care—are presented in considerable detail. Illegality intensifies dependence on patrons and power brokers in the established Irish community, creating vertical rather than horizontal alliances in the workplace. Employment conditions generally fall outside the regulatory apparatus governing tax, health, safety, and minimum wage laws. Working largely within the Irish ethnic enclave, the illegals are often victimized by unscrupulous employers. However, their ethnicity confers upon them privileged status in the labor market when compared with other immigrant groups, both legal and illegal. Despite illegality, many Irish workers have succeeded in penetrating the formal labor market, while those confined to the informal sector tend to occupy the higher status, better-paid jobs.

Community and culture formation are perused in chapter 5, which focuses on the centrality of the bar in Irish immigrant culture. The bar is more than just a cultural icon, however, serving as a home away from home, a job and accommodation advice bureau, a bank, newspaper vendor, and fundraising venue. The ethnic identity of the new Irish is rooted in the social and economic conditions of emigration. Regional, county, and local affiliations are enormously important in both the worlds of work and leisure and create cleavages within the new Irish community. Thus, although the new Irish tend to be perceived as a cohesive or homogeneous group, in reality this community is characterized by a high degree of provincialism and internal fragmentation. Social and personal relations within the new Irish group are largely instrumental, reflecting the constraints imposed by illegality. Friendship is replaced by acquaintanceship, and personal relationships are characterized by the absence of commitment and trust.

Chapter 6 raises the issues of identity and ethnicity and explores the relationship between the new Irish and the home culture, the host culture, and the ethnic culture. Although the new Irish share in some elements of the ethnic culture, they are different, and this difference is heightened by their illegality. While they have the potential to revitalize the Irish-American community, their illegal status poses a threat to the respectability of that community. The strong ties that they maintain among themselves and with the country left behind further precludes a cultural coalescence with Irish Americans.

In chapter 7, the experiences of illegal Irish immigrants are examined through the concept of a deviant career. Illegals undergo a normalization process, which helps them to adjust to their undocumented status. The emergence of a variety of institutional support systems within the community has helped to alleviate some of their problems. In the process, they have succeeded in conferring a quasi-legal status on undocumented Irish immigrants.

In the concluding chapter, a structural context for understanding the Irish illegal immigration problem is presented. At the international level, the reorganization of the world economy has repercussions for the mobility of capital and labor. In the case of Irish emigration, structural factors at both ends of the migratory process prove to be decisive. Ireland's uneven industrial development (in part stemming from tendentious injections of foreign capital) and the demand for labor-power in New York's informal economy are determinants of the clandestine emigration trail. The particular configuration of these economic processes in the 1980s created conditions that supported a large-scale exodus from Ireland to the United States. It follows that these economic processes must be taken into account in assessing future trends in Irish emigration.

SIGNIFICANCE OF THE RESEARCH

Current debates about illegal immigration have focused almost exclusively on undocumented workers from Central and South America, who constitute the majority of the estimated two to four million illegals in the United States (Levine, 1985: 10; Passel, 1986: 188). Yet, as Passel points out, Central and South American illegal immigrants are clearly not representative of all undocumented groups: "Undocumented immigrants are not a monolithic group. They come from different countries, arrive in the United States via many different routes, and have very different social and economic characteristics" (1986: 192).

Little attention has been paid to the illegal immigrants who come from such countries as Italy, Poland, Yugoslavia, and the Republic of Ireland, all of which have had long histories of emigration to the United States (Cafferty, 1983: 76). This study constitutes the first sociological analysis of the most recent wave of Irish immigrants. It explores the structural factors that are conducive to high levels of Irish emigration and examines the personal motivations of the emigrants. The analysis of the Irish immigrant's work experience illuminates the internal workings of the ethnic enclave and the avenues it provides into the formal and informal labor markets. This research contributes to a greater understanding of the social and economic relations between an immigrant group and their host culture and the processes through which those relations are formed. Focusing on a European group allows greater scope for contrasting their experiences with those of South American and Caribbean immigrants.

Furthermore, since the study population consisted exclusively of undocumented immigrants, we are afforded a valuable insight into the interplay between illegality and ethnicity in the host country. The success of Irish illegals in the New York labor market is contingent on their ability to market their "Irishness." In the context of the illegal underworld, ethnicity becomes a crucial distinguishing factor. The internal stratification based primarily on race and English-language skills greatly favors the Irish illegals. As the same time, their position as outsiders—as transients without a commitment to the host country—creates a cleavage between them and the Irish-American community. Illegality heightens the importance of ethnicity (although not necessarily ethnic solidarity) while simultaneously interrupting the assimilation process. The findings of this study call into question the appropriateness of traditional migration models for examining contemporary migration processes.

Chapter 1

The Sociohistorical Context of Irish Immigration to the United States

This chapter examines two themes. First, the sociohistorical background to contemporary Irish emigration is sketched. This provides a context within which to examine contemporary Irish emigration trends, with a particular focus on Irish immigration to the United States. Second, the literature on Irish Americans is reviewed and assessed in terms of assimilationist and pluralist perspectives. Finally, an attempt is made to outline the approach to ethnicity adapted in the current study.

IRISH IMMIGRATION TO THE UNITED STATES IN HISTORICAL CONTEXT

A pattern of Irish immigration to the United States was established during the late sixteenth century, when the first Irish immigrants arrived in the colonies (Blessing, 1985: 12). In the early decades of the seventeenth century, indentured servants and transported vagrants and felons from Ireland formed a significant part of the labor force in the Caribbean islands and on the tobacco plantations of Virginia and Maryland (Kirkham, 1990: 82). The population flow from Ireland eastward was greater, however, with Irish merchants, mercenaries, and clergymen journeying to Europe throughout the seventeenth century. During this period, Irish laborers were establishing the first of many immigrant communities in large British cities (1990: 83). The pattern of emigration continued into the eighteenth century with an estimated 350,000 people leaving Ireland in the 75 years preceding the American Revolution (1990: 85). The push factors underlying this early wave of emigration included widespread economic and political disruption caused by poor harvests, depressed agricultural prices, and British colonialism. As the cost of the passage to the United States declined in the latter part of the eighteenth century, emigration became an option for a wider pool of people. Those who did not have the fare could travel to the United States as indentured servants, who worked for a period of four to five years in return for their passage. According to Miller, as many as 150,000 Irish people immigrated to the United States in the period from 1783 to 1814 (1985b: 169). The rate of emigration accelerated thereafter. From 1815 to 1844, an estimated 800,000 to 1,000,000 Irish emigrants sailed across the Atlantic to settle in North America (1985b: 193).

Successive failures of the potato crop—the staple diet of the Irish peasantry—from 1845 through the early 1850s devastated the Irish countryside. More than one million died of starvation and tens of thousands became destitute. In such circumstances, emigration was the only avenue of escape. In the aftermath of the Great Famine, emigration from Ireland escalated at a startling rate. (See Table 1.) Between 1848 and 1925, overseas emigration from Ireland to the United States alone totaled 4.75 million (Lyons, 1973: 45). The majority of these emigrants were the sons and daughters of peasant laborers. About 70 percent of them were drawn from the 12 to 40 age group (Joyce, 1976: 30).

The numbers of Irish immigrants entering the United States slowed considerably in the 1920s and 1930s. The introduction of restrictive immigration legislation in 1924 had little effect on the level of Irish immigration, but the onset of the Great Depression followed by World War II stemmed the westward flow of Irish people to a trickle.

Increasingly, emigrants turned toward England for their livelihood. By the 1930s, three out of four of those leaving the country chose England over the United States as a destination—a pattern which persisted until the 1970s (Blessing, 1980: 540). During the war years and in the postwar period, migrant workers were in great demand in England. Prospective emigrants received encouragement from friends, relatives, and holidaying emigrants. A week's wages paid the fare, and frequent trips home were possible because of the proximity of the two countries (Ryan, 1990: 50). Over the forty year period from 1931 to 1970, only 133,337 immigrated to America, an average of 3,300 per year (McCaffrey, 1982: 40).

The civil rights movement in the United States created an impetus for the reform of immigration law, which culminated in the Hart-Celler Act (1965). The provisions of the act, which came into full effect in 1969, served to equalize the numbers of immigrants from the Western and Eastern hemispheres. National quotas based on the principle of family unification and a preference system of green card allocation replaced the more discriminatory national origins system of admission. European emigration plummeted while the numbers admitted from Asia, the Pacific, and Latin America rose dramatically. The effect of the act was to limit the number of legal Irish im-

Table 1
Irish Immigration to the United States, 1841–1980

Period	Number	Percentage Total Arrivals
1841-1850	780,719	45.6
1851-1860	914,119	35.2
1861-1870	435,778	18.8
1871-1880	436,871	15.5
1881-1890	665,482	12.5
1891-1900	338,416	10.5
1901-1910	339,065	3.9
1911-1920	146,181	2.5
1921-1930	220,591	5.4
1931-1940	13,167	2.5
1941-1950	26,967	2.6
1951-1960	57,332	2.3
1961-1970	37,461	1.1
1971-1980	14,130	n.a.

Note: n.a. stands for not available.

Source: U.S. Immigration & Naturalization Service (INS), *Annual Report* (Washington, DC, 1975); *INS Statistical Yearbooks* passim.

migrants to the United States. During the 1970s, Ireland averaged just over 1,000 immigrants per year, with the number falling to 902 in 1981.

THE SOCIAL BASES OF IRISH EMIGRATION

Over three centuries, emigration became incorporated into the Irish way of life. Miller attributes the accelerated rate of emigration in the late nineteenth and early twentieth centuries to the commercialization of Irish agriculture, which disrupted the traditional rural economy (1985b: 102). Indeed, he has argued that it was the acquisitiveness of affluent middle-class Catholic farmers (rather than oppression at the hands of Protestant landlords or British officials) that was primarily responsible for the high level of emigration among the rural laborers class (Miller, 1990: 91). Since Irish cities and industries could not absorb all of the displaced workers, most had little alternative but to emigrate. Strictly speaking, they were economic refugees, but as we shall see, the prevailing ideology portrayed them differently.

According to Lee (1989), high levels of emigration were perceived by the

Irish governing elite as a functional prerequisite for the stability of the social system. The reduction of population through emigration controlled the numbers on the land and safeguarded the relative prosperity of those who remained behind. The subdivision of small holdings that had occurred in prefamine Ireland, and which continued to be a feature of Eastern European agriculture, was no longer necessary once the disinherited could be dispatched overseas (Lee, 1989: 71). The systematic removal of the youth from Irish society safeguarded an inheritance system based on primogeniture and reduced the possibility of a challenge to that system.

In the aftermath of the famine, land became an increasingly scarce resource as landowners moved to consolidate their holdings. In the process, millions of peasants were dispossessed. One institution affected by this dispossession was marriage. Steinberg points out that marriage was traditionally linked to inheritance of land, and as land became a scarce commodity, a tendency to postpone marriage ensued (1981: 164). In postfamine Ireland, the average age of marriage increased, while the rate of marriage actually decreased. Given the retarded nature of Ireland's industrial sector, this left a surplus labor force which had little option but to emigrate. According to Steinberg, these trends were particularly harsh on women and help to explain why more women than men decided to emigrate (1981: 164). Among the Irish arriving in America between 1899 and 1910, there were 109 Irish women for every 100 Irish men (1981: 162). Most of these single women ended up in domestic service. Irish immigrant women were much more likely than either German or Italian women to emigrate and were much less likely to be married (Diner, 1983: 30–31). This explains their higher level of participation in the immigrant labor force in the late nineteenth and early twentieth centuries.

As early as the nineteenth century, mass emigration from Ireland was framed by an ideology of exile, or what Miller terms "involuntary expatriation." According to the ideology of exile, both individual and community had little choice and no control over emigration. The mass leavetaking of generations of Irish youth was ascribed to relatively nebulous factors, such as fate and destiny, or to the material deprivations resulting from "British misgovernment" or "landlord tyranny" (Miller, 1990: 92). These sentiments informed many of the popular ballads of the time in America and Ireland and explain the popularity of the nationalist movements among Irish Americans in the late nineteenth and early twentieth centuries (Miller 1985b: 427–28). Miller argues that only a small minority of emigrants (political rebels and evicted tenants) left under duress, but their mantle of noble exile was extended to all Irish emigrants. Vaughan's contention, however, that as many as 90,000 evictions occurred between 1847 and 1880 suggests that forced emigration was widespread in the Irish countryside (1984: 16). Indeed, he argues that the threat of eviction was an ever present reality. Irish estates (and their tenants) suffered as a consequence of landlord indifference, which manifested itself in a reticence to reinvest rents in the estates like their English counterparts (1984: 25).

Given the extent of the exodus from the land, the notion of exile became central to Irish culture and lent romanticism to the often sordid reality of emigration. Emigration for many became a rite of passage, but as "exiles" they maintained a strong emotional bond with the homeland.

Throughout the nineteenth and early twentieth centuries, Irish emigrants sent remittances and donations to family and community left behind (Miller, 1990: 104). So strong was the emotional bond that an early guidebook for Irish emigrants, produced by the Catholic Publishing Society of New York, admonished the Irish for their "wishful preoccupation with Ireland and their past sufferings," counselling them to adopt a more forward looking view (Byrne, 1873: 12). The prevalence of the exile motif in Irish culture across two centuries served to legitimate emigration, even as Ireland's socioeconomic and political landscape underwent dramatic change.

After the establishment of the Irish Free State in 1922, successive governments pursued policies of economic protectionism. Poor growth and economic stagnation characterized the economy during this period. High emigration continued to keep unemployment down and helped maintain higher standards of living among the fledgling state's middle class.

The degree to which the Irish professional and political elite rationalized the high rate of emigration is exemplified by the following quote from a statement by a leading prime ministerial advisor in the mid–1950s:

High emigration, granted a population excess, releases social tensions which would otherwise explode and makes possible a stability of manners and customs which would otherwise be the subject of radical change. It is a national advantage that it is easy for emigrants to establish their lives in other parts of the world not merely from the point of view of the Irish society they leave behind but from the point of view of the individuals concerned whose horizon of opportunity is widened (quoted in Lee, 1989: 381).

As Lee points out, this statement is based on a number of empirically untested assumptions about the socioeconomic realities of Irish life. Although reference is made to Ireland's population excess, for example, the country at that time boasted one of the lowest population densities in Europe.

Furthermore, implicit in this statement is the notion of emigrants not as exiles but as adventurers who are bent on broadening their "horizon of opportunity." The exile motif (which stressed political oppression and colonial exploitation as precipitating causes of emigration) had been made redundant when the Irish state achieved independence from Britain in 1922. Politicians, who had no solutions for the problem of economic stagnation and unemployment, grasped at the notion of emigrants as adventurers rather than exiles. Structural factors which give rise to emigration could remain unexamined, as long as the decision to emigrate was interpreted as a matter of free choice.

In Ireland today, politicians regularly invoke a similar refrain as a rationalization for high emigration. They stress the individual benefits accruing from emigration, such as better opportunities, the chance to gain work experience, and development of expertise. The collective necessity of emigration for those who see no future for themselves in Ireland is consistently underplayed. The dominant political discourse has over the past six decades transformed the Irish emigrant from an exile to an adventurer.

CONTEMPORARY IRISH EMIGRATION TRENDS

In the sixty years since the foundation of the state (1922), Ireland has on average lost 0.5 percent of its population through net emigration. In the 1950s, the emigration rate rose to 1.5 percent of the population, a rate of outflow that was previously surpassed only in the 1840s and 1880s (Walsh, 1988: 2). This rise prompted a long overdue political response. In November 1958, the government published a *Program for Economic Expansion*, which heralded a major shift in Irish industrial policy away from protectionism and toward free trade. In addition, foreign investment in Ireland was to be encouraged through a package of incentives, which included tax-free status for foreign firms and capital grants. The opening of the Irish economy to investment by multinational firms brought a significant increase in the growth rate and a rise in living standards. Average net emigration fell from 43,000 per annum between 1956 and 1961 to 16,000 between 1961 and 1966, and to 11,000 between 1966 and 1971, or from an annual rate of 14.8 percent to 3.7 percent (Lee, 1989: 359–60).

Between 1971 and 1979, Ireland experienced net immigration of about 109,000 people, mainly Irish emigrants returning from Britain to take advantage of opportunities in the resurgent economy. This reversed a trend, two centuries old, of high emigration. But significantly, even in this period, net emigration from Ireland persisted in the 15 to 24 age group and among men in the 25 to 34 age group (Tansey, 1989: B8). This suggests that many newly created jobs went to returned emigrants who brought with them skills and experience, while Ireland's youth continued to seek work abroad.

The relative prosperity that marked the 1960s and early 1970s was short lived. The worldwide recession of the late 1970s propelled the Irish economy (and the rest of OECD economies) into decline, and Ireland has been the slowest to recover during the 1980s (Walsh, 1988: 4). Consequently, the gap between the performance of the Irish labor market and those of the United States, Britain, and other Western countries has widened. The underperformance of the Irish economy in the eighties has been widely blamed on poor economic management by successive governments in the 1970s (Walsh, 1988: 5). The high growth rate of the seventies masked a disquieting trend—

Table 2
Net Irish Emigration, 1980–1990

Year Ending April	Net Emigration
1980	8,000
1981	(2,000)[1]
1982	1,000
1983	14,000
1984	9,000
1985	20,000
1986	28,000
1987	27,000
1988	32,000
1989	46,000
1990	31,000

[1]Figure in parentheses denotes net immigration.

Source: Central Statistics Office, Dublin.

massive foreign loans were required in order to sustain a higher standard of living. The slump of the eighties was in part a consequence of the "boom" of the seventies (Lee, 1989: 515). Fiscal expansion was replaced by a profound economic contraction during the 1980s (Walsh, 1988: 5). This period of fiscal rectitude has given way in recent years to a level of economic growth comparable with some periods in the 1960s. This growth has, however, been coupled with high unemployment (average 20 percent) and high net emigration, both of which remain well above any level that could be accepted as a long-term norm (Baker, Scott, and Kearney, 1989: 5).

According to Tansey, driven by rapid rates of past population growth, the population of working age people and the labor force began to expand rapidly during the early 1980s (1989: B8). The growth in the labor force could not be accommodated with new jobs in a contracting economy. Emigration, which had slowed in the preceding decade, began to re-emerge. This occurred slowly at first but began to accelerate after 1984. The annual average migratory outflow rose to nearly 34,000 between 1986 and 1990. This coupled with the decline in natural increase resulted in an overall population decrease in the 1980s (*The Economic and Social Implications of Emigration*, 1991: 52–54). (See Table 2.)

Ireland is not unique in its net outflow of population. According to the National Economic and Social Council's report on the *Economic and Social Implications of Emigration* a number of southern European countries, particularly Greece and Portugal, experienced net outflows in the 1960s that were comparable to, or in some instances greater than, the net rate of outward migration in Ireland at that time (1991: 61). In mainland Europe, the trend in the 1970s was toward lower rates of net outward migration in donor countries as the oil crisis precipitated recession in northern indus-trialized countries. More recently, even peripheral countries such as Greece, Portugal, and Spain have experienced small net inflows of population. Ire-land, however, has become the European Community exception in that it is the only member country in the 1980s that continues to experience a significant net population loss through emigration (1991: 62).

Since 1980, net outward migration has totaled 216,000, equivalent to over 6 percent of the population, with the bulk of emigrants leaving after 1985. This followed a decline in manufacturing and building employment during 1984–85 and a comparatively large fall in the numbers at work in agriculture (Holohan and Brown, 1986:1). Estimates show that the overall population level declined steadily to reach 3.515 million in April 1990. On the basis of the Central Statistics Office (CSO) figures, about one in twenty of the pop-ulation is estimated to have left the country between 1982 and 1989. A breakdown of the 1986 figures shows that two-thirds of all emigrants come from the 15 to 24 age group (Taylor, 1989: 7).

The CSO figures have been disputed, however, on the basis that they do not adequately reflect the actual level of emigration (Courtney, 1989). The net migration figures measure the number of emigrants less immigrants. The CSO net migration figures, therefore, are disguising the full extent of the outflow of people from the country each year. For example, net emi-gration figures for the year to April 1989 estimate that 46,000 people emi-grated (the difference between those who entered and those who left).

According to Courtney's calculations, based on Labor Force Surveys and official statistics, the gross figure is closer to 65,000 for the year April 1988 to April 1989 (as cited in Tansey, 1989: B8). If true, this would suggest that as much as 8 percent of the country's population emigrated during the 1980s. Given that emigrants are traditionally clustered in the 15- to 24-year-old age cohort, it is likely that it is this age group that constitutes the bulk of those who emigrate. In addition, to the official underestimate in calculating em-igration trends, these figures do not reflect the extent of Irish immigration to the United States—which has been predominantly illegal—over the same period.

The primary destinations of Irish emigrants in recent times, as in the past, have been Britain, the United States, and Australia. Given the geographic proximity, ease of access, and historical ties, the majority of Irish emigrants continue to go to Britain. Between 1946 and 1976, over half a million Irish people emigrated to Britain. Of those who left Ireland in the 1980s, ap-proximately 70 percent went to Britain, with the majority settling in London (Ryan, 1990: 46–47).

There are several distinct communities of Irish emigrants in Britain. In recent years, Britain has attracted a significant number of Irish university graduates who are part of the international "brain drain" (Sexton, 1987; Walsh, 1989). Trained and educated at Ireland's expense, Irish graduates are recruited directly to Britain in the annual "milk round" in which prospective British employers descend on Irish campuses offering competitive salaries and fringe benefits. Britain also continues to attract traditional emigrants, such as construction workers, many of whom do seasonal work in British cities in order to support their families at home. A disturbing trend in the last decade has been the increase in the numbers of young, unskilled emigrants arriving in London without any funds or resources who often end up sleeping in the streets. They travel to Britain on the strength of one week's dole money without adequate preparation or support.

Since entry to the United States is considerably more restrictive even for graduates, and since the cost of a ticket is often prohibitively expensive, the typical U.S.-bound emigrant in the 1980s tended to be quite different. Generally, Irish immigrants to the United States are well educated and have previous work experience, since most had to save toward the fare and the funds they needed to get established in the first few weeks. Crucially, emigrants traveling to the United States generally have access to a pre-existing network of contacts who can smooth their passage once they arrive. In sum, personal contacts, resourcefulness, and sufficient funds are prerequisites for the emigrant heading westward to a much greater degree than for the majority of emigrants traveling to Britain.

CONTEMPORARY IRISH IMMIGRATION TO THE UNITED STATES

Following the general upward trend in Irish emigration in the 1980s, legal immigration to the United States rose steadily during the decade. (See Table 3 and Table 4.)

Prospective Irish emigrants were the main beneficiaries of a short-term scheme to increase the flow of immigration from countries that had been adversely affected by the provisions of the 1965 immigration act. The NP–5 visa program, which was enacted as a provision of the Immigration Reform and Control Act (1986), offered 40,000 special visas over a four-year period from 1987 to 1990 to the 36 countries who had been traditional sources of emigration to the United States. The visas, popularly known as Donnelly visas after the congressman who initiated the scheme, were offered to applicants who were randomly selected from a mail registration list. Unlike normal visas based on the family reunification or preference system, these special NP–5 visas did not require applicants to have special skills which are in short supply in the United States or to have a job offer from a U.S. employer. Due to an intensive publicity campaign, Irish applicants secured

Table 3
Immigrants Admitted to the United States by Country or Region of Birth, 1980–1986

Fiscal Year	Irish Nationals
1980	1006
1981	902
1982	949
1983	1101
1984	1223
1985	1397
1986	1839

Source: 1984 INS Statistical Yearbook, and Irish Consulate, New York.

Table 4
Immigrants Admitted to the United States from Ireland, 1987–1990

Fiscal Year	Irish Nationals
1987	2,921 (of which 1,812 were NP-5 visas)
1988	3,458 (of which 2,367 were NP-5 visas)
1989	9,894 (of which 8,846 were NP-5 visas)
1990	4,479 (of which 3,554 were NP-5 visas)

Source: American Embassy, Dublin.

more than 16,000 (41 percent) of the total visa allocation. According to American Embassy officials in Dublin, about one-third of the successful applicants were illegal immigrants already working in the United States.

Official statistics, however, do not reflect the true extent of recent Irish immigration to the United States. Throughout the 1980s, tens of thousands of Irish people entered the United States legally on temporary visitors' visas. When the visas expired, the holders simply failed to return home, jeopardizing their legal status by seeking work without the proper documentation. Hence, they became "illegal aliens" or "undocumented workers." It has proven impossible to estimate the exact numbers of undocumented Irish residents in the United States. The evidence that is available suggests that this practice began in the early 1980s and reached a high point in the period 1985 to 1986. In 1987, the Irish Bishops Commission on Emigration estimated (on the basis of parish and diocesan reports) that as many as 136,000 young Irish people were illegally resident in the United States. In contrast, a more conservative estimate of 44,000 Irish illegals was proffered by the U.S. Catholic Conference (*Migration*, 1988: 10). It seems likely that the former figure (136,000) is an overestimate and the latter figure (44,000) an underestimate.

According to U.S. labor economists, roughly seven million people enter the United States legally every year on nonimmigrant visas. Government officials estimate that between 10 to 20 percent of those overstay the specified period of admission (Ehrenberg and Smith, 1985: 321). If between 10 and 20 percent of all those who entered the United States on tourist visas (temporary visitors for pleasure) in the period 1981 to 1987 overstayed, that would suggest an estimated range of between 50,000 and 100,000 undocumented Irish. Given the fact that the numbers staying on illegally declined after the passage of the Immigration Reform and Control Act in 1986, that at least some of the illegals have been able to regularize their position, and that some will have returned to Ireland, it is likely that the number of Irish illegals is closer to the lower estimate in this range. That is, the figure of 50,000 is probably the most accurate, although the true figure will never be known. Most of these new immigrants have settled in New York, Boston, Chicago, and San Francisco, where vibrant "new Irish" communities have emerged in recent years.

The full impact of this exodus from Ireland in the last decade has yet to be assessed. Apart from the increase in emigration, Ireland's demographic structure has been further transformed in the eighties by the decline in the birth rate, which intensified as the decade progressed, resulting in a slower rate of natural growth (Tansey, 1990: 28). In effect, a combination of rising emigration and a declining birth rate prompted population decline after 1987. According to Tansey, emigration is at least partly responsible for the fall in the birth rate in Ireland. Young marriageable adults constitute the majority of emigrants. It is likely that they will either postpone marriage and a family until they return to Ireland or that they will start a family elsewhere. One way or the other, their departure reduces the national birth rate (1990: 28). According to Walsh, the provisional results of the 1991 Census of Population indicate a continuation of the trends established in relation to fertility and migration in the early 1980s: "In contrast to the 1970s when there was widespread population growth the geographical pattern of change for the late 1980s is one of widespread decline in the immediate hinterlands of the largest cities" (1991: 116).

Apart from the demographic impact, which has been particularly acute in the areas along the western seaboard, high emigration also affects the social fabric of the communities left behind:

The absence of the emigrants, especially when they are predominantly the young teenagers and 20 year olds, leaves a void not only in family homes but in communities where their vitality and enthusiasm for life would normally be reflected in renewal and regeneration, rather than in a society which is conservative, conformist and dulled (D. Courtney, quoted in *Irish Independent*, November 6, 1989).

A bishop who has seen his diocese decimated by emigration puts it more graphically: "It's a shocking scattering—the numerical loss is bad enough but worse is the loss of youth, the loss of energy from the local community, the loss of communal sustenance in a population sandwich with a very young underside and a very aged crust" (Dr. Joseph Cassidy, quoted in *Irish Times*, February 7, 1991).

As in the past, the population flow outwards has been to the advantage of countries like Britain and the United States. The loss of a young, skilled, and educated workforce from Ireland is transformed into a gain for the recipient countries. In addition, the arrival of a new generation of Irish immigrants in the United States bodes well for Irish ethnic revitalization.

THE IRISH ABROAD: IRISH AMERICA PAST AND PRESENT

Nineteenth-century Irish immigrants were primarily of peasant stock. From 1851 to 1905, four out of every five emigrants departing for the United States were from an unskilled rural background (Blessing, 1985: 19). On arrival in the United States, most were absorbed into the industrial labor force. In 1890, for example, less than 15 percent of the Irish in America were engaged in agriculture—the majority of immigrants found employment as unskilled labor in factories, mines, and domestic work (Brown, 1976: 329). Modell and Lee's comparative research on nineteenth-century London and Philadelphia reveals that apart from a small number of artisans "most Irish males carried bricks, portered goods or produced textiles and clothing" (1981: 364). Although of peasant stock and predominantly Irish speaking, three-quarters of Irish immigrants could read and write, according to the U.S. Census of 1850. By 1910, 95 percent claimed literacy in English (Blessing, 1985: 19). In addition to emigrants of peasant origin, the United States attracted a significant number of skilled artisans, professionals, and merchants from Ireland. This latter group more closely identified with the social and economic values of the democratic market society and, thus, more readily adapted to that society (1985: 20–21). These immigrants, who were more literate and modernized than their predecessors and their peasant counterparts had created, by the turn of the century, a privileged immigrant sector (Foster, 1989: 358).

The largest Irish community was established in New York City. In 1890, at the height of Irish immigration to the United States, a quarter of the city's population (409,924 of 1,215,463) was Irish (Moynihan, 1970: 219). Blessing reports that from 1850 to 1920 the majority of the Irish resided in the most industrialized region of the country, the Northeast. Nevertheless, a significant number of Irish immigrants—over one-third—settled in areas other than the East Coast, principally in the expanding Midwest and along the Pacific coast (1985: 21). Furthermore, Blessing points out that although the numbers of Irish residing in the major U.S. cities declined in the twentieth century, the proportion living in metropolitan areas actually increased because of a decline in the overall numbers of Irish in the United States. In 1920, newcomers from Ireland were almost twice as likely to live in a city as the U.S. population as a whole (1980: 530). Despite rapid suburbanization, the Irish remained concentrated in the metropolitan hinterlands of the traditional industrial regions of the United States. In the 1970s, over 60 percent of Irish Americans continued to live in the six states of the Northeast and the three Mid-Atlantic states (Fallows 1979: 66).

Postfamine Irish immigrants were largely absorbed into the industrial labor force, "typically providing much of the heavy labor, and through the employment of young women in service, many of the household amenities which the growth of [industrial] cities required" (Modell and Lee, 1981: 365). These immigrants were exposed to all the vagaries of nineteenth-century urban life—child labor, slum living conditions, and high crime rates. They labored under dehumanizing conditions without the protection of labor unions or regulated industrial practices. The Irish were regarded by Anglo-Saxon Protestants as "shiftless and drunken" and consequently they were "subjected to severe discrimination in employment and were despised by genteel society" (Schlesinger, 1992: 29).

The historical evidence suggests that by the 1870s and 1880s, a significant number of this famine generation had begun to make important economic and political advances (Joyce, 1976: 153). Hershberg et al. point out that "the emergence of a new industrial order [based on the growth of the manufacturing sector] created a widening of opportunity for whites and provided in particular for German and Irish upward mobility" (1981: 470). Meagher cites evidence from the United States Census of Population in 1900 which shows that American-born Irish—the second generation—were overrepresented in modestly respectable low white collar positions, such as clerks, salesmen, teachers, and bookkeepers: "They were underrepresented in poorer jobs which had once been the marks of their people's degraded status" (1986: 8). On a national level, the church, political machine, and labor unions provided a framework for the Irish to assume an American-Irish identity (Mitchell, 1986: 68). By the turn of the century, the Irish had begun to make advances within the American Catholic Church (Handlin, 1973: 117–18; Foster, 1989: 358). Irish Americans were joining political parties, entering the professions, and establishing themselves in the world of business (Brown,

1966: 45). Miller sketches the emergent class scheme within the Irish-American community—a handful of millionaire businessmen and professionals formed the upper-middle class; an increasingly large suburbanized middle class or "lace curtain" Irish preoccupied with status; and the still large contingent of "shanty" or proletarian Irish immigrants from whom the other groups strove to keep their distance (1985a: 89).

A longitudinal study (1880 to 1935) of schooling and occupational attainment in Providence, Rhode Island, demonstrates the pattern of upward mobility that proved the key to Irish-American economic success. Irish-American households in Providence during this period were overwhelmingly working class, concentrated in semiskilled and unskilled work. The mean occupational score for Irish Americans, compared with white Anglo-Saxon Protestants and several other ethnic groups, rose gradually between 1880 and 1915 and more sharply thereafter. By 1925, almost one-quarter of all Irish household heads were white collar workers, about the norm for the city as a whole (Perlmann, 1988: 45). Job and language skills, as well as good connections, helped to place the Irish at a distinct advantage over the unskilled immigrants who arrived from Southern and Eastern Europe in the years after 1900.

Perlmann's data show that in 1880 almost no Irish children attended high school in Providence, compared with a Yankee enrollment rate of 23.7 percent. The high degree of cultural and political accommodation of the Irish between 1880 and 1900 made for a dramatic increase in enrollments. By 1925, 73.5 percent of sons of Irish immigrants were enrolled in high schools in Providence, a considerably higher percentage than that among Italians and blacks in the city (1988: 56).

By the first decade of the twentieth century, much of the poverty, ignorance, and powerlessness of the early years had been overcome. Addressing the American Fleet in 1908, Cardinal Moran of Australia lauded the achievements of Irish Americans: "To those (Irish) exiles the United States became the Promised Land, they found freedom, contentment, and happy homes and it is pleasant to remark that in every walk of life these emigrants and their descendants have proven themselves grateful and energetic and enlightened citizens" (quoted in *Irish World*, October 31, 1908: 3).

Handlin points to the crucial role which the church played in sustaining and integrating early generations of immigrants (1973: 106–7). Blessing argues that the successful establishment of a familial institutional life in Irish neighborhoods, in politics, and in the church was crucial to the adjustment process (1985: 31). Apart from parish and ward networks, the Irish organized into associations and societies, which provided the opportunity for socializing, recreating a social matrix reminiscent of rural life in the "old country."

The Irish built their success largely through involvement in politics and government. Political astuteness, exercised through a tightly controlled clientelistic system, became an Irish ethnic hallmark. The legacy of this cultural good can be recognized in the success of Irish politicians and lobbying groups in Washington, DC, most recently in relation to immigration law reform.

Gutman points out that strong familial and kinship ties made possible the transmission of cultural values from Europe to America, where they were adapted or discarded as required by the immigrants. Furthermore, mythic beliefs helped to cement ethnic and class solidarities (1973: 563). In general, the Irish, who came from a highly conservative, traditional agrarian society, did not share the articulated class consciousness of other urban immigrant groups like the Jews. Instead, their ethnic solidarity was founded, first, on religion and, second, on a form of romantic nationalism. Light's case study of the Irish in late nineteenth-century Philadelphia emphasizes the importance of the church and ethnic organizations (many concerned with Irish nationalism) as vehicles for structural and cultural assimilation. The Catholic church, for example, sought to control the "unruly" working class and guard against labor radicalism. To this end, it devoted much energy to maintaining and extending its constituency within the working class. Most of the Irish ethnic organizations in Philadelphia "embodied the ideals of Catholic devotion, Irish nationalism and bourgeois respectability" (1985: 132). According to Light, the growth of a self-conscious and coherent Irish ethnic community was a consequence of successful structural assimilation. In addition, the values the organizations promoted had the effect of assimilating many immigrants into the dominant culture (1985: 135). Irish nationalism provided the Irish-American community with a vehicle for achieving respect and respectability as a recognized political constituency in the United States. Brown describes Irish-American nationalism as "an affair of the spirit, a state of mind rather than a matter of birth or religion" (1976: 337). Irish nationalism provided Irish Americans with a cause which could exercise their political skills (Fallows, 1979: 55). With the recognition of the legitimacy of the Irish claim to self-determination, the Irish Americans hoped that they too would enhance their legitimacy in the eyes of other Americans. According to Moynihan, the emotional appeal of nationalism "was powerful enough to hold together the divergent sectional and class interests of the American Irish" (1970: 241).

By the turn of the century, the Irish had come to define their ethnicity in terms of their religious affiliation (the church acting as an instrument of solace and integration) and in terms of their commitment to Irish nationalism (the achievement of which would confer legitimacy on the homeland and on the diasporic communities abroad).

IRISH ETHNICITY ASSESSED

The Assimilationist Perspective

Research on Irish immigrants is generally informed by either an assimilationist perspective or a pluralist perspective. Assimilation theory, first postulated by Robert Park, holds that all immigrant groups pass through successive stages of adaptation in the host country which ultimately result in full assimilation (Hraba, 1979: 36). To test the validity of the assimilation thesis, Warner and Srole analyzed social class mobility patterns. They concluded that differential rates of assimilation among immigrant groups resulted from differences in such factors as class, race, and culture (1945: 285–86). Gordon, in his elaboration of the assimilationist perspective, distinguishes between cultural and structural assimilation, arguing that the amount of assimilation that can occur is determined by culture and structure (1964: 33). Gordon views assimilation as a dynamic process which varies from group to group in the degree to which it occurs. Acculturation is one common indicator of assimilation, but structural assimilation—the entrance of an ethnic group into primary social relations with the host society—is considerably more difficult to achieve.

According to McCaffrey, the twentieth century was a period of consolidation for the Irish in America. The entry of the Irish into union organizing, local politics, and the civil service is seen as pivotal in the process of structural and cultural assimilation. The establishment of the Irish Free State in 1922 severed the tie between nationalists on each side of the Atlantic, freeing Irish Americans to involve themselves exclusively in urban and national American politics (1976: 146). In the aftermath of World War II, the Irish made great strides in terms of educational attainment and upward social mobility. The G.I. Bill of Rights, which provided free education for war veterans, afforded hundreds of thousands of demobilized Irish-American men the opportunity to attend college. McCaffrey points out that the education that these young men had received at Catholic high schools meant they were eminently well placed to take advantage of the bill's provisions (1976: 158). He argues, however, that the conservative, Anglophilic orientation of the Catholic education system accelerated the rate of acculturation among the Irish, who lost their connection to their history and culture.

Fallows provides a sociohistorical analysis of the Irish in the United States. She sees the progressive movement of the Irish into the middle class since the late nineteenth century as evidence of economic assimilation. Data gathered during the sixties and seventies by the National Opinion Research Center consistently show the Irish Catholics above all other ethnic groups (excluding the Jews) in education and income and only marginally below white Anglo-Saxon Protestants in occupational prestige when compared on the national average (1979: 66). The integration of the Irish into American society is also indicated by high levels of interethnic marriage. Alba's analysis of the ancestry data in the 1980 Census shows that just over 10 percent of Irish Americans in the cohort born after 1950 married within the ethnic group. Sixty percent married entirely outside of the ethnic group (1990: 13). The high rate of intermarriage is also reflected in the numbers of marriages that cross religious lines. National survey data shows that half of young

Catholics—those who have married in recent years—have married non-Catholics (1990: 15).

Both McCaffrey and Fallows agree that Irish overconformity—or the loss of ethnic identity—was the price paid by the Irish for educational and financial success. Their case is somewhat overstated, as the Irish, like other white immigrant groups, have by no means been wiped off the ethnic landscape. Alba points out, for example, that while the older structural bases for ethnic differentiation—such as labor market niches and informal segregation—have been undermined by the process of assimilation, they have not completely disappeared (1990: 4). Those who have remained in the ethnic neighborhoods have homogeneous networks and tend to maintain attitudes and behavior that reflect the social and economic constraints that characterize inner-city communities (Yancey, Ericksen, and Leon, 1985: 112). The distinctly Irish profile of the neighborhoods examined in this study attest to the persistence of (white) ethnic communities in New York City.

The Pluralist Perspective

According to Zunz, "assimilation is somewhat of a misnomer, an abstraction that reflects only fitfully a pluralist and fluid reality" (1985: 84). Pluralists hold that assimilation is not necessarily inconsistent with cultural retention. Ethnicity can persist after immigration, although old ethnic patterns and new ethnic practices may be blended to form a new kind of ethnicity. Glazer and Moynihan examine ethnicity from the purview of the 1960s. They focus on the changing position of ethnic identity and cohesion among second and third generation immigrants, arguing that as occupational identity has been undermined, ethnic identity has grown in salience. In particular, they contend that ethnicity serves as a "real and felt basis of political and social action" (1970: xxxviii). From this perspective, the Irish are viewed more as a political interest group than a self-consciously ethnic group. Glazer and Moynihan's argument has been critiqued by Steinberg who maintains that the revitalization of ethnicity much heralded in the sixties, may be better interpreted as a response to the racial polarization and conflict of the decade, than to the reawakening of ethnic consciousness (1981: 61). In a similar vein, Gans argues that the practiced culture of newly arrived immigrant groups is transformed over the generations into a form of symbolic ethnicity which requires little more than identification with a symbolic collectivity (1979: 12). Ethnicity in this sense may be viewed as a vessel for the transmission of folk memories and cultural values across generations. Thus, the ethnic identity of new Irish immigrants—described in chapter 6—is influenced by filaments of the Irish-American ethnic ethos as well as contemporary Irish and American culture.

Shannon (1973) and Moynihan (1970) argue that a distinct cultural residue has persisted among Irish Americans, which has thwarted their efforts at assimilation. In his study, *The American Irish*, Shannon traverses history somewhat eclectically, exploring the various influences that shaped the Irish character in America. He singles out three formative influences: the close tie to the land, the subordinate political and economic relations with Britain, and the dominance of the Catholic church. Irish Americans, Shannon argues, are inherently traditional and conservative as a result. Although Shannon acknowledges the success of the Irish in politics, he claims that their underrepresentation in science and business is a product of their conservative peasant mentality. Similarly, Moynihan claims that success (in terms of class position and social status) has eluded the Irish because they were willing to settle for less. He argues that the Irish were trapped by their (low-level) success as ward heelers and policemen, climbing out of the working class only to settle on the lower middle-class rung (1970: 256). Excessive drinking, a fatalistic Catholic mentality, and a sense of displacement derived from the decline in Irish political power are cited as factors contributing to the Irish ethnic malaise (1970: 262).

In 1973, Greeley pronounced that the American Irish were the only European group to have overacculturated, in the sense that they had renounced their ethnicity before ethnic diversity became acceptable in the 1960s (1973: 263). Eight years later, Greeley revised his earlier thesis, rejecting the overconformity model developed by Fallows and McCaffrey on one hand, and the pessimistic prognosis of Shannon and Moynihan on the other. Greeley offers evidence from several studies to show that in terms of behavior and attitudes, Irish-Catholic Americans are still significantly different from other Americans in their religion, politics, family structure, political style, drinking behavior, and world view. Given the legitimacy conferred on ethnic identity by the new pluralism of the 1960s, Greeley predicts that the Irish will return to a higher level of self-consciousness about their Irish identification (1981: 204–06). This prediction is to some extent borne out by the successful mobilization of the Irish-American community around the issue of immigration law reform in the late 1980s.

According to more recent studies (Yancey, Ericksen, and Leon, 1985; Alba, 1990), the assimilationist and the pluralist perspectives are both partially right. Despite the decline in objective ethnic differences—educational levels, occupational achievement, rates of ethnic and religious intermarriage—many white Americans continue to identify themselves in ethnic terms (Alba, 1990: 73). Although the majority of white ethnics (in the Capital Region of New York State) experience a high degree of social integration for example, a significant number of respondents in Alba's study retain strong ties to ethnic social structures (1990: 250). Furthermore, a majority of respondents reported one or more friendships with persons of similar ethnic background. A significant number are affiliated with organizations whose membership is largely homogeneous in ethnic terms. Crucially, Alba sees ethnic identity as *voluntary* among whites: "[Ethnic identity] can continue to play an important social role only insofar as people choose to act in ethnic ways. Such choices hinge on personally meaningful identities" (1990: 4).

Yancey, Ericksen, and Juliani attribute ethnic persistence to structural rather than cultural factors, arguing that the salience of ethnicity at any given time is directly related to structural conditions (such as occupation, residence, and institutional affiliation) which are in turn linked to the industrialization process (1976: 391). Furthermore, they suggest that ethnicity should not be viewed as an ascribed attribute but as a continuous variable— that is, the effect of ethnic identity will vary depending upon the specific structural circumstances faced by the group. The role of ethnicity may thus be seen as instrumental or "situational"—ethnic affiliations may fluctuate considerably and change their meaning, according to the particular situations in which the individuals or groups find themselves (Smith, 1984: 452).

Following Yancey, Ericksen, and Juliani and Smith, ethnic identity as it is examined in this study is conceptualized not as "a fixed essence," but as "a shifting, if fundamental, boundary perception" (Smith, 1984: 455). For Irish illegals, ethnicity is highly salient in terms of *social allocation* and *social solidarity*. According to Alba, social allocation involves the channeling of individuals into locations in the social structure based on their ethnic characteristics (1990: 17). While in general this aspect of ethnicity has weakened steadily across white ethnic groups, it assumes heightened importance for the undocumented Irish seeking to gain an initial foothold in the labor market of the ethnic enclave.

The politicization of the Irish immigration problem has had consequences for ethnic solidarity between the various constituencies in the Irish-American community. Ethnic solidarity manifests itself when "group members mobilize themselves to influence the outcome of a political issue . . . the solidarity notion implies . . . a consciousness of 'something' that is shared by members and requires their mutual co-operation" (Alba, 1990: 17).

The degree to which Irish illegals have been able to mobilize support in the Irish-American community attests to the persistence of ethnic loyalty among an otherwise integrated group. While ethnic identity among white ethnic groups is predominantly symbolic, this does not preclude them from voluntarily engaging in activities and relationships of a distinctively ethnic character, as the need arises.

The new Irish bring with them a European ethnicity which is in many respects different from Irish-American ethnicity. While the two groups have forged alliances (both in the labor market and in the political sphere), culturally they are unlikely to coalesce. Many of the immigrants (who see themselves primarily as transients) are more oriented toward the homeland than toward either the ethnic culture or the host society.

Hastings, Clelland, and Danielson's reformulation of Gordon's assimilation paradigm provides a useful framework within which to examine the orientations of Irish illegals. The concepts of communality (pluralism) and insularity are introduced as alternatives to assimilation. Those who are oriented primarily to the immigrant or ethnic community (rather than the host society) are termed *communal migrants,* while those whose primary commitment lies with the homeland are described as *insular migrants.* The latter remain distinct from the ethnic community and the host society. Hastings, Clelland, and Danielson suggest a classification of immigrants on the basis of their primary orientations in terms of ideas held, self-identification, behaviors displayed, and institutional affiliation (1982: 117).

In terms of their economic consciousness, the new Irish display signs of incipient assimilation. They reject the economic policies pursued in Ireland and resent their own position of subordination within the ethnic enclave. However, they strongly adhere to the ideal of meritocracy and what they perceive as the openness of the U.S. economic system (even though they are excluded from it).

With regard to political consciousness, the new Irish have followed a model of communality or ethnic pluralism by fostering ties with the ethnic community particularly around the issue of immigration reform. They harbor considerable resentment toward the Irish political system from which they are (at least temporarily) disenfranchised. Since they are outside of the U.S. political system, they express no allegiance to it, although they admire the principle of political accountability.

On social values and norms, the Irish illegals appear most insular, with little sign of assimilation or adaptation to the host society (outside of the economic sphere). This is at least in part a consequence of the insular lives that they lead within the ethnic enclave. It is important to note however, that the internationalization of American popular culture means that many illegals—especially those from urban areas—may have already incorporated aspects of the host culture into their attitude and behavior prior to their arrival in the United States. That is, a degree of anticipatory assimilation may have already taken place. Nevertheless, these immigrants remain strongly attached to the homeland, often idealizing the family and community left behind. Their social ties to the ethnic community are weaker and tend to be instrumental, while their attachments to the host society are weakest of all. A variety of organizational supports—the Irish Immigration Reform Movement, Project Irish Outreach and the *Irish Voice*—affirm the illegal Irish community and help them maintain a sense of ethnic dignity in the face of exploitation by older immigrants in the ethnic community and stigmatization by the host society.

At the cultural level, then, there are signs of assimilation within the new Irish community, but these are countered to a great extent by the continued identification with the homeland and the possibility that at least some of them will eventually return home.

According to Hastings, Clelland and Danielson, the less the assimilation into the economic opportunity structures, the greater the degree of insularity or communality in other spheres. Furthermore, the greater the insularity, the greater the possibility of return migration (1982: 202). For Irish illegals, structural assimilation is much more difficult to achieve because they are confined to the informal economy in which there is little opportunity for upward mobility. Since it is the powerful brokers in the immigrant community who control access to the labor market, the illegals tend to be tied to communal relations—which are very often unequal.

In terms of participation in primary groups and institutions of the host society, there is virtually no assimilation. Irish illegals tend to participate in ethnic organizations and events, but at the same time maintain strong provincial and local ties, reinforcing the orientation toward the homeland.

The manner in which Irish ethnicity will evolve given the influx of a new generation of Irish immigrants remains to be seen. Their arrival has had the effect of reactivating segments of the Irish-American community, but whether the increased ethnic activity will persist depends at least in part on the future of the illegals and the degree to which they will become an integral part of the Irish-American community. If the illegals eventually become settlers, the specific form their ethnicity will take will depend on the position they occupy in the political, economic, and social structure. In contrast to their predecessors, they will not have to forfeit their cultural links with Ireland in the process of structural assimilation. It is likely therefore, that they will move (as the generations before them) from insularity to assimilation, while retaining a unique sense of their own ethnic identity.

Research Design and Methodology

The idea for this project was first conceived in the summer of 1985, when I had just completed my first year as a graduate student at Columbia University, New York. Overseas students are not normally permitted to work in the United States, but after considerable effort I had succeeded in gaining authorization. Ironically, the best paying job I could get during the vacation was in waitressing, and the owners of the restaurant cared little whether I was legally permitted to work or not. The staff was composed almost exclusively of Irish and Mexican illegals. The former worked in the restaurant and bar, while the latter were employed as kitchen staff. Our conditions of employment were unregulated, and the employers were highly authoritarian in their exercise of power and control. Our timecards recorded first names only, and the nominal weekly wage came in a brown envelope with no payslip. None of us paid taxes or social security contributions. As an "off the books" employee, I had become part of the informal economy.

My co-workers became friends, and through them I came to experience the burgeoning communities of Irish illegals in the boroughs of the Bronx and Queens. In the spring of 1986, I conducted a participant observation study in a local bar in Queens, using the contacts I had cultivated to gain access to a largely inaccessible community. The success of my preliminary forays into the Irish community prompted me to expand the scope of the study. In the summer of 1987, I set out to study the way of life of the illegal Irish community in New York.

Residential concentration is an important factor in the maintenance of ethnic solidarity (Yancey, Ericksen, and Juliani, 1976: 396). This is particularly so for illegal immigrants who rely to a great extent on ethnic networks/communities into which they can be absorbed relatively quickly. The established ethnic communities offer work and leisure opportunities and, in addition, the psychological assurance of safety in numbers. The number of apprehensions of Irish illegals is negligible, and those that have occurred have been the result of a spotcheck or a tip-off from a disaffected source. The Irish have never been the target of a planned apprehension operation, such as those regularly put into effect by the Immigration and Naturalization Service (INS) along the U.S. borders.

The new Irish in New York are primarily located in three neighborhoods: Irishtown in Queens and Erinvale and Gaelside in the Bronx.* The research was primarily conducted in Irishtown, where I resided for 12 months (August 1987 to August 1988), but frequent visits were made to other Irish communities including those in Erinvale and Gaelside.

IRISHTOWN

Irishtown is a multicultural neighborhood located in northwestern Queens, which as late as the mid-nineteenth century retained a rural profile. Its expansive estates were used as weekend and summer retreats for the city's mercantile class. The opening up of direct routes to New York City (via the Astoria Ferry) and to Brooklyn (via the Long Island Railroad) spurred the rapid development of Irishtown in the latter half of the nineteenth century. The extension of the subway system from Manhattan throughout Queens in the early twentieth century opened up the borough for further commercial and residential development. The neighborhood, with several Catholic churches and Gaelic playing fields was particularly attractive to the Irish, but Germans, Poles, and Italians also moved in.

Irishtown was chosen as the principal research site for several reasons. First, it has the biggest concentration of new Irish in comparison with other neighborhoods in which the Irish have settled. Irishtown retained a strong Irish profile at a time when other traditional Irish neighborhoods were undergoing demographic change. Its pleasant ambiance and proximity to the city and the outer suburbs, such as Long Beach, makes it attractive to newly arrived immigrants. Irishtown has not had to contend with the urban blight faced by rundown Bronx neighborhoods, such as Gaelside, whose Irish population has been severely depleted in recent years by the flight to the outer suburbs. Of the three neighborhoods, Irishtown is probably the most identifiably Irish, and consequently, it has become the center of the new Irish community. Second, the large number of quality bars in the vicinity of Irishtown makes it the focal point of social activity for the Irish throughout the boroughs of Queens, the Bronx, and Brooklyn. Visitors from the Bronx or Brooklyn regularly came to Queens to stay with friends for the weekend's

*All names of neighborhoods, bars, and informants have been changed to protect anonymity.

social activities. Third, through my earlier research in the neighborhood, I had become familiar with Irishtown and its environs. In addition, I had already developed contacts with local Irish immigrants, and these were to prove useful in conducting the research presented here.

The heart of the Irish section of the neighborhood centers on a 20-block stretch traversed by three main thoroughfares, the central one overshadowed by the elevated subway line. Housing stock consists of one- and two-family houses, rentals, and co-operative buildings. Average current rent ranges from $700 to $900 for a two-bedroom apartment. The class profile of the neighborhood is lower middle class/working class. The ethnic profile was historically European, but in recent years there has been a significant influx of Hispanic and Asian immigrants. Their presence is reflected in the area's business and retail outlets. According to a local Catholic priest, however, the Irish remain the largest ethnic group in the locale. Their numbers have been greatly augmented in recent years by the arrival of the new Irish who have favored this neighborhood above others because of its strong ethnic profile and the range of facilities it offers.

There are more than 20 Irish bars located in the general vicinity of Irishtown, at least five of which have opened since 1986. Sixteen of these are traditional drinking establishments where no food is served; the other four provide full restaurant service. Musical entertainment is provided on a regular basis at most of these venues. With few exceptions, the clientele in all of these bars is distinctively Irish, with some internal segregation on the basis of county or region of origin (see chapter 5). A variety of stores line the main shopping streets, and newspaper vendors stock a whole range of ethnic newspapers. Restaurants and markets abound and cater to a wide variety of ethnic tastes. The Irish bars jostle for space alongside a plethora of other businesses including American-style diners; Columbian coffee shops; Spanish, Chinese, and Cuban restaurants; pizzerias; Korean import stores; fruit and vegetable stores; various travel agencies; and real estate offices. In recent years, a traditional Irish bakery, an Irish import store, a Celtic craft shop and a couple of delis selling Irish produce have also opened along the main strip. Aside from the three Catholic churches that cater primarily to Irish and Hispanic parishioners, there is also a Korean Presbyterian church serving the community. The Irish Immigration Reform Movement (IIRM), founded in 1987 to lobby for legislative reform of American immigration policy, had its original base in the Irishtown community, and the Emerald Isle Welfare Center continues to operate from there.

The arrival of a new generation of Irish immigrants into neighborhoods like Irishtown and Gaelside, is generally viewed as a positive development by older Irish residents, a view they have communicated to the local priests. For them the influx of the new Irish restores the racial balance in the community, setting in motion a process of stabilization. According to one local priest, "The Irish are more welcome here than other newcomers, because the older Irish community did not want more blacks and Hispanics. They have been made welcome and are considered a strength, contributing to the overall stability of the community."

Relations between the older Irish ethnics and the new Irish are by no means harmonious, however. The willingness of the former to have the latter settle in their territory is probably less an expression of ethnic solidarity than a desire to keep other racial groups at bay.

ERINVALE AND GAELSIDE

The neighborhood of Erinvale in northwestern Bronx is middle class (bordering on an affluent suburb) and predominantly white. Erinvale retains its distinctively Irish identity because it is home to Gaelic Park, and many of the New York Gaelic football and hurling teams train in the adjacent parkland. The buoyancy of real estate prices in this relatively up-market suburb makes rent prohibitively expensive for newly arrived immigrants. Consequently, they do not settle here in large numbers. Gaelside, in northeastern Bronx, is more heterogeneous. The local parish priest estimates that his parishioners are 50 percent Irish and 50 percent Hispanic. As in Irishtown and Erinvale, the large number of Irish bars, diners, and delis on the main shopping streets provides ample evidence of the presence of a significant number of Irish immigrants in the neighborhood.

Informants often ranked the three major Irish neighborhoods in terms of their general desirability/locational preference. Irishtown and Erinvale were considered most desirable in terms of quality of life issues, such as good accommodation; access to quality bars, restaurants, and recreational facilities; and general safety. The Gaelside neighborhood was considered the least desirable on all three counts. According to local informants "the neighborhood is shot." Unlike the other Irish enclaves, it has become a racially heterogeneous area, in which the Irish are no longer in the majority. This puts the Irish on the defensive. In addition, high crime rates lower the area's general desirability. One informant recounted the tale of how he was stabbed outside a bar, and others told of being mugged in the neighborhood. There have also been a couple of incidents of open antagonism in this neighborhood between new immigrants and the local (Irish-American) community.*

All three neighborhoods share the characteristics of "urban villages": there are concentrated networks and organizations among residents of similar ethnicity, strong kinship ties are maintained, there is a primary dependence on local institutions, and personal connections are used to obtain jobs (Young and Willmott, 1957; Yancey, Ericksen, and Juliani, 1976).

---

*Although this study focused primarily on the neighborhood of Irishtown, I made frequent trips to the Bronx, and seven of the sixty interviews that I conducted were with Erinvale and Gaelside residents.

RESEARCH DESIGN

There are few large scale data sets in which undocumented aliens can be identified on an individual basis. Hence, most of the information about them comes from small scale studies, surveys, and case studies. Cardenas cites Gamio's *The Life Story of the Mexican Immigrant* (1931) and Nelson's *Pablo Cruz and the American Dream* (1975) as examples of studies that innovatively use life histories and in-depth interviewing in order to illuminate the lives of illegal aliens in the United States (1976: 139). More recently, Massey, Alancon, Durand, and Gonzalez (1987) used an ethnosurvey—a combination of quantitative information and life histories—to analyze the social process of Mexican migration.

The nature of my population—which is both illegal and officially invisible—suggested the use of the following qualitative approach to data collection: (1) participant observation at several designated locations, and (2) in-depth, informal interviews with 60 illegal Irish immigrants selected through purposive sampling.

The advantage of participant-observation is that it allows the researcher to get close to people in their natural social settings, while at the same time creating the opportunity to build trusting relationships with informants over time. A relationship based on mutual trust is crucial to the success of a study focusing exclusively on a "deviant" population. This principle influenced my strategy throughout the research period.

In August 1987, I moved into the neighborhood of Irishtown. My roommate, also an Irish immigrant, became a key informant and friend over the following 12 months. My decision to reside in Irishtown enhanced my credibility among a community largely fearful of outsiders. Yancey and Rainwater point to at least two other advantages to living in the community: (1) the researcher has a ready means of establishing relationships with informants because living in the community provides the opportunity to integrate the roles of observer and participant, and (2) living in the community ensures complete immersion in the day-to-day aspects of life in the neighborhood, which might not be considered important enough to be reported by the informants (1970: 256–57). Similarly, Whyte points out that to really become part of a group, particularly one that congregates regularly, the observer has to be in almost daily contact with them (1951: 498). During the course of my study, I made full use of Irishtown's facilities, services, and social life.

For the most part, the Irish tend to congregate in the neighborhood bars, particularly on weekend nights. In terms of gaining access to the community then, the bars were an important point of departure. I tended to socialize there, in order to familiarize myself with the immigrant culture and develop contacts in the illegal community. I also used my existing contacts in the community to broaden my circle of acquaintances and to establish my role as a researcher in the neighborhood. For example, a friend who had worked in New York illegally for several years put me in contact with the woman who became my roommate for the duration of the research. She in turn introduced me to her circle of friends, many of whom were working illegally and were willing to talk about their experiences. A construction worker with whom I had become friends during the earlier period of research introduced me to the other members of his construction gang and they and their girl-friends in turn became informants.

I was also fortunate in the timing of my study, as the IIRM had been formed by a group of immigrant activists a couple of months before I began my research. I introduced myself to the organizers who expressed a will-ingness to co-operate with my research. Several of their members proved to be an invaluable source of information and advice. The IIRM initiated a series of monthly meetings for illegal immigrants, which regularly attracted several hundred people. In a sense, the IIRM represented the first attempt to institutionalize what was until that point a very amorphous population. At the monthly meetings, I was brought into contact with a whole segment of my target population to whom I might not otherwise have access.

In the early months of the research project, I was also able to rely on the contacts I had developed over my previous three years living and working in New York. Participant observation was carried out on an ongoing basis. As a resident of the community, I observed the routines and practices of people's everyday lives. As a participant observer, I visited the homes of informants whom I had come to know over the course of the research. I shared meals with them, watched television with them, occasionally engaged in recrea-tional activities with them. I attended meetings, demonstrations, and fun-draisers organized by the IIRM. I frequently visited the organizers in their offices, and I socialized with them afterwards in the bars. I also attended church services, Irish festivals, and a variety of sports and cultural events.

My observation and participation at each of the above locations brought me into contact with a relatively wide range of illegal immigrants. I had access to people as they conducted their social lives (bars); celebrated rites of passage (weddings, twenty-first parties); engaged in leisure time pursuits (sports, musical entertainment, fundraisers) and as they became politically motivated or mobilized (through the IIRM).

While much of the data was collected through participant observation, the in-depth interviews form a major part of the study. After making initial contacts and establishing myself in the community, I selected a purposive sample of 60 informants. No official, complete list of potential informants exists for an illegal population. As with studies of other deviant groups, "the researcher must draw his sample from a universe whose limits, units and locales are known to him only fragmentarily" (Becker, 1970: 31). The main criterion that guided my selection of informants was that they should be drawn from the widest range possible, so as to reduce the probability of excluding particular sectors of the illegal population.

Sixty people were interviewed, 35 men and 25 women. The vast majority of the informants were between 20 and 29 years of age at the time of interview:

19 & under: 1
20–24 years: 17
25–29 years: 32
30 years plus: 10

The youthful profile of these immigrants is characteristic of other illegal immigrant populations, such as Mexicans (Passel, 1986) and Dominicans (Grasmuck, 1984). Given the precarious nature of life as an illegal in New York, it is uncommon for entire families to emigrate from Ireland without appropriate documentation. It is much more likely for the breadwinner of the family to travel to the United States alone, although the expense and distance involved are prohibitive. The fewer commitments the immigrant has, the more self-sufficient and mobile he or she will be. Hence, most of the immigrants I met in the course of the study were single, which is reflected in the sample of informants, 54 of whom were unattached. (I am aware that the single status and youth of the sample provides only a truncated view of their full trajectory of experience as immigrants. While I can speculate about their future prospects based on the extensive interview data, this speculation is necessarily cautious and requires appropriate qualification. At the same time, the data provides a unique insight into the lived experiences of Ireland's "lost generation" of the 1980s.)

Fifteen (of the twenty-six counties in the Irish Republic) and two (of the six counties in Northern Ireland) are represented in the sample, but most of the interviewees are drawn from the western seaboard counties (Kerry, Mayo, Donegal, Cork) and Dublin City. This distribution is not unusual given past and current legal emigration trends. The west of Ireland has traditionally had a higher emigration rate than the rest of the country, and much of that emigration was to North America. The kind of networks that the illegals have been able to tap into were established by their predecessors over several generations. Dublin City has recently experienced an accelerated rate of emigration, particularly to Britain, which has been the traditional destination of emigrants from the east coast and the Midlands. It is possible that the more affluent emigrants—particularly those who were in employment before leaving—turned their attention further afield toward the adventure and opportunity offered in the United States. The informants chosen for the study also differed on a range of variables including social class origin, educational attainment, and occupation in New York.

Interviewees were chosen on the basis of acquaintances, third-party contacts, and often selected on the basis of informal approaches made at some of the sites previously mentioned. The interviews were unstructured in format and lasted on average about two hours. They were conducted at a variety of locations including the homes of the interviewees, my home, local bars, and restaurant/diners.

The representativeness of my sample is strengthened by the selection of informants from a range of different sites, based on characteristics that distinguish them from each other. I believe that the sample reflects the demographic and socioeconomic diversity of the target population. For example, the sample includes urban and rural immigrants, university graduates and high school drop-outs, individuals from middle-class and working-class backgrounds, individuals who have a history of joining organizations and involvement in political/trade union associations, and individuals who are not "joiners" and have no involvement with immigrant groups active in New York. My aim was to gather information from the various constituencies within the immigrant community: the institutionalized (those actively involved as either organizers or members of the IIRM, the semi-institutionalized (those who met regularly for social activities in bars, attended sports, and other entertainment events), and the noninstitutionalized (those who were not actively involved in the illegal community but were themselves illegal). Since I focused the study deliberately in the immigrant Irish neighborhoods, I did not have access to illegals living and working beyond those confines in the outer suburbs of New York or in Manhattan. Irish illegals who do not rely on the Irish community for leisure and livelihood are much more likely to assimilate quickly into American society. Quantifying their numbers and identifying their whereabouts is a task beyond the scope of this study.

I evaluated my nonprobability sampling as suggested by Honigmann (1973). This involved cross-checking information received from different sources, using the data to test the soundness of my hypotheses and analytical constructs and examining the database continuously for inconsistencies, contradictions, and incongruities (1973: 272). In each interview, I covered the same core areas—reasons for leaving Ireland; circumstances on arrival in New York; work experience; relationship to home and host society; relationship to ethnic culture; views on illegality; and attitudes toward religion, politics, and so on. The material provided by each interviewee was analyzed in detail and similarities and differences between interviewees were noted. These formed the basis for constructing analytical categories that were used to frame the data. Data based on a sample of one—a statement from only one informant which could not be substantiated through another source— were discarded. Where possible, I checked the accuracy of my interpretations of data with key informants.

A number of additional interviews were conducted with those involved in providing services to the illegal Irish population. For example, I interviewed the director and staff members of Project Irish Outreach (Catholic

Charities, New York), consular officials, diocesan priests, and immigrant chaplains working in the new Irish communities. During a return visit to New York in May 1990, a number of key informants and people involved in helping agencies were contacted and interviewed again. In addition to the field work, a variety of documentary sources were drawn on in the final analysis. Newsletters, flyers, handbooks, and various other documentation produced by the IIRM and Project Irish Outreach proved extremely useful as supplemental data. In addition, the *Irish Voice*, an ethnic newspaper published in New York and directed primarily at the new Irish community proved a useful source. From its rousing first issue in December 1987, the *Irish Voice* challenged the official invisibility of the new Irish by lobbying for immigration reform (see chapter 7). After leaving the field, I continued to obtain copies of the newspaper that were invaluable in keeping me abreast of developments from a distance.

To minimize intrusion, I decided against using a tape-recorder in the field. During interviews, I made shorthand notes, which I reconstructed and transferred onto a word processor as soon as possible after leaving the field. This yielded three separate sets of data amounting to approximately 800 single-spaced typed pages:

1. A field diary in which I recorded my observations at all of the social events and other activities that I attended during the course of the field work, notes of incidental conversations with informants, and observations on my own progress in the field.

2. Extensive notes on all of the monthly meetings held by the IIRM between August 1987 and August 1988.

3. Transcripts (from written notes) of interviews conducted with 60 informants over the research period, and interviews conducted with personnel providing welfare, information, and pastoral services.

Demographic data about each interviewee was culled from the transcripts and transferred onto an index card. After repeated reading and rereading, the data was cut and filed into color coded folders, which allowed for a preliminary categorization in accordance with the general questions that I had set out to address. On subjects such as reasons for leaving, contact with home, and work experience, I filed data on men and women separately as I suspected (rightly) that there may be gender differences. I then reread the sorted data, making notes on the themes that emerged and grouping themes and sets of data accordingly. It is important to note that in an ethnography the analysis of data is not a distinct stage of the research. Analysis is always ongoing: "It begins in the pre-fieldwork phase, in the formulation and clarification of research problems, and continues into the process of writing it up" (Hammersley and Atkinson, 1983: 174).

The analysis takes shape in the continuous working through of the research data, but that process is in itself informed by the researcher's ideas, hunches, and emergent concepts. In the tradition of grounded theorizing, the collection of my data was guided strategically by the developing theory (Hammersley and Atkinson, 1983: 174).

This study could not have succeeded without the unconditional access that was granted to me by the new Irish community. Looking back I feel that two factors in particular were crucial in gaining the trust and cooperation of my informants: our common nationality and my nonthreatening status as a woman in the field. Together these factors created an opening that allowed people to present themselves and their views candidly and without fear of repercussions. As an Irish person, I was perceived as an insider rather than an outsider. In the company of Irish immigrants I found myself almost unconsciously accentuating my Irish accent. I spoke freely and openly of my family, friends, and life in Ireland. In contrast, I referred as little as possible to my other role as a graduate student at Columbia University. My informants related to me therefore, as "one of their own," although they knew that I was not an illegal immigrant. However, my experience as a waitress in a Manhattan restaurant that had put many unfortunate Irish illegals through its hands created some common ground.

As a woman, I could relate to the immigrants in a nonthreatening way. A man in this situation would have had to overcome suspicions that he might be an immigration official or some kind of informer. I did not have such difficulties as my gender alone negated any residual doubts about my motives. My approach was always warm and empathic and aimed at gaining people's confidence. This was especially the case in interviewing men, who were unaccustomed to talking frankly about their backgrounds, perceptions, and experiences. Many of them told me that, while they were apprehensive at the outset about talking to a relative stranger, they felt a sense of satisfaction on the completion of the interview. I believe that these in-depth conversations were therapeutic for the participants. While most may have reflected privately on their immigration experience, their thoughts and feelings would not have been articulated, even among friends. Thus, I feel that an element of reciprocity was built into the research design. While the interviews and casual conversations provided me with valuable data, they created space for these Irish immigrants to engage in some self-reflection and analysis.

Chapter 3

Departure and Arrival: The Route to New York

> There are many lost souls in this city. People come over in not the best of circumstances . . . they don't even have to justify it anymore. The question more likely is, "Why don't you go?"
>
> Illegal Irish immigrant, New York 1988

This chapter explores the circumstances that influenced young Irish people in the 1980s to leave their families and communities and embark on an uncertain journey to the United States. As previously noted, this decade in Ireland was marked by the return of mass emigration, on a scale reminiscent of the bleak 1950s. In addition to the exodus recorded in the official figures, a new clandestine form of immigration to the United States had emerged. What explains the readiness of the Irish to adopt the status of undocumented workers in the ethnic enclaves of New York City? What are the circumstances of their departure from Ireland and their arrival in New York? Can this wave of emigration be characterized as a forced exodus or leavetaking by choice?

The root causes of Irish emigration go deep, extending back into the economic deprivation and disruption associated with Ireland's colonial past. But the specific character of any particular wave of emigration will vary according to current circumstances. Therefore, the anatomy of Irish illegal immigration to the United States can only be understood, if we look at the underlying push and pull factors.

It is *not* simply the absence of work that prompted these people to leave. In fact, no one in the study had experienced long-term unemployment. (This finding is consistent with Grasmuck's (1984) study of Dominicans in New York City, which found that the overwhelming majority of documented *and* undocumented immigrants surveyed had been employed prior to departure). In the Irish case, it is more likely that the terminally unemployed will immigrate to Britain rather than the United States because it is vastly cheaper and easier to do so. Prospective immigrants to the United States must be able to afford a return ticket and have at least some savings to help them establish themselves. The high level of homelessness and destitution among the Irish in cities such as London suggests that Britain is the primary destination for those at the lower ends of the socioeconomic structure (Connor, 1985). A recent study conducted by the Action Group for Irish Youth in London found that only 7 percent of the Irish surveyed were in professional occupations, and the majority were concentrated in low-skilled work characterized by insecurity and a lack of employment rights. Of those questioned, 76 percent said that they would have stayed in Ireland if suitable work had been available (Randall, 1991: 24). A government appointed committee recently reported that compared with other ethnic emigrant groups, the Irish in Britain are disproportionately over-represented among the homeless (*Irish Independent*, January 4, 1993). Britain, then, continues to act as a safety valve for Ireland's surplus population, particularly the semiskilled and unskilled located at the lower reaches of the socioeconomic structure.

Those in the New York study who saw themselves primarily as economic refugees cited underemployment, seasonal unemployment, and business failure as factors precipitating the decision to leave. For many of the Irish illegals, however, years of dead-end, boring work; limited promotional and entrepreneurial opportunities; and an overextended taxation system were cited as factors that provide an impetus to leave. A sense of adventure and a desire to meet new challenges also serve as motivational factors. Finally, some illegals treat their period away as little more than a working-holiday, which can be terminated at any time.

All of these may be viewed as *precipitating factors*; that is, they are the primary motivational factors that prompt the decision to leave. In most cases, these precipitating factors interact with a set of *facilitating factors*—a set of personal conditions or circumstances that make emigration seem a feasible and reasonable option. Facilitating factors are contextual. They refer to the particular individual's work history, family history, and social location. For example, prior work experience abroad, a pre-existing kin/friendship network, and cultural norms that endorse emigration combine to facilitate emigration while not necessarily causing it.

In terms of the precipitating factors, the immigrants tend to fall into three categories:

1. Those who leave because of adverse economic circumstances—the *bread and butter immigrants*.

2. Those who leave to seek adventure because they are bored with the routine of their lives and poor working conditions—the *disaffected adventurers.*

3. Those who simply desire a temporary change of scene—the *holiday-takers.*

Among those interviewed, approximately one-half of the women immigrants saw themselves predominantly as holiday-takers with the remainder divided equally between the other two categories. Among the men, the configuration was slightly different, with approximately equal numbers falling into each of the three categories. These constituent groups of Irish illegals differ from each other not only in terms of primary motivations but also in terms of their future prospects and return plans. They do not conform to the traditional conceptualization of the settler nor do they fully conform to the status of sojourner. In fact, Irish illegals, depending on initial motivations and experience of immigration, are located at different points between these two classifications.

Settlers are immigrants who intend to become permanent residents in the host country because they have been forced to sever ties with a homeland or because they have chosen to do so. Sojourners, on the other hand, are immigrants temporarily resident in the host country who plan to return to the home country (Bonacich, 1973: 584; Passel, 1986: 183). Traditionally, Irish immigrants to the United States have been settlers. In the past, their departure from Ireland was marked by an "American wake"—the departing emigrant was feted by the community because it was unlikely that he or she would ever be seen again. Like all immigrants, many dreamed of the triumphant return to Ireland. But while they may have perceived themselves as sojourners, few actually made the return journey.

The circumstances surrounding emigration, however, have changed dramatically in recent years, not least in terms of the ease and speed of international travel, and the development of satellite telecommunications systems. The United States and Ireland are less than six hours apart in flight time, which facilitates the speedy transportation of newspapers and videoed television programs to the immigrant community. Satellite link-ups bring far-away events into the neighborhood bar. Universal telephone ownership in both countries makes frequent communication possible. Consequently, it is increasingly feasible for immigrants to live and work in one culture, while maintaining strong emotional attachments to another, a theme explored in some detail in chapters 5 and 6.

Illegal immigrants by definition live uncertain lives, and the Irish are no exception. The lives of the undocumented Irish are characterized by temporariness, transience, and marginality. In this respect they resemble sojourners rather than settlers. They have little incentive to develop lasting relationships with the host society but have every reason to perpetuate regional and ethnic ties (Bonacich, 1973: 586). However, in one key respect illegals and sojourners differ. Sojourners come to the host country with the expressed intention of going back. Unlike the illegals (the bread and butter immigrants and disaffected adventurers, in particular) they are marginals *by choice.*

The future of the new Irish community is equally uncertain. In the long-term, many of the Irish illegals may return home under duress (at the behest of American law enforcement agencies). Some may return at their own volition having saved enough to create new opportunities for themselves in Ireland. Others may become settlers if their legal position changes. How-ever, since this group is likely to maintain stronger ties with the homeland than any previous generation of emigrants, they may continue to resemble sojourners rather than settlers in terms of their culture and way of life. In order to clarify these categories, let us now take a more detailed look at each of the three immigrant groups.

BREAD AND BUTTER IMMIGRANTS

Jack, a native of Cork, completed a carpentry apprenticeship with the State Training Agency but he could only get two weeks' work in the three months following the course. He and his wife and child were living on unemployment assistance. When a friend of the family advised him to go to the States, it seemed the sensible thing to do. According to his wife, Tina, who joined him several months later, "We couldn't survive the way we were. He had to go."

Jack and Tina are representative of those among the illegals who feel they have been *forced out* of Ireland. If they had the security of a breadwinner's wage, they would have stayed at home. They differ from the majority of illegal immigrants in that they constitute a family unit attempting to cope with additional adjustment problems. They fled a life on the dole in Ireland but ironically they still find themselves on the margins in New York. Jack's attempt to set up a business on his own was beset by problems primarily because of his illegal status and his inexperience in construction work. Jack's weekly income is quickly eroded, with little or nothing left over to save for a better apartment or a new car. They have already fallen into a poverty trap in New York—the same sort of poverty trap they tried to escape. Jack earns more money than he ever did in Ireland but the family now has additional expenses. For example, they incurred extra medical expenses when Tina had her second child in the local hospital, and they have fees to pay for their daughter who attends a private Catholic school in the locality. (They did initially contact the local public school but found the teachers unresponsive and the conditions very overcrowded. The public school was not willing to accept their daughter for the school year because she was three days short of the age limit, although she has already completed one year of school in Ireland. The Catholic school was willing to stretch the point and accept her.) Tina outlined their financial situation:

The rent alone is $7,000 for the year. After that you have gas, electricity, and the car plus insurance. Add to that the day-to-day expenses plus the cost of diapers and baby milk, money for school uniforms, shoes, boots, tights. At present we are in a break-even situation.

Nevertheless, they are able to afford "luxuries" that they could not afford at home. Tina was anxious to point out that even though they are just "scraping by" they have more (commodities) than they ever had at home:

We never had a car because we couldn't afford it. We never had a video, and we only had an old black and white TV. We didn't have a phone. We just couldn't afford any of those things.

While their standard of living may have improved somewhat in New York, they are still very much on the margins of a society where opportunity and the right kind of breaks continue to elude them. Bread and butter immigrants on the whole tend to be the least resourceful and the least skilled of all three groups. Hence, they are more likely to fall on hard times.

Those who have marketable skills invariably fare better. Margaret and her husband Derek came to New York in 1985, a month after they were married. They have since had a child. Prior to emigration, Margaret had a secure job in the civil service. However Derek, a skilled carpenter, could only get seasonal work in Ireland. The move to New York has provided them with financial security and access to more consumer goods than they had before:

I never see my husband now because he is always at work, but I guess that is a good thing. We have a nice home on Long Island and considerably more money and spending power now.

As a skilled artisan, Derek was able to begin the process of legalization through the sponsorship provided by his employer. Once his sponsorship is approved (a process that can take up to four years), the family will probably settle permanently in New York. Derek's considerable skills, which he accumulated in Ireland but was never able to fully utilize there, will provide him with a secure livelihood for the foreseeable future. It is an irony of Ireland's industrial policy that great emphasis has been placed on training and the acquisition of skills, but there are too few job opportunities in the Irish marketplace to absorb skilled labor.

Many others like Derek and Jack found it impossible to get full-time secure employment in Ireland after completing training/apprenticeship courses. For example, Seamus spent four years serving his time as a bricklayer:

After finishing my apprenticeship I could only get patchy work, nothing secure and I was spending more than I was earning. So I went to London (and later New York). If I had had steady employment in Ireland I would have stayed there.

For those without skills, the possibility of escape from the dole queue proved seductive. Josephine was actively encouraged by her sister (who had already emigrated) to join her in the United States. Examining her own situation, Josephine found there was little to keep her at home:

I wasn't doing anything with my life. I was working in a chippie, and in a night club a couple of nights a week and claiming the dole. My father was also unemployed and we used to go down to the dole office together. That really was no life.

Subsequently, Josephine's father joined his two daughters in New York, and her mother, the only one of the family with a secure job in Ireland, was contemplating emigration at the time of our interview. According to Kate, a school-leaver like Josephine, emigration was a way of escaping the only two options that seemed open to her in her home town:

I could have stayed at home and waitressed for sixty pounds a week, but I didn't want to be stuck in County Clare forever. A lot of my friends were on the dole. When I had the ability to work, I really wanted to work. My biggest fear was not being able to work.

Among the bread and butter immigrants are a minority of professional and skilled workers who lost their jobs or saw their businesses fail in Ireland. They tend to see their options in stark terms—dependence on the welfare system or emigration. The latter is for them the preferred alternative. Pauline had a Business Studies degree, but like the rest of her graduating class, she found it difficult to find work commensurate with her skills. She eventually secured a position with an American multinational company in Ireland, but a personality clash with her superior lead to her losing her job. Her spontaneous reaction was to go abroad for a while and try and decide what to do with her life. Another immigrant from Kildare, who had seen a lucrative business decline in the space of 18 months, recalls the demoralization of the unemployment office:

The worst part was meeting people I had known from school on the same line. Although I was entitled to the dole, I couldn't bear to collect it and so I stopped going after a few weeks.

In such circumstances, emigration is often a hasty decision, a shock response to job loss and the fear of being unemployed. Those who failed in business were particularly critical of the lack of support in Ireland for indigenous entrepreneurial ventures. They pointedly argue that the business environment is unsupportive of initiative or creativity. The Industrial Development Authority (IDA) in Ireland was singled out for special criticism when people complained about the lack of support for indigenous talent at home. The IDA was accused of ignoring grass-roots attempts to innovate.

It was also accused of catering almost exclusively to foreign interests, to the detriment of local entrepreneurs. The perception of many in the illegal immigrant community was summed up by the caustic words of one informant who claimed that the high-level bureaucrats in the IDA "pull out all the stops for the Germans and the Japanese, but we're only Paddies in their eyes." This lack of confidence in the state's industrial policy as it is perceived at ground level gives grave cause for concern. Potential entrepreneurs who encounter difficulties are, in such circumstances, more likely to leave than to stay. The kinds of criticism voiced by Irish immigrants have been echoed in the recently published report of the Industrial Policy Review Group, *A Time for Change: Industrial Policy for the 1990s*, which calls for more emphasis on developing indigenous industry. Indeed, the report recommends the disbandment of the IDA and its replacement by two new agencies, one aimed at attracting overseas industry and the other to foster home industry (*Sunday Tribune*, May 10, 1992: C9).

In sum, bread and butter immigrants tend to have experienced the insecurity of unemployment, underemployment, redundancy, or business failure. Unable to find work in their locale, they are willing to uproot and emigrate. The opportunity to work and the lure of a regular income generally outweigh concerns about illegal status.

Of the three categories of Irish illegals, this group has had the least choice in terms of making the decision to emigrate. They are the most likely to make a permanent commitment to the host country, given the opportunity to do so. They see no real alternatives for themselves in Ireland and are more likely, therefore, to put down roots in New York. Those with the least skills and/or credentials will be most dependent on the United States for a livelihood. The bread and butter immigrants most closely approximate the settler immigration pattern that has characterized Irish emigration to the United States in the past. The United States offers them the opportunity to work, an opportunity frequently denied them at home.

Throughout the 1980s, a small number of families left Ireland for an undocumented existence in the United States, and these generally fall into the bread and butter immigrant category. As they begin to have additional children and their families settle into the community and schools, it is increasingly unlikely that they will uproot themselves and return home. These immigrant families want to settle in America, but legal barriers currently prevent them from doing so. They are most likely to take advantage of any legislative initiatives that encourage legal immigration. As such, they may be thought of as involuntary sojourners. If they are ultimately unable to regularize their legal status, there is a possibility that they will have to go home. Given the continuing high level of unemployment in Ireland, the contraction of the British economy, and the recent changes in Eastern Europe, which have brought millions of new workers into the European Community labor market, the prospects will not be good for these returnees.

They will probably be exchanging positions of gainful employment, albeit illegal, for life on the dole.

THE DISAFFECTED ADVENTURERS

The second group of Irish illegals left Ireland not because of direct economic necessity, but because of a growing sense of disillusionment with the quality of Irish life. The scarcity of jobs in Ireland has resulted in a stagnant labor market. People with jobs have no prospect for promotion, career advancement, or skills development. For example, in the teaching profession in Ireland, it is almost impossible to secure a permanent position in a school. A recently published survey, conducted by the Higher Education Authority in Dublin, traced the career paths of graduates with Higher Diplomas in Education. Only 4.1 percent of the 1989 graduating class secured permanent positions as teachers in Ireland. A further 43.2 percent found part-time, temporary, or substitute teaching posts only (*Irish Times*, February 6, 1991: 1). As Michael, a former schoolteacher turned construction worker, explains:

I was a secondary schoolteacher at home, but because of the cutbacks, I was never able to get a permanent job. I became very disillusioned with my status as a *second-class citizen* because I was employed temporary full time for five years. That meant no pay at Christmas, Easter, and during the summer holiday period. I started coming out to New York to work in construction during the summers.

As an illegal, Michael remains a second-class citizen, but his financial remuneration as a construction worker is higher than it would be at home. As each summer sojourn in New York passed, Michael became more culturally assimilated, so that his ultimate decision to leave was an informed one. It was also a decision that was one of *choice* rather than of force, but a choice made in the context of limited options.

As fewer people move in and out of jobs in Ireland, upward mobility has become increasingly difficult in both the private and public sectors. Promotion channels have been closed off, which has caused frustration among junior staff. Reluctant to see their opportunities stifled, more and more white-collar workers decided to generate a challenge for themselves elsewhere. In a sense, the challenge denied them in a dead-end boring job is replaced by the challenge of surviving in a less sheltered but ultimately more rewarding environment, at least in monetary terms. Surviving as an illegal in New York becomes a challenge against which they can pit themselves and their resources. This is particularly true for those working in civil and public service jobs in Ireland, a sector that has been badly affected by austerity policies. The Civil and Public Service Union (CPSU) maintains, for example, that junior grade civil servants are on such low salaries relative to other sectors that they cannot marry and begin a family (*CPSU Conference*

Report, 1990). As a way of reducing staff costs, a leave of absence scheme was introduced throughout the civil service in 1984. The scheme provided career breaks for civil servants for a period of up to five years. Once the period of leave without pay has expired, the staff member returns to the civil service to fill whatever position is currently vacant at that grade. The individual's job is assured, but he or she loses seniority for the period of absence. In February 1989, the policy on granting career breaks was revised to permit leave for educational or domestic purposes only. Between 1984 and 1988, more than 3,500 civil service officers took leave of absence to travel abroad (Personal communication, Department of Finance, September 24, 1990). The scheme was also extended to the public sector, which includes local government employees, health care personnel, the police force, and teachers. Career breaks were taken up predominantly by clerical grades in the civil service and by teachers working in the public sector. Similar schemes (offering shorter career breaks) have also been available in recent years to employees in the private sector. It is not clear yet how many of the civil and public servants will eventually return to their posts since most left after 1985 and have been able to extend their period of leave up to five years. Individuals on career breaks form a significant constituency within the Irish immigrant community in New York.

Jim is a case in point. After leaving school, Jim, from the southwest of Ireland, worked for nine years as a local government employee:

And then one day I was 27 years of age and I felt that I had done nothing with my life. I felt it would be a challenge to go to a strange country and try to succeed. I wanted to see if I had the neck for it. I just knew I wanted to do something different.

Brigid, a former civil servant, also took leave of absence from her job in order to go to the States:

Kilkenny was a good town, but it was too comfortable. I felt that I had spent my life running away from challenges. I figured I wanted a change.

Others complained of the repetitious nature of their work and the absence of any opportunity for advancement. Once one member of an office left on a career break, several others followed shortly after. Many had taken career breaks to satisfy parental concerns about giving up "a secure job." They did not intend returning to Ireland, at least in the short-term, or to the jobs they had left behind. Some did not take up career breaks even when available, so sure were they severing their ties.

Mark had a job with a state-sponsored body before emigrating to the States. He said "he had it made" because the job was permanent and pensionable:

But it was a dead-end job. I was a semiskilled laborer and I couldn't really work my way up. The work was boring and I never liked the boss's attitude. Overall I would say that the conditions under which I worked were not favorable. The money was good but the tax took a huge slice out.

I was 25 years old and couldn't see a future for myself in that situation unless I were to get married, get a mortgage, and then just wait for a family to arrive, and hang on in there to get the pension. That scenario held no attraction for me.

Similarly, John, a former employee in a supermarket chain store in Ireland, felt cramped by the limited opportunities for advancement and the limited returns even if promotion was in the offing:

I just got fed up with the job. The money was lousy and I worked like a slave. You were paid for a 40-hour week even if you put in 80 hours. There was no overtime, no thanks. I was there three years and there was the possibility of becoming a manager, but there would be a lot more pressure. There would be more money, too, but the tax would kill you.

Barry worked for a multinational firm in the West. It was a good place to work, he said, but there was little opportunity for advancement, and the high level of taxation undermined his incentive:

The problem for me was that everything was static. It was a personal decision on my part to leave. The company was good but I just didn't want to wait around for three years for promotion. I think the big problem in Ireland is taxation. It was like the company was paying and the government was taking. There was no incentive to work hard.

This sentiment regarding the oppressive tax system destroying any incentive to work was repeated over and over in the course of the research. People could quote to the last penny the percentage of their weekly wage deducted by the government. Taxation is a thorny issue in Ireland. A recent analysis of the Irish taxation system, which draws on the comparative Organization for Economic Co-operation and Development (OECD) study *The Public Sector: Issues for the 1990s*, shows that in 1986 Ireland had by far the highest first tax rate of all member countries (Barrett, 1991: 11). Although the starting tax rate has been reduced from a figure of 35 percent in 1986 to 27 percent in 1993, it is still one of the highest in the OECD. Ireland's rate of reduction in the top rates of tax since 1986 has been one of the lowest in the OECD. Low-income workers pay tax at one of the highest *standard* rates of countries in the OECD. According to Barrett, the imposition of high taxes on low incomes gives rise to the poverty trap. In addition, high tax rates create a "tax wedge" between the cost to the employer of taking on an employee and what the employee gets to take home in pay (1991: 11–12). The grievances expressed by the Irish illegals are not ill-founded given the onerous nature of Ireland's taxation system.

In terms of relative deprivation, Irish illegals saw themselves as worse off than their contemporaries living on social assistance. Stories like the following were common:

The guy next door didn't work, he was on the dole. But he did a couple of days work on the side during the week. And he was doing much better than me. I felt a lot of resentment toward the system because of that. On Sunday night down in the pub he would jibe me: "Mark, make sure you get home early so you are up for work tomorrow. I need all the tax money you can pay."

For some immigrants, this early aversion to excessive taxation developed into a pattern of tax evasion in the host country (see "The Normalization Process" in chapter 7).

For the disaffected adventurers, then, the challenge of surviving as an illegal is a primary motivational factor. Bored with the predictability of life at home, they feel they have little to lose by facing the uncertainties posed by an illegal existence in New York.

Unlike the bread and butter immigrants, the disaffected adventurers have never suffered the economic hardship or psychological demoralization of unemployment. Yet, the kinds of jobs they held in Ireland provided poor remuneration, militated against the use of initiative, and provided little opportunity for advancement. Many of these immigrants use their time in the United States to work hard and save money. Like the sojourners Bonacich describes, they are future-oriented in the sense that they accumulate capital with a view toward making good investments in the years to come. Most express the desire to invest their savings in property or in business in Ireland, but in a stagnant and uncertain economic climate, those options remain limited at least for the foreseeable future.

Of all three groups, the disaffected adventurers come closest to the sojourner model outlined by Bonacich (1973). Their situation is complicated, however, by their illegal status. On the one hand, they are unlikely to go home unless they can substantially improve their economic position there. On the other hand, the longer they stay in the United States, the more frustrated they will become by their inability to penetrate the formal labor market. I believe this will serve as a discouragement to remain in the United States.

In the event of their legalization, they will have the opportunity to utilize previously unused skills and credentials in the host country. This does not mean, however, that they will then sever ties with the home country, since their primary ties in the United States will have been developed in the ethnic enclave, and they will have nurtured the ties with home over the preceding years. In fact, many of the disaffected aspire toward a transnational existence—a lifestyle that would allow them to enjoy the advantages of the home and host cultures. Thus, they speak of developing work/business interests that would allow them to commute on a regular basis between both countries. Therefore, they would not have to make a firm commitment to either place. Such aspirations are idealistic and, in the long term, probably unrealistic, especially if they begin to marry, settle, and start families. This expression of a desire for a transnational existence indicates that for this group their status as immigrants remains an unresolved dilemma.

THE HOLIDAY-TAKERS

The third category of immigrants may be described as extended holiday-takers—people who come from relatively wealthy middle-class families, who will eventually inherit a farm or a small business when they return home. They see their time in New York as an extended working holiday before settling down to adulthood and its attendant responsibilities. If they happen to make some money along the way, then it is an added bonus. The trip to the United States involves no risk (even if they are unlucky enough to be apprehended) because they have every intention of returning, and more importantly, they have a livelihood to which to return. Dermot, for example, spent all of his life in the South West working a farm, which he will eventually inherit. He and his wife, Sara, came to America shortly after they were married:

I was happy and content in what I was doing. But farming is a job that goes from morning to night, seven days a week, 365 days a year. I had never been away from Ireland, although I had read widely. I loved Michener's novels about Chesapeake. To retrace his steps would be the highlight of my life.

We were getting married and were faced with the choice of settling down or postponing that for a while. My decision to come here was purely a matter of choice. My father gave me five years to make up my mind about working the farm.

Sara saw her husband's visit in slightly different terms. She felt that leaving was a way of expressing independence from a domineering father who had maintained tight control over the land:

Dermot was working on the farm under the strict control of his parents. He literally lived on pocket money, as he had no independent income. So for him, emigration was a liberating experience. He had never been away from home before.

When Sean came out in 1985, he already had three brothers and a sister working in the United States. He came on a football trip but decided to stay on, as did half of those who came on that particular tour. As the youngest of a family who have all emigrated, he will inherit the family farm. His father took a pragmatic approach to his decision:

My dad's attitude was "do your own thing, but the farm is there. I don't expect you to settle down so young. It's better to do your traveling now and not think that you missed something later."

Gerard, from the Midlands, had been a secondary school teacher at a North Dublin school before leaving. He describes himself as being in a rut and says that he simply "wanted a change of scene." Interestingly, he explicitly rejects the notion that his decision to leave was an economic one. Rather, he wanted to see some of the world while he was free from the constraint of family ties and commitments:

I had spent eight years in Dublin and I felt it was the same people and the same porter all the time. I wouldn't class myself as an economic emigrant. I was living fairly comfortably and drinking plenty. The fact that I had nothing to tie me—no family or children—helped in making the decision.

Another informant had a business in the Midlands that was turning over a profit, but he often had to work 16-hour days, seven days a week. He sold his business and headed off for New York:

I guess I saw it as an adventure, a way to make money. It could have been Australia for that matter. I just wanted a different lifestyle.

Brian, the son of a wealthy publican in the southeast of Ireland, also came out of choice rather than necessity. For him the route across the Atlantic was fueled by the American dream:

You need a lot of motivation to leave. People are in a rut at home, and it takes a lot of guts to break out of it. Success comes from having money and success breeds success. This is what America is about.

Indeed, most of the immigrants in this study subscribe to the American success ethic. Irish history provides ample evidence of the achievements of the Irish in America. The folklore surrounding the Kennedy success story in the United States has long since passed into the national consciousness. The national and international print media and American television in Ireland are replete with American success stories. Indeed, some of the highest profile figures in the Irish media are American-based Irish millionaires, such as Tony O'Reilly, chief executive of Heinz, Inc. Wealthy Irish Americans descend on Irish towns and villages every summer fueling the image of the United States as the land of opportunity.

The new Irish believe that a set of hurdles (of which illegality is the most formidable) must be negotiated in their bid to get "the right break" and their share of the American dream. As we will see in chapter 4, the pursuit of "the right break" influences all of their choices, once they have gained an initial foothold in the labor market.

For the holiday-takers, then, living as illegals in the United States represents the challenge of uncharted territory, without any real element of risk taking. They are insulated from the worst effects of illegality because they have the option to go home at any time. Ultimately, all of the illegals may return home but the holiday-takers are in the position to determine when and under what conditions they will do so. Their commitment to the host society is ephemeral, since they are merely marking time before getting down to the real business of adulthood and its attendant responsibilities. They are merely in transition between two stages in the life cycle—adolescence and adulthood. For them, the sojourn in the United States is little more than an extended holiday, which inevitably will come to an end. Holiday-takers tend to have an abundance of capital (in the form of property or land that they own or will inherit) and/or cultural capital (high educational qualifications and marketable skills). Their real commitments lie at home in the family farm or business or in the career prospects that are open to them in Ireland, Britain, and continental Europe. For this group, emigration from Ireland was purely a matter of personal choice. They are neither settlers nor sojourners, but temporary visitors for whom a period as an illegal alien in the United States is little more than an aberration in an otherwise conventional life structure.

In contrast to the holiday-takers, the bread and butter immigrants and the disaffected adventurers do all the risk taking in making the journey to New York. They have a much greater stake in making a success of their time in the city and ultimately will have more to lose when and if they have to return home. The practical circumstances of emigration and future outlook, however, are different for all three groups. Indeed, an element of class stratification is implicit in the typology. The bread and butter immigrants, drawn primarily from the working class, are closest to the economic refugee model in that they feel forced by economic necessity to leave. They are most likely to settle in the United States given the opportunity to do so. The disaffected adventurers, on the other hand, are representative of a disillusioned lower middle class. They see themselves as having made a choice, exchanging the exigencies of life in Ireland for the uncertainties of life in New York. In fact, they have made a *circumscribed* choice in that their real options (particularly for security and advancement in the Irish labor market) are extremely limited. Whether they will settle or return home depends on several factors, including the prospects for legalization and economic trends in both the United States and Ireland. The third category of immigrants— the holiday-takers—have incurred no real risk by coming to the United States. As members of the middle and upper-middle classes, most of them have access to important economic goods, such as educational credentials and/or property. Of all three groups of illegals, they are the most likely to return home.

FACILITATING FACTORS

Although economic hardship, alienation, and a sense of adventure are primary motivating factors, other important facilitants to the current wave of emigration must also be taken into account. Indeed, on closer examination these facilitants tend to normalize emigration and, in doing so, grant it a degree of legitimacy as just another "fact of Irish life."

Family History of Emigration

One striking feature of those interviewed in the course of this study was the high proportion of people who came from families with a history of emigration. Well over half of the women and the men in this sample had at least one relative (such as parent, aunt, uncle, grandparent) who had immigrated to the United States or elsewhere. In addition, almost two-thirds of the women and just under half of the men had at least one other member of their immediate family (usually a brother or sister) living and working abroad. A significant number of Irish immigrants are children of Irish immigrants, who returned to Ireland from either Britain or the United States in the 1970s.

A facilitant to emigration is the influence exerted either by friends at home and/or by friends and relatives abroad, which often gives rise to chain migration. There is some evidence to suggest that chain migration occurs, although it is much more common for women to follow another family member than for men. Social historians have long recognized the importance of chain migration, which Charles Tilly defines as a process involving sets of related individuals or households (who move) from one place to another via a set of social arrangements in which people at the destination provide aid, information and encouragement to new immigrants (quoted in Zunz, 1985: 62). "Migration chains" were first described in the sociological literature by Park and Miller (1921) who identified networks of friends as one of the key mechanisms by which migration is structured (Yancey, Ericksen, and Juliani 1976: 393). Chain migration is an integral part of the migration process but its importance is heightened for those groups, such as illegals, who cannot rely on institutional support systems. Thus, the pattern of immigration for the illegal Irish closely approximates the chain migration model.

Familial contacts are of heightened importance, indeed virtually a prerequisite, for newly arrived immigrants seeking work without adequate documentation. It follows that those most likely to become illegal immigrants have a pre-existing network of kinship ties to draw on. The prevalence of these kinship networks among the illegal population testifies to the embed-dedness of emigration as a way of life for generations of Irish families. The fact that the illegal can rely on these networks substantially reduces the level of risk, at least in terms of being assured some shelter on arrival in the host country. This is crucial to the newly arrived immigrant for two reasons: It minimizes day-to-day living expenses thus giving them more time to search for a job, and relatives provide immediate access to the ethnic community within which they will begin to develop the contacts necessary for securing work. Of those interviewed for this study, well over two-thirds traveled from Ireland to members of their immediate or extended family or friends, who could provide accommodation during the initial adjustment period. Only a tiny minority had to rely on their own efforts to secure accommodation.

From this research, it appears that there is a significant amount of chain migration within nuclear families, with many immigrants having at least one sister or brother living in New York. While the extended families were generally helpful in providing accommodation, they were much less impor-tant in terms of helping the illegal Irish to secure jobs. Many of these relatives, especially the upwardly mobile ones who had moved out of the ethnic enclave, had few connections in the immigrant labor market. In addition, as law-abiding, tax-paying citizens, they were likely uneasy about recommending "illegals" for positions. Thus, for the most part, the help they gave was limited to providing a temporary home until the immigrant is established. The immigrant's own efforts and the efforts of friends on his or her behalf are much more likely to result in securing a job.

Encouragement from Family and Friends

The advice, help, and example proffered by friends and relatives also can act as an inducement, which the prospective immigrant feels he or she must act on. Prospective immigrants may be offered accommodation and/or a job by a member of the extended family or by a friend. He or she may see close friends and family members leaving and begin to ask themselves whether there is any point in staying.

Enda inherited the family business in a South Western town in the early 1980s. For a couple of years all was well until the recession started to affect the surrounding farming community on whom his business depended:

I watched the money I had ploughed back into the business all but disappear. Everything crumbled around me. At this stage many of my friends had gone to Germany, Australia, or England. I was beginning to ask myself what I was doing here—banging my head off a stone wall. My friends can't all be wrong. So I decided to give it a shot.

Sara, a former civil servant, explains one of the reasons that influenced her and her husband to leave:

Dermot's cousins worked the adjoining farm. They traveled to New York two years consecutively and saved enough money to furnish their house and expand their farm. I think that sparked a feeling in Dermot. If his cousins could do it, why shouldn't we—make a few dollars in a few years to set ourselves up in Ireland.

Claire worked as a secretary before coming to New York:

My best friend left a year earlier and she loved it. That put pressure on me. I had nothing to hold me in Ireland. I was disheartened because so many people I knew were leaving. My friend pushed me. I was afraid of my life, but I decided to go.

Statements like these suggest the existence of a culture of emigration, particularly among young people in Ireland. Leaving is equated with courage and the will to explore new frontiers. This sometimes entailed leaving a job and going against the will of their families. Staying, on the other hand, implied stagnation and the inability to extricate oneself from "the rut," represented by a low-paid, boring job and the onerous tax and social security contributions involved. In addition, since many towns and villages in Ireland have had their populations decimated by emigration, those that stay behind find that they have few companions in their own age groups. The population structure, particularly in rural Ireland, is skewed in such a fashion that there are disproportionate numbers of people at the younger and older ends of the scale. This increases the pressure on young people to leave.

Some of the immigrants distinguished between their own observations of the numbers leaving and their perception of the exodus derived, at least in part, from sources such as the media. Declan, a native of the North West, lived and worked in the same town for several years. Like Enda, he was influenced by his perception that his entire generation was leaving:

Things had more or less come to a standstill with the job. Everybody was going, or so the papers said, and I started wondering if I wasn't missing something by not going.

Pat, who is also from the North West, worked in Dublin for six years before emigrating:

It was a good living in Dublin, I was doing well. For me, leaving was purely a matter of personal choice. I left a job and the promise of a job should I go back. I guess I came to see what it was like because everybody else was going.

The frequent representation of successful emigrants in the Irish media (in particular, portrayals of Irish emigrants as adventure seeking, talented, and ambitious) has fostered at least a tacit acceptance of emigration among the general public. Since the mid-eighties, all the national newspapers have given consistent coverage to emigration and related issues. The *Irish Times*, for example, carried three major series on the subject of emigration in June 1988, January 1989, and December 1989. Scores of other articles appeared in the national media on a range of topics, including rates of emigration and current emigration trends, "the brain drain," illegal immigrants in the United States, and impoverished Irish immigrants in Britain. In addition, all of the dailies gave extensive coverage to statements on emigration made by leading politicians, clergymen, and policy experts. While the thrust of these contributions has been on emigration as a social problem, some leading commentators have intellectualized the "problem" of emigration by redefining it as a solution to the widespread disaffection in Irish society. According to this logic, it is only by going abroad that the Irish can suspend "the sense of internal exile, the sense that Ireland has become somehow unreal, unrecognizable" (O'Toole, 1989: 10). Looked at from this perspective, America appears as a panacea, a place that offers a future, an anodyne for Ireland's cultural ills. America is described by O'Toole as "a place that is less complicated, less haunted by its own past." More recently, another prominent Irish newspaper columnist has argued that Ireland is "no country for young women or young men" (Waters, 1992: 12). Emigration is redefined once again as a solution to Ireland's myriad problems; the dislocated in Irish society must simply relocate elsewhere.

In addition to print media coverage, the national broadcasting station RTE has given extensive coverage to the subject, sending crews to the United States and Australia for current affairs programs and documentaries on contemporary emigration. A radio program directed specifically at Irish emigrants in Britain began broadcasting in 1987. This program also carries regular reports from and about Irish immigrants all over the world. The popular media has also responded to the new wave of emigration with chart-topping songs about the new generation of emigrants, such as the Wolfe Tones's "Flight of the Earls," Luka Bloom's "I.R.I.S.H. in the U.S.A.," the Pogues's "Christmas in New York," Christy Moore's "Missing You/Voyage," Dolores Keane and Mick Hanley's "My Love Is in America," and most recently Brendan Grace's "Illegal Aliens." New Irish writing pages in the national newspapers have also featured short stories and poetry with emigration as a major theme.

Available evidence suggests that emigration in the 1980s has come to be seen as an inevitable aspect of Irish life. In August 1987, a survey conducted among 16 to 24 year olds found that 70 percent of those questioned felt that Ireland did not offer young people a good future. Sixty percent said that they had contemplated emigrating (Kirby, 1988: 124). A more recent survey conducted by the Market Research Bureau of Ireland (MRBI) for the *Irish Times* showed a relatively high tolerance level for emigration among the general population (*Irish Times*, November 28, 1989: 8). The survey analysis headlined "Emigration Has Merit" revealed that 44 percent of the respondents saw some good in emigration, although it is important to note that well over half of those surveyed said that emigrants of the past three to four years have only temporarily left Ireland. These findings suggest that as long as emigration is perceived as a short-term option, and emigrants are seen primarily as sojourners, public tolerance will remain high.

The dominance of the economic refugee/adventurer motifs masks some of the real social problems that also underly the current high rate of emigration. Indeed, high emigration serves to legitimate leavetaking as a solution to personal or familial problems. In such instances—the break-up of a marriage, family violence, or the death of a loved one, for example—emigration is often viewed as an acceptable response to the tragedy or trauma at hand.

Eamon's story is illustrative. Married with one child, the family lived in a Western Ireland community. After eight years of marriage, his wife took their daughter and went to the United States. Eamon had a nervous breakdown and had difficulty picking up the pieces of his life: "A certain stigma attached to me—I was seen as an outsider—because I was a separated man." Eamon is a casualty of what he perceived to be the restrictive community life in the West of Ireland. He chose an "out-of-status" life as an illegal in New York, which at least guaranteed him anonymity, over an "out-of-status" life in Ireland resulting from his ambivalent marital status.

Paul's marriage to his long-term girlfriend broke up after less than a year. Both of them had become unemployed shortly after the marriage and this put additional strains on their relationship. Paul initially moved to England but later went to the United States:

I gave no thought to going to the States until a couple of my friends were coming over. It was a last minute decision. I guess my reason for coming was to relax . . . and get my life together again.

Interestingly, cultural tolerance of emigration contrasts rather ironically with Irish intolerance of marital breakdown.

Prior Experience Abroad

A significant number of illegals have already traveled or worked abroad, and this prior experience prepares them for the journey across the Atlantic. For example, well over one-third of the men interviewed had lived and worked abroad, mainly in England, prior to their arrival in the United States. Some of these immigrants become acclimatized to going abroad for work at an early age. In the West of Ireland particularly, there is an established tradition of seasonal migration that prepares people for a lifetime of nomadic work abroad.

Most of those with prior experience abroad had previously worked in England. Generally, it was agreed that one could make a good living there. However, that had to be balanced against two important factors: the inferior status of the Irish as an ethnic group in England and the prejudicial attitudes with which they had to contend on a daily basis. (For a discussion of anti-Irish prejudice in England see chapter 6).

For example, Seamus, a Dublin-born bricklayer, arrived in New York after a sojourn in London. During his three years there he became increasingly disillusioned:

After finishing my apprenticeship I went to London. After three years there I returned to Dublin with the idea of going to America. I was fed up with the status of Irish people in England. There was a certain stigma attached to being the paddy/navvy going to England, working for the English, and making your contribution in England which made me resentful.

Harry, from the west of Ireland, dropped out of college and worked in construction in various European countries for six years before returning briefly to Ireland. When a business venture failed to materialize, he went to England and onto the construction sites once again:

But I couldn't take living in England. On TV you were constantly hearing Irish jokes. You would get all dressed up and go down to the pub only to hear the same jokes about the Irish and it would ruin your Saturday night. It really got to me because you would see van loads of Irish going all over working, while the English sat on the dole.

For these young men, life as undocumented workers in New York, with all its disadvantages, was preferable to the prejudice and discrimination to which they were subject in English cities. Prior work experience abroad also makes these Irish workers acutely aware of the value of their labor. They are, therefore, in a better position to bargain over wage rates than immigrants with less experience. They know the ropes and seek to extract from prospective employers the best possible terms, given the constraints of their illegality.

In particular, Irish construction workers form part of a floating population of labor, moving sporadically from one country to another and, more often than not, from one construction site to another. When work doesn't come to them, they go where the work is. They become acclimatized to the idea of living and working abroad from an early age. If they return home, it is merely to touch base before embarking on another trip. Their nomadic lifestyle prevents them from putting down roots or from forming strong ties or committed relationships. Not surprisingly, these men generally postpone marriage and remain unattached into their late twenties and early thirties. (For a discussion of personal relationships see chapter 5.)

SUMMARY

Precipitating factors provide the emigrant with a rationale to emigrate. He or she may be tired of a dead-end job, frustrated by the tax system, and/ or frustrated by a stagnant promotional structure. Alternatively, the immigrant may simply long for adventure or for the opportunity to take on a challenge and overcome the obstacles of a new working environment. Facilitating factors, such as prior work experience abroad, family history of emigration, and encouragement from relatives or friends, more often act as the catalyst in making the final decision.

The tenets of an ideology or value system that endorses contemporary Irish emigration are recognizable in family histories, in the perceptions and experiences of Ireland's youth, and in representation of emigration in the media and popular culture. The "American Dream" mediated through private family histories (which abound with stories of successful emigrants abroad) and popular cultural forms offers an escape (however fleeting or temporary) for the bread and butter immigrants and the disaffected adventurers, and an incentive for the holiday-takers.

This ideology functions in much the same way as its historical antecedent. Miller (1985b) and Lee (1989) argue that the ideological endorsement of emigration as "political exile" in the past virtually sealed the fate of generations of emigrants who accepted emigration with passive resignation. The ideology underpinning contemporary Irish emigration is one that endorses the notion of the emigrant as a highly skilled, inner-directed, robust entrepreneur/adventurer who cannot be contained within the confines of national boundaries. He or she will go abroad to hone skills and talent and gain experience that will eventually be brought back to Ireland. The reality is that only a small number of Irish emigrants fall into this category and those that do are unlikely to go back home once they have tasted the rewards abroad.

Irish Illegals in the New York Labor Market

> When an individual sells his or her labor power within the nation of which he or she is a citizen, it is done within the network of legal protection which that state normally affords its nationals. When individuals cross national boundaries to work, they become part of an international work force. Yet, they remain governed or restricted by national policies and legal codes, since there exists no significant international body of laws and regulatory agencies which maintain jurisdiction over an international labor market. (Petras, 1981: 51)

In this chapter, the work experiences of illegal Irish immigrants in New York City are examined. The three employment sectors in which Irish illegals primarily find work are the construction industry, the restaurant and bar trade, and private child care/home care service. Newly arrived immigrants who previously worked "on the buildings," in farming or in other manual occupations generally seek work in the construction industry. White-collar workers and those who worked in the services sector at home gravitate toward jobs in restaurants and bars or work as care-givers in private homes. These distinctions are by no means definitive, and one will find teachers working as laborers and former laborers working as bartenders. The majority of men, however, work in construction, while most women work as nannies and home companions. A smaller proportion of both sexes work in the restaurant and bar trades.

A tendency to operate (albeit to varying degrees) in the informal economy is a characteristic of all three employment sectors. (For a detailed analysis of the buoyancy of the informal economy and its relationship to the internationalization of the production process, see chapter 8.) The informal economy has been defined as "the sum total of income-earning activities with the exclusions of those that involve contractual and legally regulated employment" (Portes and Sassen-Koob, 1987: 31). Although this definition encompasses illegal activity, the term *informal economy* is generally reserved for the production and sale of goods and services that are legal, but which are produced and sold outside the regulatory apparatus governing health, safety, tax, minimum wage law, and other standards (Sassen-Koob, 1986: 1). While the informal economy is similar in description to the secondary labor market or competitive sector of a dual economy, Portes and Sassen-Koob point out that the latter is composed of *legal* enterprises while the informal economy operates at the very margins of the law (1987: 31–32). In fact, the boundary between formal and informal economic activity is somewhat anomalous and begs analytical specification.

Castells and Portes argue that "the absence of institutional regulations may rest in *different elements* of the work process: the status of labor, the conditions of work, the form of management" (quoted in Sassen, 1991: 81, my emphasis). There are different levels of formality and informality in any given workplace. On the one hand, an illegal worker with false documentation may secure a position in regulated, unionized employment. On the other hand, a legal worker who is either a citizen or a resident alien may work in an unregulated sweatshop. In practice, undocumented Irish immigrants (who are by definition informal workers since they do not enjoy the legal protection that the country normally affords its nationals) are found in both the formal and informal economies. This is particularly the case in the construction industry.

THE CONSTRUCTION INDUSTRY

The construction industry in New York has seen a steady expansion in the past few decades. According to New York State Department of Labor statistics, New York City had over 10,000 registered construction firms in 1988 (Sassen, 1991: 88). The average number of workers in these firms is 11, with over 80 percent of all firms employing fewer than 10 workers. A major trend in this sector (as in many other industrial sectors) is a decline in unionized employment and a parallel expansion in informal, "off-the-books" job opportunities, which are increasingly taken up by new immigrants.

Construction work in the city is organized on a two-tiered system, with one sector of the industry operating in the formal economy and the other in the informal economy. Construction outfits working on commercial buildings in downtown Manhattan and on public contract projects, such as maintenance of the subway system, tend to be unionized and highly regulated. In Manhattan, for example, construction union locals, which are ethnically controlled, jostle for control of new construction jobs. By prior arrangement, Irish-run locals operate on the west side of the city, while Italian-run locals operate on the east side. In contrast, commercial and residential alterations and renovations are almost the exclusive preserve of independent contractors or subcontractors who rely to a great extent on nonunion labor. Many of these firms are unlicensed and carry out construction work without the necessary permits (Sassen, 1991: 88). Since they already work outside the regulatory apparatus, they are more likely than the larger licensed operators to hire undocumented aliens. For employers in the informal sector, immigrants constitute a "reserve army" of labor whose wages can be held down because of the ever-present threat of replacement (Portes and Sassen-Koob, 1987; Edwards, 1979). The flexibility of these workers is heightened because of the ability of the employer to fire "undesirable" illegals at will. The employers also profit from tax and social security obligations, which they do not honor. These are the primary factors that give companies in the informal sector their competitive edge and that have contributed to their proliferation.

The majority of Irish men who came to work illegally in the United States in the mid–1980s found work in the booming construction industry. Not all ended up in the informal sector, however. Those workers with hard-to-find skills and with good union contacts gained access to the unionized jobs in the formal sector. A key link in this process is the union agent or gang foreman (see next section on The Role of the Broker). At the other extreme, those with limited contacts and limited skills (the "JFK carpenters," whose credentials materialize rather dubiously at the point of arrival) generally work for small contractors or set up on their own. These workers are confined within the informal economy. Despite their different locations within the industrial sector, both sets of workers find that they are subject to excessive surveillance, exploitation, and control because of their illegal status.

ACCESS TO EMPLOYMENT: THE ROLE OF THE BROKER

Almost all immigrants rely on their own efforts or the efforts of friends in gaining their initial foothold in the labor market. In addition, experienced immigrants operate as brokers in the ethnic community, matching recent immigrants (clients) with prospective employers (patrons). The power of the broker lies in his access to people who control resources, such as land, jobs, or money. Brokers are the intermediaries in a clientelistic system (Bonacich, 1973: 583; Hazelkorn, 1986: 327). They mediate transactions between patrons and clients, ensuring a reciprocal exchange between both parties. The prototypical broker in the Irish construction sector has established himself as a valued employee (usually a gang foreman) or is a union agent. He uses his own position to negotiate jobs for others, just as the broker in the padrone system imports contract workers for industrial agents (Yancey, Ericksen, and Juliani, 1976: 393). Clientelism has been and continues to be an integral part of Irish political culture. Its persistence has been explained in terms of the uneven pattern of Irish economic and political development (Gibbon and Higgins, 1974: 43). Clientelism flourishes in the ethnic labor market of New York because of the dependency of Irish illegals on that labor market for economic survival:

I know a guy who is a very good welder. There are only a small number of guys in Ireland who can do gas welding as it is a particularly specialized job, and it is difficult to get someone to do it here. The foreman asks M. if he can recommend anybody for a job. M. says he has a friend in New Jersey who might be interested. He calls Ireland that night and tells one of the lads to get over on the next flight. That guy starts work on Monday morning. That's how it works.

A friend of my cousin's was a delegate for the [construction] union. He told me that if I was ever unemployed to give him a ring. So I did. By the following Monday, I had become a member of the union and had a union job in the city.

It has been the practice to hire Irish illegals on the basis of a recommendation from a union agent or power broker. The prospective employee will be asked to produce some documentation, such as a social security card, but the authenticity of the documentation (which is almost always false) is not questioned. There is an implicit rather than explicit acknowledgment of the illegal status of the employee. This is important because unionized companies are highly regulated and must conform to the letter of the law.

An industrious broker can use his position to displace other immigrant workers with hand-picked workers from his own ethnic group, as one beneficiary explains:

Peter had been a construction worker in both Ireland and England before coming to the States. He got work with a subsidiary of a major construction company, which has a big contract with the Transport Authority. Peter was initially the only Irishman on the construction crews, which were made up of immigrants from Antigua, Trinidad, Jamaica, Spain, Italy, and Portugal. A vacancy came up and Peter got T., a mutual friend, onto his construction crew. More workers were needed, and the foreman asked if there was anyone else Peter could recommend. He phoned some lads in Philadelphia, and they came up and joined another crew. The amount of work increased and extra help was hired. Another Irish guy and myself were taken one. Within 10 months, nearly 20 of the 80 men on the crews we worked with were Irish, most having got their jobs through Peter.

In some cases, brokers operating in Ireland secure jobs for people emigrating to New York, but these tend to have contacts only in the informal economy:

My cousin called his son Maurice in . . . NJ and told him I was going out. I left my town in the spring of 1984 and 15 people left the same week. When I contacted Maurice he picked me up in his truck and put me to work six days a week, from 7 A.M. to 7 P.M. for $275. He also fixed me up in a dogbox of an apartment which was very cramped and unsanitary. There were two other guys from my town there, who Maurice had invited over when he visited Ireland the previous summer.

Since the kind of jobs available in the informal economy tend to be less attractive, access is more easily obtained by new immigrants, especially the less skilled. Positions may be obtained on the basis of a casual encounter or contact. For example, Paul was a butcher in Ireland and his first job in New York was as a butcher in a meat factory in Brooklyn. He soon tired of the long hours and the length of his commute and switched to construction work:

I happened to be in a bar one night with a friend who's a carpenter and we got talking to the bartender who introduced us to someone who was starting a construction job. I didn't let on I had no skills, and we were both hired for the job.

Just over a year later, Paul was working as a foreman for an American construction company. Having picked up the rudimentary skills of construction in that time, he has plans for expansion:

I have started to get some of my own jobs through contacts as well. I am doing houses at the moment, subcontracting off a guy with whom I play golf. He was backed up on the job, and so contracted some of the work to me.

Once ensconced in a job on a construction site (or in a bar or restaurant), the immigrant becomes part of an occupational matrix which is tightly woven into the larger ethnic community. News of jobs travels largely through word of mouth, so it is incumbent on the immigrant to extend his or her network of contacts. Ethnic contacts and ties must be cultivated because of the exigencies of survival and the structure of job opportunity in the illegal immigrant market. The interviews conducted for this study are replete with advice on the importance of contacts. Brian sums up this highly instrumental view of the labor market:

People you meet at work are of no consequence except as job contacts, that is what it boils down to. You are friendly with them only because they are potential job contacts.

Many immigrants who work as contractors (usually unregistered) doing residential or renovation work find themselves in a bind. The amount of work they can secure is limited because their illegal status impedes them from advertising their skills openly. An illegal who advertises his or her services openly runs the risk of attracting the attention of tax officials and/ or immigration officers. Illegal entrepreneurs must rely almost totally on word of mouth—on the personal recommendation of a current client who can refer them to the next client. It is not just the structure of the labor market that can be described as informal. The interactions that occur between employers, brokers, and employees on the one hand, and contractors and their customers on the other are all characterized by a high degree of informality.

For example, when Seamus and Diarmaid started taking on jobs in construction, their landlady proved to be a crucial contact. They had renovated an apartment for her and she had a business partner who was able to pass on some jobs to them. Once people saw their work, word traveled fast. They did not advertise but relied strictly on word of mouth and referrals from people for whom they had successfully completed jobs. Similarly, when Sonny and Brendan decided to go into business together informally, Sonny contacted someone for whom he had worked two years previously repairing sidewalks. The contact put them in touch with their first job doing a sidewalk on Lexington Avenue. Their work was complimented by another builder on the block who asked them to help with renovating a building nearby.

Contacts in the extended community are the crucial ones:

With regard to contacts—you need the right ones. Americans and Irish Americans are the good contacts. It's the people of your own kin that can't really help you and are really no good to you.

As with all immigrant groups, the Irish illegals make use of the ethnic network to improve their position. They move beyond the obvious first-order contacts to make use of second-order contacts, which are ultimately more influential in the community. Because they are without documentation, however, advancement is limited, and they are largely confined to the ethnic enclave.

Advancement within the ethnic enclave tends to be incremental, and most of the interviewees—whether in the construction industry or in the restaurant and bar trade—changed jobs frequently, with a view to bettering their position and increasing their earning power. This practice confirms the evidence gathered from other studies of undocumented immigrant groups that found that the illegals' wage rates rose steadily with increasing migrant experience (Massey, 1987: 268). Wage rates are generally lower than in the formal sector, but special skills and experience are rewarded through a differential wage structure. Legislative changes in the mid–1980s, however, have restricted access to jobs for the undocumented and have indirectly depressed average wage rates in the new Irish community. Consequently, many illegal construction workers who enjoyed the benefits of employment in the formal economy have found themselves demoted to the informal economy.

IMPACT OF IMMIGRATION LAW ON ACCESS TO JOBS

The picture painted thus far is of an immigrant labor force constantly in flux, at least in the case of male immigrants. At the time of this research, this fluidity was beginning to change. The change can largely be traced to the introduction of the Immigration Reform and Control Act (1986), which paved the way for the imposition of fines on employers who knowingly hired illegal aliens after November 1, 1986. Under the provisions of the act, all employees who were hired after May 31, 1987, are obliged to complete a form verifying their employment eligibility and identity (Form I–9). Those who were hired between November 7, 1986, and May 31, 1987, had to complete the Form I–9 before September 1, 1987. The employee is required to furnish his or her employer with *two* pieces of original identification, such as a passport, social security card, birth certificate, alien registration form, and driver's license. Since passage of the act, there has been a decline in the level of job mobility within the immigrant community, not just in the construction sector, but in the restaurant and bar trade too. During one week in November 1987, for example, the IIRM received over 80 phone calls from Irish immigrants who had lost their jobs because they were unable to complete the I–9 form. Those who were in jobs before the sanctions on employers took effect have been inclined to remain in those jobs as the prospect of finding another has become increasingly daunting.

The desire to be retained in employment often entails greater risk-taking on the job. Not only are construction jobs dangerous, but the Irish are more willing than others to volunteer for the dangerous tasks:

Irish guys work hard. They take a lot of chances I think because they are afraid of losing their jobs. They will push harder to make a name for themselves so that they don't get laid off. But sometimes they push so hard they end up getting injured and having to stay off work for weeks at a time. They'll take the chance on dangerous work, not because they are crazy, but because they want to be kept on. The Irish guy goes home each evening and worries if he is going to be back at work tomorrow.

The work ethic is thus positively and negatively reinforced: People work hard because of the monetary rewards but also out of fear of losing their jobs.

According to one immigrant activist, the effect of the law is to marginalize the illegal Irish within an already marginal sector of the New York labor market:

The law hasn't had the desired effect. The kids can still get jobs but the possibility of exploitation goes up, and there will be lower pay. The law is driving all of us further underground.

Smaller construction companies operating out of the suburbs will continue to need labor and are unlikely to be selective about their employees. Such companies are unlikely to fall within the ambit of the immigration authorities, who have targeted their efforts (publicizing the provisions of the act) at larger employers. As job opportunities decline, the small contractors will be able to exercise even more control over the immigrant labor market. As employers "of last resort," they will consolidate their position of powerful patronage in the community. Irish workers face lower wages in this sector and no union benefits. The larger construction outfits, such as companies with city contracts, that offer more secure, regulated employment will be increasingly closed to immigrants who cannot complete the I–9 form.

The provisions of the Immigration Reform and Control Act have exacerbated the situation of illegal Irish immigrants whose tenure was already precarious. The law has contracted the immigrant labor market still further. The most coveted jobs within the construction sector (skilled, unionized, secure positions) are now the least accessible. Moreover, the overall demand for construction labor is in decline, given the recent downswing in the New York construction industry. In early 1990, new construction starts in Manhattan reached the lowest point since the mid–1970s. The chief source of the depression is attributed by industry experts to a major slowing in commercial office projects (*Irish Voice*, March 17, 1990: 1). If the decline in the construction industry is a sustained one, it may have serious repercussions for the illegal immigrant work force. They may be forced to move elsewhere within the United States (there is already indications of a flow to California and the Sunbelt cities of the South) or they may have to return to Britain or Europe.

POWER, CONTROL, AND EXPLOITATION

Illegality intensifies dependence on patrons and power brokers in the established Irish community. As undocumented workers, the Irish are dependent on employers who won't ask awkward questions. Hence they gravitate toward Irish contractors and the Irish-owned bars and restaurants. The employer may hire and fire at will, for his or her employees have no recourse under the law. Dependence on clientelistic relations for survival contributes to the heightened parochialism among the new Irish community. The greater the extent of the clientelism—of personalistic relations in the workplace— the more difficult it is for the illegals to organize around their own interests.

The new Irish are generally regarded as willing and compliant workers. As a local priest in Irishtown remarked:

The new Irish have a great name for work. They are in the prime of life, they make good wages, and they adapt well to the production line methods where you simply can't sit around. They do the work in half the time.

Despite this excellent reputation, all Irish illegals—by virtue of their irregular status—are subject to excessive control and exploitation on the job.

It is generally the smaller construction firms who are most culpable in this respect. Work on construction sites, which is physically demanding, is often tightly controlled:

The foreman would stand over us, and it really got on my nerves. The work was complicated but I really resented the constant supervision . . . when the whistle blows you start working. When the coffee break comes you don't sit down because you are on company time. The foreman stands over you and shouts. . . . I think for most of the guys, it's a case of leaving your brain at home when you leave in the morning.

In Ireland, the lads show up on the construction site five minutes late. Here the workers are there half an hour before they are supposed to start. Coffee breaks are taken standing up.

Other workers are denied any sense of security or continuity in the job:

Membership of a [construction] union does not confer a right to work . . . it is always up to the company to decide whether or not you will work. They hire on a day-to-day basis.

As an illegal looking for a job, the immigrant has little choice but to accept the terms of employment as laid down by the potential employer. As the labor market tightens, the immigrant has less and less bargaining power. The relationship between employer and employee becomes increasingly exploitative. Employers have little sense of loyalty to their employees. As legitimate members of their own community, they are frequently unwilling to involve themselves in the underworld of the illegal immigrant. If the latter is faced with a problem, the employer generally tries to disengage immediately:

I was working as a mechanic and getting sponsored by my America boss. I had a lawyer on the case and had already paid him part of the fee. After my accident the boss completely disowned me, even though we had been on friendly, sociable terms. He owed me three days' pay when I had the accident, and he paid me for three days, not even a full week, even though I had worked many long hours for him on weekends and evenings without pay. I lost the job and my sponsorship at the same time.

The most common forms of complaint have to do with rates of pay and length of the working day. Undocumented construction workers may be paid at a lower rate than other unionized and nonunionized workers, although they are all doing the same tasks. However, it should be pointed out that Irish immigrants generally fare a lot better than nonwhite illegal immigrants. For example, undocumented Dominican workers tend to be concentrated in small firms, in nonunion jobs. Their earnings are 40 percent less than those of documented Dominican workers. Men averaged $150 per week in

1988 (Pessar, 1988). In contrast, even the lowest-paid Irish construction worker earned twice that amount per week. Those who did not pay taxes could take home even more.

Several interviewees pointed out that non-English speaking Europeans were less well paid than themselves because they had difficulty negotiating with employers. Undocumented Mexican workers were generally the worst paid of all. Even on a job in which all the workers are unionized, two differential rates of pay may apply—one for legal workers and one for the undocumented. The union knows that the latter have no recourse under the law and therefore cannot complain. (Labor racketeering practices in some New York construction unions in the 1980s made it possible for some contractors to hire nonunion labor in return for bribes paid to union agents. Thus, a contractor could have as many as four categories of workers under his control: unionized legals, unionized illegals, nonunionized legals, and nonunionized illegals. Rates of pay varied accordingly.)

Immigrants in the informal sector do not constitute a homogeneous group. They are stratified according to race, ethnicity, skills, and experience, as well as legal status, and that stratification determines to a great extent their labor market experience. Indeed, Massey argues that legal status in itself is not the principal determinant of differential wage rates:

On average, undocumented migrants do earn lower wages than legal migrants, but they do so not because they lack legal papers, but because they compare unfavorably to legal migrants on variables that determine wage rates. U.S. wages are principally a function of English language ability, time spent on the job, skill level, and close kinship with a legal migrant (1987: 267).

This explains why Irish immigrants—with good English, a high level of skill, and close ties to Irish-American power brokers—tend to do better in the migrant labor market than their European and Central American counterparts, both of whom have access to a much smaller pool of affluent employers. It also explains why Irish illegals have been successful in penetrating the formal labor market and why other immigrant groups have been unable to do so.

Differential treatment of undocumented workers precludes the development of interethnic solidarity groups. It also prevents the formation of a workers' coalition that might organize around shared interests. Even within the Irish ethnic group, the existence of clientelistic linkages between employer and employee precludes the emergence of intraethnic solidarity, as illegal immigrants strive to ingratiate themselves with their employers in order to safeguard their own interests, and vertical rather than horizontal alliances characterize the immigrant workplace.

It is the "old timers"—the Irish-born bosses and foremen—who receive the most criticism from new arrivals. Most independent contractors and construction union agents in the Irish enclave are first generation immigrants who came to the United States in the 1950s and early 1960s. Lacking formal education and skills, they went into the construction industry, where the successful ones worked their way up in the union hierarchy or set up their own contracting businesses. They are, therefore, the "gatekeepers" who control access to jobs in key areas of the construction industry and upon whom the illegals are most dependent. The second- and third-generation Irish are much less likely to be involved in blue-collar work, having had the opportunity of a college education denied their parents or grandparents.

Employers in the informal sector maintain their competitive edge by extracting the maximum amount of labor at minimum cost. For example, a group of employers operating in the same geographic region may form a cartel to lower their labor costs. According to one informant, five construction outfits (three of whom were Irish) in a New Jersey city got together and decided to fix wages. They dropped the carpenters' pay from $100 to $80 per day and laborers' pay from $80 to $60 per day. The informant called a meeting of his co-workers, exhorting them to withhold their labor until they got the right price, but nobody wanted to rock the boat. The general sentiment was that if they protested, the employers might turn them into the immigration authorities.

Occasionally, some of the smaller construction companies have cash-flow problems, and it is generally the employee who suffers the consequence:

I was working for a furniture removal company. All I wanted was a job. I didn't know if it was good money or bad money, at least I was earning money. And then the checks started to bounce. You would work an 80-hour week and be owed $500 and he would give you $300 and owe you $200. There was always money on the long finger. He hired Irish illegals exclusively and really took advantage. We were totally overworked yet there was no such thing as time and a half when you did overtime.

Companies can siphon off part of the employee's pay in other ways, as Barry learned when he took a job in a demolition company:

The pay was $35 per day. The guy was supposed to be withholding some of the money to help me get a green card, but it was a big rip off. He wasn't doing anything at all.

The employers use a variety of strategies to extend the working day and thus get more return from the labor:

The Irish companies will always try and squeeze a bit more out of you, tacking on an extra half-hour here or an hour there. As a bricklayer, I can earn a minimum of $150–$200 per seven-hour day. The Irish companies pay by the hour though—$20 per hour—so you have to work a seven-and-a-half-hour day to get up to $150—the average wage.

The only reason the Irish are employed is because they [the employers] have a hold over them. So on the job there is no double time, no time and a half. They know the score, but they are more interested in getting people without papers. It costs less to hire illegals.

Safety and health regulations are frequently flaunted. At successive meetings of the IIRM, lawyers and others present pointed out that workers were being exposed to unnecessary risk in the workplace. For example, workers were allowed to go on scaffolding in dangerous weather, even though they had no insurance coverage for injuries received at work. Construction work in particular is fraught with danger. In the absence of adequate supervision and training, workers are at greater risk of injury. Without proper treatment, some injuries can become chronic conditions, which may ultimately make the injured party unemployable. Other workers may be exposed to hazardous substances without being aware of the consequences. One informant who has been working with an Irish construction firm, specializing in the removal of hazardous substances, criticized the exploitative work practices in the Irish-run firm for whom he worked:

On the job they try to cheat you out of your lunch break and your coffee break. If they give you an hour they try to take it back somewhere along the line. They constantly expose the workers to hazardous substances but if you complain you are out the door. They violate the regulations by not issuing enough protective clothing and mouth filters. Since I raised objections about this, I haven't been called into work. The money is not the issue. The issue is the way the operation works. They get people to work Sundays, all through Christmas vacation to finish a job. And then in January there is no work. There is constant pressure to get the job done quickly and cheaply and little concern about exposure to hazardous substances.

Here, the profit motive takes precedence over considerations of ethnic loyalty or solidarity across generations.

Another technique for extracting the maximum effort from immigrant workers is to stimulate the pace of work by covert means. Construction companies may hire a "pushman" to increase overall productivity. Terry and his partner currently employ about 10–12 workers. Laborers get paid $100 per day, bricklayers about $150 per day. One of the bricklayers is a personal friend. Unknown to the other workers, the latter negotiated separately and is being paid $300 per day. However, he will only work on the job for a week or two. He is what is known in the trade as a pushman—working in one corner of the building, he will put the blocks up quicker, speeding up the pace all round. The pace the pushman sets allows the foreman to put pressure on the other workers. The week the pushman worked, they laid 4,000 blocks. The following week they laid 1,800 blocks and the job went on over the weekend:

It's a dirty way of cheating, but you get the job done quicker. It's more efficient to pay the pushman $150 extra per day and to get the job done than to pay all the tradesmen an extra $30 each as added incentive.

Not surprisingly, there is a high degree of alienation among Irish construction workers. They complain of the lack of autonomy on the job and the necessity of "switching-off" mentally during working hours. Work is viewed primarily as a means to an end—a weekend of drinking before the treadmill starts over again on Monday morning. One construction crew observed closely over the period of research regularly binged on the weekends. They worked night shifts doing underground construction work, so their working week finished on Saturday morning. Some of the crew would go straight to the bar after work—dirty, exhausted, and with a full pay packet in their pockets. They would drink steadily throughout the day and night and into the following day. Sometimes these binges would go on until Monday morning, ending only because the working week was starting over again. They explained the weekend drinking-bout by pointing to the drudgery of their work:

When I'm on site all week the only thing that I think about is when is this going to be over and what am I going to do at the weekend. You work and sleep for five days each week, and you have to have release at the end of it.

The experience of work is occasionally tinged with a sense of unreality— with immigrants speaking of their working selves as if it is in some way detached from their "real" selves:

Often when I sat down for coffee on the 56th floor, I would survey the city and wonder what the hell I was doing there. It's not really until you get a chance to look around that the scale of the thing really hits you.

In the immigrant's social and cultural milieus, this fractured sense of self is reflected in the close affinity and orientation toward "home," which is almost always conceived of as Ireland and almost never as New York.

OCCUPATIONAL IMMOBILITY

After the initial adjustment period, many immigrants discover that although they can find remunerative work, there is little sense in which they can structure a career path for themselves. Ironically, many left jobs in Ireland because promotion prospects looked bleak. They felt unchallenged and unrewarded by their work. As immigrants without legal status their occupational mobility is equally inhibited. While there is a high degree of lateral mobility—moving from one construction firm to another, for example—there is little upward mobility on the job. In the short term, the monetary rewards are more attractive, but material gain in itself does not smooth the path toward the attainment of occupational goals. Illegality, the intervening factor, is an ever-present barrier to upward mobility. Few regard construction work as a lifelong career yet, as illegals, most other channels of work are closed off. Advancement and security can only be provided through occupational paths to which they have no access:

There is no work open to the Irish, except in construction and, for the girls, jobs as nannies. Some guys are happy at that because the money is good. But it is only temporarily good. Twenty years from now you would need something more to fall back on. We have a lot to contribute to society through government jobs and city jobs, but we can't. . . . I am very frustrated at the fact that I can get laid off and that I have to stick with the union and with jobs in the construction industry. The money is good but there is no future. In a few years you are totally burnt out.

Even if opportunities become available at work, there may be a reluctance to accept additional responsibility. For example, accepting promotion may involve an immigrant in further lies and subterfuges to conceal his identity. His relationship with his superiors becomes a tenuous one, because he has breached the trust placed in him. His authority may also be impugned by subordinates who find out his real identity or illegal status:

One of the business partners asked me to be a foreman. At first, I didn't want the responsibility. I suggested that they promote an American co-worker who is older than me. I didn't want to get into something which might complicate my situation further.

When I was a foreman for a company I did a job for a guy. The job ran fast and everything was done according to his specifications. The guy was recently looking for a manager and he offered me the job. It would have suited me great, but I couldn't take the job because of my legal status. I have had a business relationship with the guy for three years and I didn't want to complicate that by asking for sponsorship. Then he would know that I was illegal up until that and he had always done things strictly above board. It really killed me to turn it down. I'm only here to get the right break and that could have been it, but I couldn't follow it through.

Setting up one's own construction business is an alternative, but the illegality issue means that this path is also fraught with problems. It is difficult to raise the necessary capital and credit rating, as well as insurance coverage:

You need a social security number in order to get a federal identification card for the company insurance. If a company doesn't have insurance then it can't incorporate, and incorporation is your only protection. It feels like you are rowing up river all the time.

Without adequate insurance coverage, the company or individual contracted for the job is personally liable for injuries, accidents, or damage that occurs on the job. The level of risk attached to the work makes independent contracting work unattractive to all but a minority of immigrants. One solution is to go into partnership with a legal partner who can handle all the paperwork, such as acquiring finance and insurance. But establishing the trustworthiness of a potential partner is difficult:

If you get someone else involved—as a silent partner to get the insurance—and the company starts doing well, they might decide they want to get in on it. You are left without a leg to stand on.

Companies cannot advertise openly in the ethnic press for fear that they will be targeted by immigration officials. Business referrals mainly come through word of mouth. Once a job is completed, they have no legal recourse if clients default on payments:

The problem for small guys setting up a construction company is that they will have difficulty getting paid. Also, they never make a contract for the job, so they don't have a leg to stand on if the terms of the job come into question.

A valiant attempt to break out of the cycle of exploitation by setting up one's own independent operation may prove costly as well as foolhardy. This acts as a major deterrent to prospective entrepreneurs and frequently leads to disillusionment with the immigrant experience.

THE LABOR ARISTOCRATS: FOOTBALLERS AND HURLERS

Gaelic sports are an intrinsic part of Irish cultural identity. The Gaelic games of football and hurling are played competitively at parish, county, regional, and national level in Ireland. For generations of Irish immigrants, Gaelic sports have provided an important connection to the past—their childhood, youth, and homeplace—in Ireland. Gaelic games have also been traditionally associated with Irish nationalism, and the cultural revival movement that thrived on both sides of the Atlantic in the early part of the twentieth century. The Gaelic Athletic Association (GAA) has historically played the role of cultural bulwark against the encroachment of Anglo and American sporting influences. Davis points out that "the remembered past like all other products of human consciousness is something that must be filtered, selected, arranged, constructed and re-constructed from collective experience" (1979: 116). Gaelic games continue to embody—through their identification with the heroic past—an important part of the Irish-American collective experience.

The Irish-American construction network and recreation networks are closely enmeshed, which works in favor of an elite cadre of Irish immigrants. The GAA in New York oversees the local football and hurling leagues. The numbers of second-generation Irish and New York natives playing Gaelic games are miniscule, so the GAA depends largely on new immigrants. An estimated 3,000 people, adult and juvenile, play Gaelic games in New York City (*Sunday Independent*, May 7, 1989). The New York teams retain Irish county names, and so a tremendous amount of county pride attaches to the teams that win the championships in September of each year. The teams actively compete with each other to attract top players onto their sides, and invariably the team with the most selective incentives at its disposal attracts the best players: "Donegal's powerful Gaelic footballers... hardly have a Donegal man among them, but the number of stars on the team is explained by Donegal's strong ties inside the New York labor unions" (McLaughlin, 1988: 142).

Immigrants who can prove themselves on the football or hurling fields are virtually ensured a well-paid job in construction and, occasionally, other perks, such as free apartments. Their sporting skills serve to insulate them against the precariousness of the illegal labor market. A recent arrival may go to Gaelic Park (or one of the training grounds in the Bronx or Brooklyn) and ask for a trial on a team. If he proves good enough, he will be helped in finding employment so that, in return, the team can benefit from his skills. One woman explained how her boyfriend filtered into the GAA jobs network:

When we were out here two weeks, Paddy's uncle arranged for him to go to Brooklyn to play a try-out game. He's a very good player, and that is what got him his first job out here and every job since then. If you're a good player, they'll all fight for you.

Another immigrant recalled the hard work that went into creating a good impression on the playing field:

If you get to play for a team you've got to run your legs off out there to impress them. Then in the dressing room after, someone will ask you if you need a job, and the next week there will be 30 pairs of ears listening out for you (McLaughlin, 1988: 142).

Alternatively, an immigrant may be induced into the system by "talent spotters" who travel to Ireland for the express purpose to bring star players to New York. These talent spotters offer selected players all expenses paid weekends in New York plus an appearance fee. In some cases, the prospect of a job is used as a selective incentive to entice a good sportsman to emigrate permanently. Many of the premier team players were first introduced to

America through the "Gaelic junket"—weekend trips to New York to play in crucial games with all expenses taken care of by the team:

One of my first trips to America was on a "Gaelic junket" to play an important weekend game. On one occasion, eleven members of our team in Ireland were flown out to play a final. When I emigrated in 1982, I started playing for the "Shamrock" team and I've been with them ever since.

The incentives to come out are good. I used to come out and play weekend games. I would leave on Thursday evening and be back on Sunday night. The weekend specials from home are killing the game here though. It makes a mockery of the guys who train and play here all year round. There is enough emigration now to supply all the teams in New York.

The competition between rival teams is so strong that the team managers will go to considerable lengths in order to "acquire"—even temporarily—a premier set of players for important matches:

They (the team managers) will pay any price to get the guys in. Money is no problem. In 1986, the treasurer of the "Harps" team went to Ireland to watch a "Gaels" versus "Harps" semifinal. "Harps" won so they had to stay on for the final, so he paid the "Gaels" team members to come over and play for "Harps" in New York and improve their chances of winning!

According to several sources, the junketing has decreased in recent years, mainly because there is a much larger pool of available talent in New York from which team managers can choose. The rise in emigration during the eighties means that it is no longer as difficult to field a team of sports stars as it was in the nadir years of the seventies. In addition, the influx of young immigrants in recent years has led to the formation of many new clubs and teams who play more for pleasure than for glory. It is now the Gaelic teams in Ireland that are witnessing a downswing in their fortunes as their numbers are depleted further each year. As one official attached to a Midlands team in Ireland explained:

No sooner have we trained a player to an adequate level of footballing skills but he's taking the boat or plane. Apart from the problem of fielding teams of mature players, we're finding it a major problem to get enough lads to coach the underage teams, so there's a vicious circle in the sense that fewer coaches will mean fewer players in years to come (*Irish Times*, January 24, 1987).

Despite the decline in junketing, top players can still name their price and may negotiate between several teams before accepting an offer. However, such is the competitive nature of the sport in New York that once a player signs for a team he becomes indentured to that team:

There is a very thin line between making it and not making it out here. Football was the key for me. . . . I got my first job and into the union through football connections. A friend at home had a brother who played with the Clare football team, so when I came out I started training with them. For me, football was a bigger asset than my four years at college. You have to be careful how you negotiate your rewards though. Lots of people will offer you a job in return for playing on their team. But once you opt for a team there is no going back, and if the job isn't forthcoming then you're in a mess.

Diarmaid is a case in point. He was spotted playing football at home in 1986 and was invited out to play for a team in Philadelphia who had used county players from Ireland on a regular basis. Diarmaid was promised airfare, a house, and a job if he joined the team. It seemed like an attractive package so he decided to go:

Once I was here the deal soured. The accommodation was very poor and two weeks passed without mention of a job. I became very disillusioned. I went to play for a rival club who offered to "buy me over." There was strict segregation between the teams—you worked, played, and hung out with your own team. A friend in New York offered me an even better deal so I decided to cut my losses and leave Philadelphia for good.

Diarmaid's last club was unhappy at his departure, and they succeeded in having a two-year ban imposed on him from playing Gaelic games in both Philadelphia and New York in retaliation for his failure to honor his contract.

Irish immigrants, estranged from the home country, retain a strong sense of loyalty to their place of origin. This loyalty is given expression at Gaelic Park every time two opposing county teams face each other on the playing field. The pattern of fiercely competitive game-playing, which characterizes Gaelic sports in Ireland, is replicated in microcosm in New York. The team members on the sports field play vicariously for their sponsors off the field. Both are engaging in a collective experience which while recalling the past, also acts as a means for expressing present "anxieties, aspirations, hopes, fears and fantasies" (Davis, 1979: 116). More important, the new immigrants exercise their considerable sporting skills in return for economic security and/or financial gain. For recent arrivals, assimilation into the Gaelic network appears to be the ultimate sinecure. But as in all clientelistic relationships, the benefits that they receive come only at a certain price.

THE RESTAURANT AND BAR TRADE

Job opportunities in the restaurant and bar trade were once plentiful for Irish illegals but have declined steadily since the passage of the Immigration Reform and Control Act. The attempt to regulate the trade by requiring all employees to complete the I–9 identification form has left fewer and fewer openings for workers without documentation. Consequently, those who do obtain jobs (often with false documentation) are even more dependent on the goodwill of their employers. As in the construction sector, insecurity, exploitation, and excessive control are features of the bar and restaurant workplace, particularly within the Irish ethnic enclave:

My boss [in the bar] has everything [figured out to his advantage]. I have been with him for seven or eight months. Everyday I call up to see if I am due in. That's the way the boss does it. You call up and you are told if you are working that day, and the next day the same again.

Even though Brian has worked full time since he started the job, the guarantee of work is never made. Thus, the boss is able to maintain tight controls over his work force. Brian describes his Irish-American boss as a tough task master—a stickler for detail and unwilling to give credit even when it is due:

You could do 150 things right, and one little thing wrong and he would pick on you over that. No matter how hard you work it is never enough.

The exercise of discretionary power as a way of maintaining control is not uncommon as Jim discovered when he went to work for another Irish-born boss who had been highly successful in the bar trade in New York. He found that both he and another Irish girl were hired for the same job. They were forced to compete against each other for the one available position, under the critical eye of the restaurant boss. Summary dismissal is another example of the discretionary power of the employer. Already marginalized because of their illegal status, immigrant employees who feel they have been unfairly dismissed have no recourse under the law:

One week the boss was grooming me for a position as assistant manager in the restaurant. The next week he fired me. The only reason he gave was that as the boss he could hire and fire as he pleased.

One morning the boss rang me and said he wouldn't be needing me anymore. I asked him why and he said he couldn't keep a sloppy register. I knew it was nothing to do with me at all. As an illegal it would not be worth losing your job over $20 or $30 short in the till, so you would always even it up. I told the boss they had the wrong man. Later I heard that they had fired the guy with whom my shift overlapped, but I never got my job back.

John's hours in a downtown bar were gradually reduced by the boss (who eventually hired his own son as a replacement) even though John was a popular bartender. When he confronted the boss, there was no explanation. "That is the way it is," he was told. While illegal labor is a valuable commodity, it is always expendable without regard to due process.

From Shrink to Pal: The Emotional Labor of the Bartender

Bartending, like waitressing, is a job that calls for emotional labor as well as considerable physical and mental stamina. Emotional labor, according to Hochschild, "is the management of feeling to create a publicly observable facial and bodily display . . . this labor requires one to induce or suppress feeling in order to sustain the outward countenance that produces the proper state of mind in others" (1983: 7).

The bartender is in constant face-to-face contact with the public and is required to produce benign feelings in his clientele. In order to do this, he must manipulate his emotions to create an ambiance in which his customer instantly feels welcome, comfortable, and at home. In effect, the bartender's personality on the job becomes the property of his employer. Failure to do the necessary emotional work can result in loss of custom, and ultimately, one's productivity is measured in terms of the till takings. For the bartender who is also an illegal immigrant, this front stage impression management is paralleled by a back stage management of doubts, insecurities, and anxieties relating to his tenuous status in the job. The emotional strain of the job is accentuated for the bartender working in these particular circumstances.

There is pressure on the bartender to cultivate customers in order to prove his worth. But a bartender cannot "make people buy drink" without first gaining their trust and making it pleasant and worthwhile for them to spend time and money in the bar:

The bar I worked in was a real low life place. A lot of drug dealers used to hang out there. As the bartender, I had to get down to their level. I drank a lot and acted the idiot but inside I despised them. The boss was happy because the takings were great. I used to keep the place open until four or five in the morning. Sometimes I would sleep over in the bar because I would be too drunk to go home.

Emotional labor may take several forms, from merely listening to the customer to providing consolation, affirmation, and advice. In all cases, however, the bartender is involved in a process of impression management— suppressing his own feelings and adapting to the illusory roles of friend and/ or confidante.

Bar work is a pain in the neck. These guys sitting at the bar expect you to talk to them all the time. There is a tremendous amount of mind pressure. People pour out their heart to you and you have to be careful with them. It is as hard on you mentally as construction is physically. You have to be psyched all of the time.

My take home pay is $650 per week. It is a lot of money but I think I earn it. Bar work can be very depressing. I open my bar at 8 A.M. in the morning. My first customer is a Czechoslovak engineer. He has six shots of whiskey before going to work. He comes in again on his coffee break and at lunch time. I get doctors, engineers, and construction workers—all types of people—going down the tubes. They fortify themselves with drink. I often find myself in the role of psychiatrist listening to their problems. When I finish my shift at 6 P.M. they will beg me to come on the other side of the bar with them and have a drink as pals. The customer wants you as a pal and there is a pressure to play the game.

The bartender is aware of the vicarious nature of his "friendship role." He distances himself from his customer by withholding true friendship, by not becoming "a pal." Indeed, the bartender is ever mindful that dropping his guard to a customer could have grave repercussions for his job, if that customer decided to "turn him in" to an employer or the immigration authorities. To a great extent, the bartender estranges himself from his real feelings. He generates a false or illusory set of feelings that form the basis of his emotional work. This estrangement is often quite conscious and is part of the bartender's repertoire for impression management. One bartender whom I observed on several occasions interchanged real and illusory feelings as a routine part of his work—he was the disgruntled employee one moment and the ever-pleasant bartender the next, as I recorded in the following field note:

Martin's behavior behind the bar was instructive. When a customer entered the bar he would murmur something derogatory about them under his breath. The next minute he would sail up and be polite, friendly, or flirtatious—whatever the situation required. For example, as one man entered, Joe muttered "this fucking little prick" or something along those lines. Then he calmly approached the man in question and greeted him warmly—"hello, how are you, looking great, God bless you."

All workers (regardless of legal status) who are involved in emotional labor have a repertoire of roles that they play as required. But for illegal workers, the distinction between the real and illusory becomes increasingly blurred. To satisfy his clientele, he must create not only the role of the bartender but also the role of himself. A "plausible self" rather than the "authentic self" must be presented to the customer who wants to become a friend.

Irish bartenders, like their American counterparts, have to remain abreast of developments in the worlds of sport and politics. The customers expect to be able to discuss such matters with the bartender and assume a generally prior knowledge of the activities of local football teams and local politicians:

Working in bars brought me more outside of the Irish community. I met people of all races. You have to interest yourself in what's going on around you in the country, otherwise, you would have nothing to talk to them about. You have to be up on the sports and all that. When they ask you what did you think of the Mets last night, you gotta have an answer!

In order to communicate with their customers, bartenders, to a much greater degree than other Irish immigrants, have to be familiar with American culture and politics. There is a greater incentive for the bartender (especially those working in nonethnic bars) than for the construction worker, for instance, to identify with the host culture. This suggests that where one is placed in the immigration occupational structure determines to some extent one's level of adaptation to the host culture.

As with the management of emotions, a bartender's opinions have to be carefully constructed to avoid antagonizing or conflicting with the customers. For example, bartenders who work in ethnic bars that cater to Irish Americans find that they have to tailor their perspective on Ireland to fit those of their customers. Many Irish Americans have a distorted or illusory view of Ireland based either on hazy memories or the traditional stereotypes that have in the past dominated the American media. This "stage Irishism"—or what is colloquially known as the "come all ya" attitude—serves as an irritant to the bartender:

When people get a lot of drink into them, they talk a lot, and you have to listen to them. A lot of them go on with the "come all ya" about Ireland, and it sickens me to hear all this baloney. My customers say things like "I guess your Dad is down on the bog now," and I agree for peace sake. But I resent the distorted view of Ireland.

The bartender also has to sustain abuse and make decisions as to when to eject unruly customers. He has to maintain control in the bar at all times. His position of authority in the bar, however, must always be balanced against the need to ingratiate himself not only with the owner, but also with the customers. Despite the pressure of emotional labor, bartending, because of its superior physical environment, is considered by many illegal immigrants as an easier option to construction work, although there is also some movement in the opposite direction:

I'm glad to have hung up my construction boots. Bar work is a better job. Your hands get soft but it is great in all weathers—air conditioned in the summer, and heated in the winter.

I was fed up with bar work. I wanted to make a change and get into construction instead. I felt I was getting soft behind the bar and that construction would toughen me up.

Moving from one occupational category to another is unusual, however. Most of the immigrants find that their location in the occupational structure and their career aspirations are highly circumscribed. As pointed out earlier, the absence of occupational mobility is a key obstacle faced by the illegal alien. Through his job, the bartender continually comes into contact with people of his own age (and sometimes similar qualifications) who are successfully pursuing careers. Comparisons with this reference group are very disconcerting and serve to heighten the bartender's sense of frustration at his exclusion from the system:

A bartender's job is talking to customers and you get very frustrated. They are on the other side of the bar with their careers, and you know that you have the same potential but they see you only as the bartender on the other side. You feel you have better capabilities and more potential than a lot of them—I know I would be a good salesman, but it can't be done.

Initial expectations are high, but few are fulfilled. These immigrants work in jobs for which they are unsuited and experience frustration because they feel they are capable of better. The earning potential attached to prestige jobs in construction and bartending, however, remains an attraction, at least in the short term. Money is an important anodyne. As one community activist put it:

I think a lot of people won't give up and go home because they are ashamed to say what work they have done. You might be earning $600 per week, but you work real hard for that. I guess there is nothing makes you feel better than having $600 in your pocket in the pub. It compensates for everything you had to do to get it.

It is unlikely that people with skills and credentials will remain in nonmobile positions indefinitely. If there is no prospect of regularizing their status, they will eventually return home.

Service with a Smile: The Waitress at Work

While domestic work attracts the majority of undocumented Irish women immigrants, a proportion continue to find employment as waitresses in the restaurant and bar trade. Waitressing work is much sought after because of its higher earning potential. (While the average wage for a nanny living out was approximately $250 per week in 1988, a waitress could expect to earn $300 plus per week.) In the service sector, women can reach parity with men, although they work harder and are subject to greater abuse in the line of duty than are their counterparts behind the bar. In the restaurant and bar trade, workers are generally paid nothing for the first couple of weeks' work while they are learning the ropes. Yet they are expected to purchase a uniform and support shoes before they can start on the job. Few waitresses are paid per shift, and if they are, it is usually a token amount. They are expected to live off their tips. An employer may hire more waitresses than he actually needs to staff his restaurant. The customer gets personalized service but the women get only a meager return for their labor.

Unlike nannies and home companions who are afforded a modicum of protection because of the privatized nature of their work, waitresses are situated in a public milieu. A casual slip may inadvertently lead to exposure as an illegal alien, so they must always be on guard:

You have to be careful in the restaurant. If any customers ask I say that I was born in America, but my family moved back to Ireland when I was young.

Occasionally it affects me when people in work ask if I am legal or if I have my green card. I always say yeah, but it makes me more conscious and careful about what I say. I never have to be careful about what I say in front of the boss because we got on so well. But what if one day we had a big fight and he fired me? Where would I be?

Even the friendliest of clients (and coworkers) have to be treated with a certain degree of circumspection. Arrests of illegal Irish immigrants have tended to be in bars or restaurants, which have a strong ethnic identification and are highly accessible. Illegals working in the service sector must constantly deal with the possibility of having their illegality exposed.

Unlike the men, who may change jobs frequently within their own occupational category, women tend to be much more cautious. They generally stay with the same waitressing job for years. This reflects the lack of structural opportunity attached to the job. Whereas a waiter may progress to bartending and from there to a managerial position, waitresses are not as upwardly mobile. Once a waitress has served her time, she gets the best station to work and thus there is little incentive to move and start over in another restaurant. A waitress does not build up occupational credentials—every time she moves to a new job, she has to prove her worth all over again. In addition, the compulsory shift work makes it impossible to structure activities outside the job (such as educational courses), which might provide a path out of service work and illegality.

All of the more prestigious restaurants (operating in the formal economy) now require completion of the I-9 form. As in other sectors, people hired after November 1986, who are unable to produce the necessary documentation to their employers, have lost their jobs. Those who were hired before that date are more secure but are unable to take up better opportunities elsewhere:

It's getting very hard to get waitressing without papers at the moment. Even though my current job is getting very monotonous there is no hope of getting another one. One of the top restaurant bars in Manhattan has been raided twice in recent weeks by immigration. They haven't been hiring for a while, and even when they were, you needed papers. As soon as you go into one of the [prestigious] restaurants, an I-9 form is put in front of you straightaway.

A nanny who was tired of her long hours and low pay tried unsuccessfully to get a waitressing job. She found one restaurant that had instituted a policy of shedding illegal workers through a process of attrition:

I tried to get into waitressing but it was just too hard—they're all looking for a green card or a social security card. Some proprietors used the new law to get rid of a lot of staff. My friend worked for one that started cutting the girls' hours here and there. They would come in for a night's work and he would tell them he didn't need them. In the end, she had to go home.

Like bartending, waitressing is an emotionally labor-intensive operation:

I am really beginning to hate waitressing. Going in there night after night and having to smile endlessly to people no matter how they treat me.

Like the flight attendant in Hochschild's study (1983), the waitress must sell her smile as part of her productive labor. Impression management is an integral part of the job, particularly in ethnic restaurants where the waitress is expected to market "her Irishness" to the clientele (see chapter 6 on identity and ethnicity).

The public expressivity of the job masks a private instrumentalism:

Every customer becomes a potential tip and you work on that angle alone. It's as if when they walk into the restaurant, your eyes light up with the dollar bills. The longer I stay here the more into the money I get.

Despite its drawbacks, waitressing is perceived by undocumented women immigrants as more prestigious work than home care, because of the sociability and high earning power attached to the job. But for most of these immigrants, increased restrictions in the marketplace mean that domestic work is the only viable option.

INVISIBLE LABOR: IRISH WOMEN AND DOMESTIC WORK

> Domestic work . . . had the earmark of feudalism. Lacking a separation between work and home, the domestic was, in effect, bonded to her employer and scarcely an aspect of her life escaped scrutiny and regulation. (Steinberg, 1981: 157)

As mentioned earlier, in the postfamine era, Irish women were more likely to emigrate than Irish men. They were also more likely to be unmarried than their Jewish or Italian counterparts when they embarked on the journey to the United States (Diner, 1983: 30–31). Given their limited alternatives, it is not surprising that Irish women went into domestic service in disproportionate numbers. As Steinberg points out, domestic service "provided them with food and lodging and carried them over until such time as they could find either husbands or more desirable employment" (1981: 164).

Given the similar contexts of limited opportunities, the parallels between the experiences of these nineteenth-century immigrants and their contemporary counterparts are striking.

Most of the women who left Ireland for America during the 1980s took positions as nannies or companions in private homes. These jobs were not necessarily their first choice, but often they were the only accessible jobs for those who lacked legal documentation. The restructuring of the American economy in recent years has created a demand for domestic labor. Two factors in particular have contributed to this increasing demand: (1) the increased number of married women in the work force, and (2) the trend toward deinstitutionalized health care.

Since the 1960s, more and more married women have chosen to remain in the work force. In 1987, for the first time, more than half of the new mothers in the United States remained in the labor force. The Census Bureau reported that in that year 50.8 percent of women with children under the age of one were either working or actively seeking employment (*New York Times*, June 20, 1988). In the absence of a national child care policy, most of these women must make their own arrangements to have their children cared for while they are at work. There is thus a high demand, especially among dual-career couples, for domestic or live-in help, which is increasingly being met through immigrant labor. In the past, "high income families exploited the captive labor of women denied sufficient alternative employment opportunities as cheap domestic help" (Hunt and Hunt, 1985: 276). The plentiful supply of domestic labor freed the American middle-class wife to engage in a public life of social and volunteer activities.

Since the early 1970s, it has become increasingly difficult for the average American family to maintain living standards on the income of a single male wage earner. Unstable commodity prices, high inflation, and decline in per capita productivity have lead to a stagnant economy and an increase in economic inequality (Levy, 1987). One consequence is that more and more middle-class women have entered the labor force in order to maintain the comparatively comfortable style of life of their parents' generation. In order to go to work, they must have some back up domestic service, and increasingly, they look to the immigrant labor pool to fill domestic positions.

Immigrant women, many of whom are illegal, are willing to take on work that provides them with some security as well as a possible path toward legalization. Domestic workers may be sponsored by their employer for legal residency. The sponsorship program, however, takes several years, and during this time, the employee is more or less indentured to her sponsoring employer. This increases employer control over the employee. As a full-time participant in the work force, the working mother is assured of reliable back-up support at home. In effect, middle class women "have escaped some of the constraints of sex stratification by using the labor of the class of women most severely limited by this stratification" (Hunt and Hunt, 1985: 276–77).

Domestic help, often live-in, is increasingly an essential accoutrement of the dual-career family.

The restructuring of the American economy in the health care sector has also created a demand for more domestic labor, in particular home companions to aged or convalescent clients. Prominent feminists have argued that under advanced capitalism, some aspects of women's work are becoming increasingly decommodified (Glazer, 1987). Recent changes in the American health care system are changing the social organization of women's work both in the hospital and in the home. Federal regulations that reimburse hospitals on a flat fee basis per operation have encouraged hospitals to pursue an "empty beds" policy by minimizing the patient's postoperative stay in hospital. Patients are redirected either into nursing homes or back to their own homes, where they require constant attention. According to Glazer, releasing people back into the community reverts primary care to the patient's household. Families who are unable to cope hire home companions (at much lower pay than for private nurses) to do the supportive labor, such as cooking meals, emptying bedpans, and administering drugs. The needs of the elderly, especially those who are in poor health, create a further demand for home help labor.

Most Irish women obtain their jobs through two principal sources: (1) newspaper advertisements in Ireland and New York, or (2) immigrant information networks. Female emigrants are more likely than their male counterparts to travel to the United States to a relative or a friend and to have employment secured in advance. This often creates problems as the terms of employment are generally laid down by the prospective employer with little or no room for negotiation. Conditions of employment may deteriorate rapidly with the result that the women almost immediately begin to seek other jobs.

An alternative strategy is to come to New York and then look for a job in the local ethnic newspapers, which run columns of advertisements for nannies and companions each week. These newspapers also act as a good source of information about work for people who are between jobs. Since few women remain in the same job for longer than six months to a year (unless they are being sponsored), there is always a floating population looking for employment or willing to leave their current position if something better comes along. Another important source of jobs is the individual's social network. Often, a sister or friend who has been in the United States for a while will phone or write home with the news of a job in the vicinity. As the nanny population tends to move around quite a bit, and as people come and go from Ireland, jobs open up and information about them is passed around the immigrant community through word of mouth.

A job that is often boring and underpaid is made infinitely better for the incumbent if there is a close friend nearby with whom the trials and tribulations can be shared. Most of the women edit out the less attractive aspects of their work when phoning or writing home. This is a tactical ploy to avoid censure from concerned parents—"If my mother knew I was cleaning out other people's toilet bowls, she would have insisted that I come home"—is a typical refrain. (As long as the reality of life abroad is concealed, the expectations of prospective nannies at home will remain high.) If you can't talk about your work to the people you work for (and live with) or to the family you have left behind, having close friends or relatives around becomes crucially important.

Isolation, Exploitation, and Curtailment of Freedom

A nanny's job is in many respects unattractive. Nannies interviewed for this study report that they are paid less than a minimum wage for a 12-hour day. The job description tends to expand once they take up residence in the household. Apart from infringements of their privacy and loss of personal freedom, some have had their personal belongings confiscated and have been threatened with the immigration authorities if they raise any objections. They find themselves almost completely subordinated to the will of their employers. Their jobs are characterized by isolation, exploitation, lack of personal autonomy, and subsistence living.

One of the biggest difficulties facing a woman who takes up a nanny job in suburban New York is that of personal isolation. The majority of the women have given up jobs in private sector or public sector offices where they mixed with people their own age and where there was a well-developed sense of camaraderie among the workers. They may have been members of sports or social clubs and were used to socializing with their colleagues after work hours. Work-centered sociability is not generally a characteristic of either a nanny or a home companion job. An Irish woman who answers an advertisement in an Irish newspaper may find that she is living on the periphery of suburban New Jersey or New York. Without a car, it is virtually impossible to commute into the city. Given the long shifts worked, even a social visit to the city in the evening would not be feasible:

My first job was upstate New York, and I was really bored. I wanted to go home. I was living in a quiet area, and I had been used to going out all the time. It was a depressing time for me—I had no one to talk to. I just wanted to go home. The only way to survive was to move to New York City.

I was up every morning at 6 A.M. and on duty from 7 A.M. to 7 P.M. It was the middle of winter and I felt very isolated. It snowed a lot and I couldn't go out. For a different kind of person it would have been okay, but it wasn't for me. I'm not a television watcher, and I wasn't used to staying home all week. I was lonesome for some fun and lonesome for my independence.

These women are often cooped up all day with a baby and no social stimulation other than the daytime soap operas on television. For some, television offers a temporary escape from the boredom of work, enabling them to share vicariously in a part of American life to which they have little or no access. For others, their dependency on television for entertainment is a constant source of frustration. They frequently complain that they are vegetating under the circumstances, consequently, getting out for a weekend becomes their sole goal. Work becomes more and more a means to an end, which is defined purely in social/leisure terms. But a subsistence income coupled with long work hours makes it impossible to enjoy a full social life. Social activities are almost exclusively confined to the immigrant bar scene. They have neither the money nor the time to travel or participate in other sport and leisure pursuits. They compare social life in New York unfavorably with social life at home.

An Irish consular official in New York, who looks after immigrants' interests, including illegals, confirms that isolation is a problem primarily associated with the kind of work that Irish women immigrants do:

I think the girls over here have much more of a problem dealing with isolation than the fellas. We have had real problems with homesickness. An 18- or 19-year-old girl comes out here and is stuck in the middle of suburbia, miles away from anything and never seeing another Irish person from one end of the year to the next.

Since the neighborhoods of Irishtown, Gaelside, and Erinvale are at the hub of immigrant social and community activity, home help jobs in the city tend to be at a premium. Most women will try to move from suburbia into the city at the earliest opportunity. The escape from suburbia is an escape from isolation. It is much easier to meet other nannies in a high-rise building or a built-up neighborhood. They meet in the lobbies, along the streets, and in the parks. Friendships are cultivated—not only with Irish nannies but with American women and other foreigners—and a network is formed. Information about jobs and immigration matters, news from home, forthcoming social events, and public meetings are publicized through this network. It constitutes a bulwark against isolation.

Home companions are often more isolated than nannies because they must care for elderly people in poor health. They wash, dress, feed, and administer drugs to their charges, as well as run errands and other tasks required by the employer. The difficulty of working with the elderly is compounded by the lack of mobility. Unlike the nannies, there are no social meetings in the park to offset the isolation on the job. Nannies can visit in each other's homes when they take their charges there on play dates, or they can congregate in the park in the afternoon. They can create a center of sociability because the children act as a point of contact. But those who work with the elderly are much more privatized and thus report higher levels of stress on the job.

Exploitation in the domestic sector includes long hours, poor remuneration, tight control, and surveillance at work. As illegal immigrants, the women find that they have little control over the terms of employment and conditions of work. The hours of work are long—a 7 A.M. to 7 P.M. shift is not uncommon—and may be extended arbitrarily at the behest of the employer. Comments like these are typical:

I was only supposed to babysit on a Friday or Saturday night. But if she knew I was staying in, she would go out for dinner, even though theoretically I had every night off. They take you for granted.

I was supposed to work 8 A.M. to 6 P.M., but often they mightn't come home until after 8 P.M. She would never say anything if she came home late. It was expected that I would stay on.

Most nannies get a nominal couple of hours free in the afternoon, while their charges are sleeping. However, unless one of the parents is home, the nanny is still ultimately responsible for the welfare of the children. As long as the nanny is around the house, the parents feel they can come and go as they please. Free time is hard to delineate in this kind of job. The presence of the nanny in the home restricts her ability to do as she pleases and expands the carefree time of her employers. She is frequently entrusted with the care of the children during the evenings, even though evenings are supposed to be time off. Her "free time" is not her own:

Even if you are not working every minute, your time is not your own. Once you are in the house, you are still responsible all the time for the kids.

The job description tends to expand as soon as the nanny takes up residence in the household. Although the primary task is to take care of the children, with very few exceptions, the nannies are also expected to help out with cooking, cleaning, laundering, and shopping:

They take you for granted. You do something once and they expect you to do it all the time. You are employed to care for the children but you end up doing all this extra work.

Objections to taking on extra work may be met with a veiled threat to report the indignant employee to the immigration authorities. In many cases, the wife is either a full-time or part-time homemaker, so there is constant surveillance of the work done:

In the morning I had to get the kids up and dressed and fed and then take them to the bus. There would be trouble if I hadn't cleaned up the breakfast things before leaving. I was expected to take care of three children, scrub floors, cook, and clean for $130 per week.

She was terribly fastidious. She saw me making scrambled eggs in a pot one day and said "don't you know that scrambled eggs are made in a pan?" Another time she told me that her husband didn't like the butter scooped out crookedly but should be scooped in a straight line.

Those who work as home companions, like nannies, find that from the outset they too are locked into a subordinate role with the employer or his/her family. The loss of control over the direction of their own lives adds to the stress created on the job. The ground rules for the employment relationship are generally drawn up in advance by the employer without prior consultation with the employee:

Although I am a qualified nurse, my employer never treated me as such. In fact, he treated me as a child, as if I was too young to take on any responsibility. He wanted me to sign a contract to stay in the job for a year and a half, during which time he would sponsor me. It annoyed me the way he tried to take responsibility for my life, without adequately consulting me.

In many respects, dealing with an elderly patient is considerably more stressful than dealing with small children. With no preparation for this sort of demanding work, home companions can become ill from the physical and mental exertion of their work. Marie's first job was as a live-in with a woman in her seventies who had just been released from a psychiatric hospital:

She was totally batty. She would go for walks every day and I would have to follow her at a discreet distance. I had to constantly watch her as she would do crazy things. She had me washing windows, hoovering, looking for dirt where there wasn't any. I had an hour and a half free each evening, and I would go for a walk through the park and cry solidly. On my one night off—Sunday—I would go down to Irishtown and get plastered. It was my only way of dealing with it. After a while I figured that one of us was headed for a mental breakdown, and she was more likely to survive since she had more experience! So I left.

In her next job, Marie lived out but again cared for a woman in her mid-seventies suffering from Alzheimer's disease. She found the work both stressful and emotionally draining. Interestingly, none of this was ever communicated to her family at home. Several others told stories of caring for elderly clients who were demanding and abusive. Kate took over a job as home companion from a contact who had gone back to Ireland. She says her 89-year-old charge was extremely difficult:

She used to scream at me and humiliate me in public. I worked a 10-hour day from 9 A.M. to 7 P.M. five days a week. If I as much as slipped outside for a minute to smoke a cigarette she would scream at me. No matter how carefully I prepared her oatmeal in the morning she complained that there were lumps in it. I used to be a complete wreck when I got home in the evenings.

Kate eventually left that job after she developed swelling in her limbs, which her doctor diagnosed as a stress-related reaction to her work.

As with child minding work, there is little scope for exercising personal autonomy in a home companion job. Surveillance is constant. Once a person accepts a position as a nanny or companion in a private home, her personal freedom is restricted, and many women find that their lives are circumscribed to a greater degree than they were previously. Home and work are located in the same place, so there is tremendous difficulty "getting away" from the job. Her social life becomes the business of her employer who may monitor her comings and goings, arguing that she needs a "good night's sleep" in order to perform her duties properly.

It was hard for me to live in. I was so used to living away from home, that I found it even worse living in than living at home. I took a job in a bar two nights a week and the family started complaining about me coming in late. They don't really approve of you going out the night before if you have work the following day. Some families like to rule your life. "Are you going out *again* tonight?" they'll say.

Ailish also found that her employer took more than a passing interest in her social life:

She was a bit of a snob really. She didn't like when I used to go off to the Bronx for the weekend. She didn't think it was nice, and she didn't approve of me traveling on the subway.

Since workplace and home are not separate, the loss of one entails the loss of the other. If the women question the authority of their employers, they find that they not only lose a job but also a home, often without notice. Several nannies spoke of rows with their employers which ended with them being literally put on the street:

After the row it was agreed that it would be best if I left. I dropped around to my friend to cool off but when I got home at 11:30 P.M., my suitcases were packed and in the hall. They hadn't even paid me my week's wages and they obviously didn't care what happened to me.

Returning home after a weekend off I found my bags packed in the hallway. They [the employers] had been through my luggage and read a letter I had been writing home, in which I had described the children as spoilt and demanding. I was allowed to make one phone call, and then I was thrown on the street.

As a guest in someone else's home, the nanny or companion is placed in the ambiguous position of being an insider who has the status of an outsider. The women are often welcomed into the home, but both sides are aware of the tenuous legal situation. An employer may threaten to report an employee to the Immigration Service should she decide to leave. This makes for an absence of trust in the employer/employee relationship. As a precautionary measure, most nannies give as little information as possible to their employer. They may keep their personal documents and effects at a friend's home and have their mail sent to another address. This makes a speedy exit considerably easier.

I was afraid that they [the employer] might get nasty, so I had to leave very carefully. The main thing is to give them as little information as possible about yourself because you don't know whether or not they will turn on you. Don't get involved, don't give any details. The less they know the better.

Alone and totally dependent on a family for shelter and work, it is difficult to protest about pay and conditions. Those who are most successful in negotiating a better deal for themselves in the workplace are the women who live out. By living out, they are in a stronger bargaining position for delineating the terms and conditions of employment. They usually share an apartment with several other women and commute to their jobs. The separation of home and workplace means that the employer possesses less of the employee, and the job is moved onto a more professional, contractual basis. The optimal situation is for the woman to control the price of her own labor, by charging the employer a rate per hour, which ensures payment for all overtime worked. But this kind of street-wise knowledge comes only with experience. As one immigrant said:

The parents walk all over you if they can. Even the nicest people will—they won't pay you a decent wage. You get better at sticking up for yourself with experience.

The longer the stay in New York, the more likely it is that conditions of employment will improve, even in the short term. However, those who are situated at some distance from the city—outside the immigrant network—and who are in live-in employment will have greater difficulty improving their position. Urban-based nannies will develop contacts through their own network and through the larger immigrant network of which they form a part. Through these contacts, they will be directed toward better-paying jobs. The more experience they develop on the job, the greater their confidence and the more likely they are to negotiate a better deal for themselves. Even so, pay levels in private home care remain considerably lower than those in the restaurant and construction sectors.

Most of the women who work as nannies find that their income (which usually falls within the range of $100 to $300 per week depending on whether they live in or out) provides them with little more than a subsistence living. Unless they take on extra work, they cannot hope to save money. Thus, one finds that nannies and home companions take on a variety of extra work in order to supplement their meager income. Two or three and even four jobs are not uncommon.

At the moment I am working four jobs. I work housekeeping 12 to 6 P.M. five days a week, I do house cleaning in the mornings, bar work several evenings a week, and I waitress all day Sunday. It's all to save money so that I can get on a computer course and then look for a job with a company who can sponsor me for a green card.

I only work three days a week with my family. They can't afford to pay me for anymore. They got me a job with another family for the other two days and that supplements my income. I also do two other jobs—it's all a bit much really. I babysit every Monday night, and on Saturday morning, I do a cleaning job.

Three nights a week, I look after a woman who is 106 years old. It is very isolating work. Two days a week I waitress downtown, and on the weekend, I go on call with an agency for home companions.

Taking on extra work restricts free time and routinizes further the nanny's or home companion's working life. It is in this respect that "women's work" contrasts most starkly with "men's work." A construction worker has his day's work finished by mid-afternoon and generally has his weekends free. He earns up to twice what a woman worker earns in half the time. Thus, he has more money to spend and more leisure time in which to spend it. Nannies and home companions, in contrast, have much less money and much less leisure time available to them. This indicates a grave inequality in the position of men and women in the immigrant work force. Irish women must take on at least two jobs to earn an income comparable with that of Irish men.

Many of these women would have held relatively good positions as white-collar workers in Ireland. Their secretarial skills go unused and the social aspects of their working lives are considerably curtailed. Whatever independence they enjoyed as single women in Ireland is transformed into dependency when they take up positions in private homes in New York. In this respect, their quality of life is seriously diminished. The advances that women have made relative to men in the Irish economy are almost totally reversed through illegal immigration. Like the men, they are unable to capitalize on their skills or take advantage of the opportunities in New York. But unlike the men, their earnings can in no way assuage the frustration of restricted mobility. Two former white-collar workers explain their frustration:

I can't get a decent job or earn decent money. I would love to have more stimulating work because I feel as if I am brain dead. I could not go back to my previous job now. My skills are gone and it bothers me. I am not making money, and what money I do make is going out on bills.

I get depressed when I compare the skilled computer work I did at home with the house cleaning I do here. The thing is that you can be better off here but you have to work for it.

Given the precariousness of their work situation, few women have managed to formulate long-term objectives. Many women accept their downward mobility because they see it as a temporary state. In the event of legalization, through an amnesty, visa lottery or a sponsorship program, they hope to re-employ their existing skills or learn new ones. In the meantime, they are prepared to put up with the drudgery of housework and the monotony of looking after other people's families, whether they are children or the elderly.

SUMMARY

Given that Irish illegal immigrants are afforded no constitutional protection in the United States and that they are increasingly concentrated in the informal sectors of the economy, their powerlessness is most acute. Only a small minority continue to successfully penetrate the formal economy, where wages and benefits are considerably better. One major effect of the Immigration Reform and Control Act (1986) has been to extend the apparatus of regulation through the I–9 identification form into small businesses, which previously were unconcerned about the status of their employees. Consequently, many illegal immigrants have been pushed further underground.

It is the tradition of patronage and brokerage within the Irish ethnic community that eases the newly arrived immigrant's passage into employment. Clientelistic controls are exercised over Irish illegals in the ethnic enclaves of the labor market, particularly in the construction sector and in the restaurant/bar trade. In extreme cases, an almost feudalist control is exercised over young Irish women working as live-in nannies or home companions. Illegality forces young men and women into unskilled work, which they are willing to do at least in the short term, in the hope that it will provide them with a path toward legality. Downward mobility, however, undermines their sense of self-esteem. For Irish nannies, long hours and little stimulation lead to lethargy, which is difficult to overcome. Difficult and often dangerous work compounds the precarious work life of the construction worker, who is more often than not working under an assumed name. Not only does he run the risk of being apprehended for working illegally, but he may also face the more serious charge of falsifying documentation. Workers in the restaurant and bar trade must also manufacture identities for themselves—their emotions must be packaged and sold as part of the labor commodity. This results in a high degree of alienation from the job.

In the absence of an alternative accessible opportunity structure, Irish nannies (like their predecessors) are prepared to do jobs that the indigenous work force are no longer willing to do. Work becomes a means to an end, and like construction workers and those in the restaurant and bar trade, they turn increasingly to leisure time to create meaning in their lives. In this regard, communal activity and participation in a shared culture helps to counteract the negative effects of illegality in the informal labor market.

Chapter 5 _____

Immigrant Culture and Community Formation

Given the number of hours and amount of energy expended at work, it is not surprising that these Irish immigrants soon learn to value their leisure time. Work is primarily viewed as a means to an end, while leisure time constitutes an end in itself. Leisure time activities, rather than work, provide the immigrant with a sense of gratification. This is particularly the case for immigrants whose work lives are highly privatized (nannies, home companions). It is primarily through their leisure time activities that they become integrated members of the Irish community.

A HOME AWAY FROM HOME: THE IRISH BAR

In common with other immigrant groups, the Irish have created their own community meeting places, which are functionally adapted to cater to the needs of that community. These meeting places frequently provide a link to the customs, practices, and social institutions of the old country. The Irish bar serves the same functions for Irish immigrants as the bodega, the cassito, the social club, and the coffee house do for other immigrant groups. It is the focal point of social interaction and community coalescence. It serves as a place for "doing business" and as "a home from home."

For immigrants recently arrived from Ireland, the Irish bar is a sociable and accessible point of entry into the immigrant community. Fallows argues that the bar played a crucial role in the adjustment of earlier generations of Irish immigrants: "Here in the saloon were the camaraderie and consolation for the workers, a forum for political and social discourse for the concerned and the calculating, and a club-like atmosphere for those who were unlikely to join more formal organizations" (1979: 51).

Stivers documented the role of the Irish bar in the eighteenth and nineteenth centuries as a focal point of the immigrant community. The pub functioned as a hiring hall, a center for commerce, and a recreation center, as well as a newsstand for the dissemination of oral and written news (1976: 23). Little seems to have changed in the intervening years. For recent arrivals from Ireland, the Irish bar remains almost the only meeting place serving recreational and business purposes. The Irish bars serve an important social function as centers of sociability and live entertainment. But more importantly, they serve a community function—it is through the various services offered by the bars and the activities that take place there that a sense of community is fostered and preserved. Since they serve as community centers as well as centers of sociability, they tend to define the parameters of social and cultural life.

Recent immigrants, constrained by their lack of documentation, are generally excluded from formal institutions and organizations, membership of which may call into question their legal status. Since they are "out of status" they are *outsiders*, unable to fully integrate into the society in which they live. Consequently, the majority retreat into the Irish ethnic community where they enjoy the status of *insiders*. The community tends to crystallize around the bars, which provide the physical space to congregate and serve as the focal point for a variety of activities. This is recognized by immigrant action groups such as the IIRM who regularly place leaflets and posters in the bars in Queens and the Bronx to announce forthcoming events. Some of the IIRM leaders were affronted when, on one occasion, a government minister visiting New York declined an invitation to come and meet recent Irish immigrants in the neighborhood bars. They felt that he was snubbing the constituency whose needs he was seeking to address.

The geographic location of Irish bars is important. They tend to be located along the main thoroughfare or arterial routes that run through the older Irish neighborhoods in the Bronx and Queens. This means that they are accessible to all of those living in the immediate neighborhood and are generally only a bus or cab ride away from those living in the outer suburbs. The new Irish tend to settle in three neighborhoods, two of which are located in the Bronx and one in Queens (for description of research site, see chapter 2).

Since the arrival of the new wave of immigrants in the mid–1980s, the Irish bar in New York has undergone something of a revival. Dank and seedy bars have been refurbished, and new bars have opened to cater to the growing Irish population. Between 1985 and 1990, for example, at least five new bars opened their doors in the Irishtown neighborhood. The decor of the most popular bars increasingly reflects the taste of a younger, more urbane clientele. For example, I first visited the Welcome Inn (not the actual name) in Irishtown in the spring of 1986. This is how I described the bar then:

On the left when you enter is an old-fashioned wooden bar, lined with high stools. On the right are some scattered tables, covered with bright colored table cloths, with candles atop. There is a cigarette machine in one corner and a juke box in the other. The latter offers a selection of contemporary British and American rock music. The walls are covered with distinctly Irish memorabilia—the kind of artifacts you are likely to see displayed in a small country pub in Ireland. The proclamation of the Republic of Ireland is framed on one wall and surrounded by mounted pictures of the seven leaders of the 1916 Rebellion. On another wall hangs a large map of Ireland and a framed photograph of Barry McGuigan, the (former) Irish world boxing champion. In addition, the walls are speckled with framed photo montages of the clientele, variously posed with some of the Welcome Inn bartenders. You get the impression that you have trespassed into somebody's private living room.

I returned to the Welcome Inn in January 1988 and found the bar utterly changed. The wooden fixtures had been replaced by chrome and mirror, the walls were stark and painted gleaming white. The juke box had been equipped with a video screen, and it was playing rock music loudly and constantly. The image is high tech rather than homely. It now more closely resembled one of the formula disco bars that have mushroomed in Dublin and other Irish cities in recent years. Indeed, the Welcome Inn, in common with many city-based bars in Ireland, bears the hallmarks of Americanization. The change in the Welcome Inn is reflected in many other Irish bars, where traditional Irish music and dancing is replaced by rock bands and disco on weekend nights. Some bars, however, retain the traditional ethos, but the clientele they attract is noticeably older and from a rural, rather than urban, background.

The bars are generally owned and managed by first-generation immigrants who came to the United States in the post-World War II era. They retain a fierce loyalty to their county of origin. Thus, the bars are often distinguished from each other in terms of their county or regional identity, and they attract a clientele on that basis. When I was leaving Irishtown, one of the most popular and successful bars was Molly Malone's (not the actual name)—a "Dublin" pub, which opened in early 1988. This bar was different in that the owners—two husband and wife teams—were part of the new wave of immigrants, and many of the clientele had known them when they worked in the bar trade in Dublin. Both of the men in the partnership had also "served their time" in big Manhattan bars. From the start, they attracted a Dublin crowd, although as the reputation of the bar grew, the clientele became more diverse. One of the attractions was live music every night of the week, with a particularly popular rock line up on weekend nights.

THE CENTRALITY OF THE BAR TO IRISH IMMIGRANT CULTURE

Bars are popular because they are accessible, they offer companionship and intimacy, and they are a relatively cheap form of entertainment. They are a safe haven where the psychological barriers (necessary for negotiating the world of work) can be dismantled and where conversation, humor, and emotion can be given free rein. As one immigrant activist put it:

If you have been working all day in construction or looking after someone else's children, you feel very dehumanized. You get off work, go into an Irish bar where there are Irish accents and a sense of home. People feel they belong just like at home. That sense of belonging is heightened here because the outside world is more alienating, and the bar offers the possibility of establishing a sense of identity.

The busiest nights for the Irish bars are the weekends. Most will have regular customers during the week, but the numbers will be greatly augmented on Friday and Saturday nights. Often people have to queue outside in order to get in to one of the more popular bars. Most of the immigrants will favor one bar over the others. This is regarded as a "local." In Ireland, people use this term to designate the bar where they go to meet friends and acquaintances on a regular basis. Regular patrons will enter a bar and make their way to the counter, where there is almost always a friendly exchange (first-name terms) with the bartender. This greeting ritual is confirmation that this bar is indeed the patron's "local." The mutual acknowledgement by the bartender and the patron is part of Irish pub culture. It also highlights the social nature of the visit to the bar for these young people. Apart from greeting people from behind the bar, the bartender or proprietor will emerge at various stages during the night to collect empty glasses. He uses this time to stop and chat to people, again reinforcing the friendliness and sociability of the bar. Bartenders who are perceived as "uppity" and who don't make the effort to engage their clientele in conversation soon find that their bar is dropped in favor of another.

Sherri Cavan in her study of bars in the San Francisco area notes that the bar counter typically serves as the focal point of the public drinking place: "It is here at any given time the maximum concentration of patrons will be found" (1966: 95). My observations in the Irish bars corroborate her finding. People come to the bar in groups or arrive alone, having arranged to meet people there. There is almost always a preponderance of men crowded around the bar counter, while in the seating area, the distribution of men and women tends to be more or less equal. Even when there is entertainment in the bar, it is usually located at the back of the room and directed at those in the main seated area. A crowd (generally male) remains standing around the bar engaged in loud and often raucous conversation. The music and musicians are merely a backdrop.

The bar functions first and foremost as a place to socialize with other Irish people. The most common opening line is "Where are you from?"—a question that may be asked legitimately of any person in the bar, attesting to its distinctively Irish and immigrant character.

Most of those with whom I spoke regretted their absence from important events in the lives of their families and friends at home. They missed weddings and christenings and birthday and anniversary celebrations. A concerted attempt is made to celebrate these events when they occur in the immigrant community, and often, these kinds of celebrations are held in the bars.

One Sunday afternoon I arranged to meet one of my informants in a local bar. We had thought it would be quiet and conducive to an interview, but it turned out otherwise:

A christening party was in progress, and a hot food bar had been set up in the center of the seated area of the bar. Stylishly attired couples sat around drinking and chatting, while children played around the tables and chairs. The atmosphere was warm and familial as the owners of the bar mingled easily with the guests. There was some food left over and one of the owners prepared plates and passed them around to those of us sitting at the bar.

Twenty-first birthday parties—an important rite of passage in Ireland—are celebrated in the bar and provide another occasion to gather family and friends around. Wedding parties often spill over into the bars, which are also the main venues for "wakes in reverse."

In the course of my research I spent a period of time with a group of construction workers who worked night shifts. Perhaps because of their unusual hours and the nature of the work (mainly underground), they had developed a strong sense of camaraderie. They shared houses and apartments and tended to socialize together particularly on weekends. When one of the group celebrated his twenty-first birthday, I was invited to the party and recorded the following field note:

I arrived around 4 P.M., and the bar was already fairly crowded with people. The band was belting out traditional ballads. Most of Joe's construction workmates were there. Some had come alone, others had brought wives/girlfriends, as well as brothers and sisters, some of whom had recently arrived over from Ireland. Everyone was standing around drinking and talking in little groups. Most people were suffering from hangovers because they had been at parties the night before for Peter and Bridie, a couple who are due to marry next weekend. The bar provided buffet food for the party, and a couple of the girls brought out an ice cream cake. "Happy Birthday" was sung and the candles blown out. The cake began to melt in the heat, while the lads gave Joe the bumps. Then it was back to drinking, which continued until late into the night.

Peter and Bridie's wedding took place the following weekend, and the reception was held at a hotel in Queens. Once again, all of the construction crew were there with partners, neatly groomed for the occasion. The dancing went on until midnight at which point the bridegroom invited everybody to join him in The Shillealagh bar, his local bar a few blocks away. Once the wedding party were ensconced there, the festivities could be extended indefinitely. I later learned that apart from a trip to a nearby apartment for a few hours sleep, about 10 of the revelers continued drinking in the bar throughout the following day and night.

A farewell party for Peter and Bridie, who were returning to Ireland, was held in yet another bar favored by the construction crew. Two girlfriends (of crew members) had arranged the party but were worried about its success because most of the men worked nights. As it turned out, most of them took the night off. A $20 contribution was collected from each person to defray the expense of hiring a musician for the night. While the women sat at the bar, scrutinizing the wedding photographs, the men stood around in little knots as usual, with one or two of them making overtures toward some of the women present. One informant described one such farewell party as "a wake in reverse"—an ironic play on the Irish tradition of holding a wake for prospective emigrants, who knew they had little chance of seeing their families again. The wake in reverse marks the immigrant community's loss. The intense sociability and communal lifestyle that is characteristic of the illegal Irish in New York could not be replicated at home. Consequently, the departure of individual members of the community is acknowledged through an appropriate social event. There is little expectation that the individual will be seen again and certainly never in the same intensely intimate circumstances.

Apart from the social activities associated with the Irish bars, many of them also sponsor soccer teams who compete against each other in a local league. The teams tend to be representative of a particular bar's regular clientele. For example, a Dublin bar will field a Dublin team and a Meath bar will field a Meath team. Apart from playing against each other, the players also compete in an ethnic league against Czech, Spanish, Greek, and Russian teams. Unlike Gaelic football and hurling, soccer is an international sport, and the soccer league is one of the few interethnic activities in which Irish immigrants engage. The different teams, however, do not socialize together away from the football field. Since soccer is not controlled by the GAA, it is not a part of the Irish-American jobs network. Hence, soccer is played primarily for leisure and not for livelihood. Within the New York-based Irish community, soccer is played almost exclusively by recent (male) immigrants from urban centers in Ireland.

HOME TERRITORIALITY AND LOCALISM

Cavan, in her study of San Francisco bars, developed a typology that included the category of home territory bars: "bars used not as a public place, but rather as though they were the private retreat for some special group" (1966: 205). The territoriality associated with bar space may be accentuated when the clientele is almost all immigrants. Cavan points out, for example, that when the patrons share one or more features of their social identity, a common bond is formed, which provides a basis for defining "who are welcome in the establishment and who are not" (1966: 206). In the case of the Irish bars, the patrons are bonded first and foremost through their common nationality, which is explicit, and through their illegal status, which is implicitly assumed. Thus, there is an unwillingness to admit outsiders, and incursions by outsiders may elicit hostile responses. One informant recalled the hostile reaction that he and his friends received when they entered a bar in Irishtown:

One night a few friends of mine came out to Irishtown for a drink. The company included a couple of Dublin guys, a Wexford guy, and a couple of Hispanics and Taiwanese guys with whom I work. We were in the . . . (bar) for a few minutes when a group of Tyrone guys came over. "This is our bar," they said, "and we don't want any fucking spicks in here." We tried to play the incident down and moved to another bar across the street. We were in the door two minutes when we got hassled again, this time by a crowd from Monaghan. "What's that Chinese prick doing in here?" they shouted from the corner. We left.

Outsiders, however, may be admitted to the bar if they are there as the guest of regulars and can be vouched for. For example, one evening I observed a group of men drinking at the bar. A couple entered the bar and engaged one of the group in conversation. The latter turned to his companions and introduced them as cousins from England who were staying with him until they got fixed up. The man doing the introductions negated his companions' nationality by introducing them as family, legitimizing their presence in the bar. Outsiders who enter the bar without a legitimate contact run the risk of exclusion. In the course of the field work, I came across several instances in which English people who entered Irish bars (without an insider connection to vouch for them) became targets of verbal abuse. In some cases, bartenders refused to serve them.

British-born Irish immigrants occupy a somewhat ambiguous position. Although they are Irish and undocumented like everybody else, they speak with English accents. They are involved in an ongoing process of establishing their identity. Kate, for example, was raised in England until she was 11 years old when her family moved back to County Clare, Ireland. When she is asked where she is from, she says County Clare but immediately adds that she was born in England—thus, she has an explanation for her English accent. Since her parents are Irish, she feels that this qualifies her apparent English status.

This incident, and similar ones which are recorded, suggest that a person's ethnic or national identity is at issue only in so far as they are *perceived* to be different by others. If the apparent outsider can explain that ethnically he or she is an insider, then he or she is ensured acceptance into the community.

Territoriality is also expressed in the self-segregation that occurs within the immigrant community. According to Bonacich, sojourner communities are often riddled with division and conflict, based on regional, linguistic, political, or religious differences found in the homeland (1973: 586). However, in relation to the host society, these differences fade before an overriding "national" unity. The undocumented Irish constitute a unified group in terms of their circumscribed existence within the host society. In the face of a threat from outside (for example, encroachment by a law enforcement agency), the undocumented Irish quickly close ranks. This cohesiveness, however, does not preclude a degree of internal fragmentation that reflects the regional, local, and urban/rural cleavages in Irish society. Indeed, localism together with clientelism forms an integral part of Irish political culture (Chubb, 1970). Not surprisingly, these cleavages are reproduced within the immigrant Irish community in New York.

County and regional affiliations, which are so crucial as an entrée to the labor market, define the immigrant's social world. Irish illegals frequently redefine themselves into constituent regional groups, underlining the local orientation of the community. For example, the "Connies" is the colloquialism for designating people from Connemara, and the "Norries" is the colloquial expression for those who have emigrated from the North. The few institutions serving the illegal Irish community tend to reinforce those internal divisions. Most of the Irish bars in Gaelside, Erinvale, and Irishtown are noted for their allegiance to particular counties, generally the proprietor's county of origin or ancestry. Bars with a high county or regional profile attract selective crowds on the basis of place of origin. For example, on several occasions it was pointed out to me that one of the bars in Irishtown was a "Connie" bar—that is, the clientele was made up of construction workers from the west of Ireland. Outsiders—in this case, Irish people from other regions—were unwelcome. Similarly, one of the bars in Gaelside was well known as a "Norrie" bar and catered exclusively to a Northern Irish crowd. These bars were described as very "clannish"—a word favored by the immigrants for designating those who mix exclusively with people from the same county or region. People from the western and southern counties are generally regarded as the most clannish of all. The territorial clannishness in the bars has implications for boundary maintenance in the immigrant community and is discussed more fully in chapter 6.

THE IRISH BAR AND COMMUNITY FORMATION

Through its various functions, the Irish bar provides its clientele with a sense of belonging to a community however transitory and internally divided that community may be. In the bar, information is dispensed on jobs and accommodations; pay checks are cashed; funds are raised for those who are ill, injured, or bereaved; and links are maintained with home.

Job and Accommodation Information

In the absence of a formal infrastructure for helping new immigrants, the Irish bars have acted as clearing houses for information on jobs and accommodation. One immigrant recalls his early days in New York and the importance of the bar in this respect:

One beer in the bar after work is a great means of contact. You could get information about jobs, apartments, and so on. There is a real communications network in the bars. You need a lot of contacts so you need to know a lot of people, and you can do that through the bar. It gives you access to the community, and to new friends.

Those immigrants who have neither relatives nor friends in the city invariably gravitate to the Irish bars. Information about jobs is always circulating in the bar, with the bartender often acting as the crucial conduit. Prospective employers and employees make their needs known to him, and he, in turn, disseminates that information among the clientele. In addition, bartenders tend to visit each other's bars during time off. They are generous in their tipping—a ritual that amounts to an acknowledgment of each other's valued custom. These informal visits allow the bartenders to keep abreast of employment and accommodation information with the community.

As one bartender explained, he automatically identifies with the Irish and will endeavor to help them out. However, his degree of commitment depends on the local profile of the individual concerned:

When I worked in the bars, guys were always coming in to see if there was any work going. If there was any inkling of a job in the grapevine, I would direct them there. It doesn't matter what county they were from, but if they happened to be from the same county, I would make a greater effort. And if the person knew someone that I knew at home, then I would try to help them even more by keeping in touch in case anything came up.

The clientele in the bars talk directly to each other, and many deals are struck and information passed on without the intervention of a third party. Several of the interviewees found that the bars could be a useful place for making contacts:

I landed at JFK and I didn't know a soul. I went into Manhattan to a bar. I met a guy who told me there was work in Jersey City, so I ended up working there.

Peadar from the South West secured a superintendent's job in a building on the Upper West Side of Manhattan through a casual encounter in a bar:

I got chatting to a man from Clare who asked if I knew anyone who was interested in a super's job on 60th Street and Broadway. He himself was moving out to a building nearby. I went for the job the next day and got it, and I have been there ever since.

I met Peadar in a local bar in Irishtown. Although he now lives and works in Manhattan, he still commutes out to Queens to socialize with friends. Social life in the city holds little attraction for him. Although there are many Irish bars in Manhattan, they tend to attract a heterogeneous clientele in terms of both class and ethnic profile. For illegal immigrants, they are not nearly as homely as the bars in the ethnic neighborhoods.

David finally found a job through a contact in a bar after exhausting all his other leads:

I used up every contact name I had, and nothing was doing. I was trying to get into the steel fitters union but it was a closed shop. I really started to feel the pinch. Although I had come out with $2,500, I was down to under $1,000. I felt that there was work out there, I just couldn't tap into it. Finally, I went up to (a bar) in the Bronx to suss out a casual contact. It was a guy who was looking for people in pipe fitting. He told me to report to the site boss the following Monday morning.

Some contractors actually solicit immigrants in the bars. These brokers are well placed to strike a hard bargain over the price of the labor because they know that immigrants seeking work in the bar either have no instrumental contacts or have exhausted whatever ones they had. An Irish-American academic who used to frequent a popular bar owned by a friend of his in Irishtown told me:

There were always people in and out making a deal, fixing people up with jobs, and so on. The archetypal broker was (the owner's) cousin who did all his wheeling and dealing in the bar. For example, renovations in the bar were done with cheap labor— illegals paid less than the union rate, no papers, no questions asked.

Information about accommodation is passed along the same grapevine. Bartenders have a store of information on people who are seeking accommodation and people who are looking for tenants or roommates. Thus, they can act as facilitators to a mutually beneficial agreement. As is the case with jobs, information about accommodation is passed around the bar clientele by word of mouth. Those in need of emergency accommodation turn to their local subgroup within the bar clientele. A newly arrived immigrant who is simply looking for a stop gap or short-term option—a bed for a few nights in order to get on his or her feet—generally relies on "someone from home" whom he or she seeks out in the bar clientele. This means that new arrivals without contacts will automatically gravitate toward their own county/regional bars. A personal contact is crucial as, generally, the newly arrived immigrant's credentials would have to be substantiated in some way.

When Terry came over, a contact that was supposed to meet him at the airport never showed. After waiting around for five hours, he took a bus into Manhattan:

I looked up the subway and took a train to the Bronx and went into a couple of bars. I met someone from home, who gave me the phone number of someone else from home who was able to put me up for a couple of weeks. Without the bar network, I wouldn't have had anywhere to go.

On his first trip to the Bronx, Bobby met two people he had known at home. As he describes it:

One was staying in Queens and was already under a compliment where he was staying. The other had a one-bedroom apartment but there was already six people staying there. Still, he said "If you're stuck, we won't leave you on the street."

There is a sense of loyalty to someone from home that overrides all other considerations. As it turned out, Bobby stayed in the overcrowded apartment for a week until he was able to find his own place. Interestingly, when Bobby was hospitalized after a serious car crash more than a year later, this friend was the only one who visited him regularly. "Friends" he had made during the preceding year in New York disappeared.

Check-Cashing Service

Several of the more popular bars operate check-cashing facilities for their customers. While some people manage to open bank accounts (by producing the required documentation or by opening a business account), many are totally dependent on a sympathetic bar proprietor who is willing to exchange the checks for cash. While there is no charge for the service, there is an expectation that the customer will spend some of his earnings in that bar on a regular basis. This reinforces the clientelistic relations between established members of the Irish-American community and the new immigrants because the proprietor knows that the customer has little chance of cashing his or her check elsewhere.

The check-cashing service usually takes place on Friday evening. In one of the most popular bars in Irishtown, for example, a small wooden booth has been erected in the back of the bar, which provides a modicum of privacy to the customer. One of the staff sits in the booth, and the construction workers stand in a line that extends the length of the bar. The bar is always packed by 6 P.M. on Friday evening, and the atmosphere is festive. It is not necessary to arrive when the booth is in operation in order to get cash, as I found out one night when I accompanied an informant to the bar:

We arrived about 11 P.M. and Conor went to the back of the bar and spoke with one of the bartenders on first-name terms. Then he disappeared into an adjacent storeroom. About 15 minutes later, he emerged with the cash and proceeded to buy a couple of drinks.

A proprietor may decide to provide a service for a select group of immigrants, usually a group whom he knows and trusts. One of the crew of underground construction workers referred to above, explains:

R. B. is an Irish American who knows our gang. One of the wives (of the workers) bartends and does his books for him. We have this system where everybody leaves their checks with him on Wednesday night or Thursday morning, and we pick up the cash on Friday morning. There is no charge, we just pick up our envelopes that morning.

Most of the group are regular customers, and some of their parties and socials are held there. The service rendered by the proprietor is generously reciprocated. When this unwritten norm of reciprocity is breached by the customer, the service may be withdrawn. On one occasion, I went to interview an informant at his local bar. He was engaged in conversation with two fellow countrymen when I arrived, but shortly afterwards they left. Pat looked at the bar where they had been sitting and shook his head:

Those two lads came in here to get their checks cashed because they said (a nearby bar) wouldn't do it for them. Their checks were cashed here but they didn't leave a tip. No wonder the (bar) got fed up with them. I leave a tip every time I am in here. That way when I come in to cash my check I can just drink a soda and that's fine. You have to remember what goes around, comes around.

Occasionally, problems arise with the system, when checks are not honored by the banks on which they are drawn. This is a risk that the proprietors of the bars offering this service take, but it must be balanced against the additional income that the service attracts. Customers tend to spend more and tip more generously in the bars that cash their checks.

Fundraising

In the absence of a formal welfare structure, people in need must rely on the generosity of their friends within the immigrant community. Fundraisers are generally organized in the bars, with musicians donating their services free for the evening's entertainment. Fundraisers are advertised in the ethnic newspapers. To encourage local support, the county or place of origin of the person in need (and that of the spouse if married) is usually included in the appeal. Fundraisers are held primarily for people who have become incapacitated—either through illness or injury. Fundraisers are also held to cover the costs of funeral arrangements for immigrants who die in New York. In the event of a death, the remains are normally flown home to Ireland for burial. This is costly, and in most cases, it is members of the immigrant community who donate the necessary funds.

Link with Home

The bars offer the immigrants their closest link with home. Many of them import Irish newspapers (local and national) on a weekly basis and sell them in the bar on Monday evening. One of the most popular bars in Irishtown also offers immigrants a full range of Irish imports in its adjacent "Irish" store. Traditional foodstuffs, such as bacon, sausages, and black pudding, are popular. Monday night is also video night, when matches played during the weekend at home are replayed in the bar. Tapes of Irish current affairs programs are also screened from time to time. For special events, live transmissions by satellite are screened in the bars. For example, in June 1988 when Ireland was playing in the European soccer championship finals and in 1990 when Ireland participated in the soccer World Cup, all of the games in which Ireland competed were transmitted live.

Such occasions provide an opportunity to express pride in nationality and reaffirm Irishness. This was particularly the case when Ireland defeated England in their first match in the European championship in 1988. In the aftermath of the Irish victory, the mood in the community was jubilant. A journalist, Terry George, writing in the *Irish Voice*, captured the euphoric atmosphere that enveloped an Irish bar in the Bronx:

Anxious fans burst into the (bar) and were greeted by the heavenly sight of FOUR TVs showing a perfect picture of both teams coming onto the field. . . . And then it happens . . . Irish man Aldridge leaps like a salmon and heads it across the goalmouth. . . . A moment of shock. Then uproar. Pints spilled, people spluttering into their drink (*Irish Voice*, June 18, 1988: 44).

Those who had not seen the match live on Sunday were able to watch video replays in the bars on Sunday and Monday nights. The following Wednesday, many people took the day off work to watch Ireland draw with the Soviet Union. On Saturday morning, I went to a local bar in Queens to watch the third match in the series, Ireland versus the Netherlands. By 9:45 A.M. the bar was packed to capacity with all eyes transfixed on one of the four television screens carrying the match live. The crowd was predominantly a Dublin one, as soccer in Ireland is almost exclusively an urban game. Every person present identified symbolically with the team and the fans attending the match in Germany:

Each time the TV cameras surveyed the sea of Irish supporters at the game, a great— almost tribal—cry of national solidarity went up in the bar. As the teams struggled to get the ball into the net, a series of whoops and cheers (when the Irish team played well) was followed by sighs of dismay and head shaking (when the Dutch went on the offensive). Ten minutes before the final whistle, the Netherlands scored. A shocked silence replaced the roaring and shouting that had filled the bar. The disappointment was palpable as people started to file out of the bar. The one consolation, according to my companions, was that England had been defeated in three games, and Ireland had triumphed over her arch rival. "At least the lads can hold their heads up high when they go home. They'll get a hero's welcome for that," concluded one fan.

This elaborate communications network enables the immigrant community to continue to identify instantaneously with national and international events and issues from a distance. They can "experience" sports events live. They can view videotapes of current affairs programs that deal with contentious issues. They can read analysis of current events in the national Irish, local Irish, and local New York press. In short, the "psychological" distance from home is minimized by the range of mass media available to them through the neighborhood bars.

The communications scholar Ien Ang points out the paradox in the development of transnational communication systems. On the one hand, they tend to disrupt existing forms of national identification (e.g., through the Americanization or Anglicization of Irish culture). On the other hand, they also offers opportunities for new forms of bonding and solidarity and new ways of forging cultural communities. She cites Gillespie's (1989) research among South Asian families in West London which confirms that

the circulation and consumption of ethnically specific information and entertainment on video serves to construct and maintain cross-national "electronic communities" of geographically dispersed people who would otherwise lose their ties with tradition and its active perpetuation (Ang, 1990: 255).

So despite the geographical distance from home, psychological identification with Ireland and the international Irish community is maintained through the ready availability of transnational cultural goods.

CULTURE AND LIFESTYLE IN THE NEW IRISH COMMUNITY

Irish culture in New York is predominantly bar-centered. This is likely to remain so, given the absence of alternative venues that are as sociable and accessible and the prohibitive cost of leisure pursuits. None of the Irish neighborhoods has a dance hall, which is a source of contention among the Irish immigrants. They point out that bars at home are visited as a prelude to going to a disco or a dance. The absence of a dance hall is cited as a contributory factor to the all-night popularity of the bars. The young people miss the atmosphere of a dance and the physical outlet of dancing. City clubs and discos hold little attraction, as Mark explains:

At discos here you get a real ethnic mix—blacks, Hispanics and Puerto Ricans—but I prefer to be with my own. There are no discos or dances catering to us.

This insularity is common in the new Irish community. Irish illegals are much more likely to attend a county dance organized by Irish Americans twice their age, than a racially heterogeneous club or discotheque frequented by people of their own age. The annual county dances (organized by the Irish-American County Associations in New York) provide one of the few opportunities for people to dress up and take to the dance floor in style. They have become increasingly popular in recent years with the influx of new immigrants. Indeed, many counties have reestablished their annual dances after years of county association decline. The biggest and most well-attended dances are the Kerry, Mayo, and Dublin events.

Although many of the immigrants would have been active in sports and athletic clubs at home, only a small minority enjoy the various leisure activities (golf, skiing, adventure sports) available in the New York area. To use recreational facilities, time, money, and transport are necessary. Those who work relatively short hours, are well paid, and own their own transport are most likely to take advantage of the facilities available. However, even those who are motivated and have the financial resources find that the erratic nature of their working hours (particularly in bars and restaurants) makes it difficult to plan ahead or establish a leisure time routine. Those who work relatively long hours, who are poorly paid, and who are dependent on public transport are least likely to take advantage of the opportunities. There is, therefore, a gender difference in participation rates. Construction workers and bartenders have the most opportunity to take advantage of recreational and travel opportunities, while nannies (even when they want to) are limited in terms of their leisure time options. Their social scene invariably narrows to the bars, as one nanny explains: "Here it is very much a bar scene. If you want to meet someone, he's generally got a pint in his hand."

This suggests that while sociability is intensified in the new Irish community through the centrality and popularity of the bar culture, the range of accessible social activities is extremely narrow. In many respects, the lifestyles of many of the illegal Irish, especially those on a low wage, are impoverished rather than enriched by the immigrant experience. It is true that bars are central to Irish culture at home, but because of restrictive closing hours, there is more participation in other forms of leisure and entertainment. In addition, social life in Ireland is family-centered, and Irish people tend to visit frequently in each other's homes. Irish illegals think of Ireland when they think of home and, consequently, see their "homes" in New York as little more than temporary way stations. Uncertain of how long they will be staying, they invest little in furniture and decor and favor commodities (like compact disc players or video recorders) that are relatively easy to transport. Often, they will put up with overcrowded conditions in order to reduce their living expenses. Their apartments are functional and do not lend themselves to relaxation or entertainment. In such circumstances, the bar becomes a refuge from home.

More recently, Irish priests working with the new Irish in New York have tried to shift the focus away from the bar culture by organizing alternative social activities and events (see chapter 7).

INSTRUMENTAL SOCIABILITY: ACQUAINTANCESHIP VERSUS FRIENDSHIP IN THE NEW IRISH COMMUNITY

The structure of the immigrant labor market and leisure time activities has definite consequences for the kinds of social relations that people form. The organization of work, whether in construction or in the home help/child care sector, follows certain precepts: Jobs are frequently short-term, conditions of work are often exploitative, and security of tenure is rarely guaranteed. Working life may be characterized as transitory and insecure. Social life is largely confined to the bars. Not surprisingly, the pattern of social relations in the new Irish community reflects the insecurity of these immigrants' lives.

Relations with others tend to be largely superficial because, as one immigrant put it, "There is no presumption of seeing that person again." People move in and out of apartments, in and out of neighborhoods, and in and out of jobs. New immigrants concern themselves primarily with building a network of useful contacts. Little energy is expended on cultivating friends. Those who can exercise leverage for securing jobs are courted regardless of their intrinsic qualities as potential acquaintances or friends. Most of the immigrants in the study attested to having many acquaintances but few friends. Since acquaintance relationships are largely instrumental, they tend to cross class and regional lines. Friendships, however, are bound by class and county of origin, and close friendships tend to have been formed long before emigration.

For illegals, friendship is defined by standards set in the old country. One would not expect to see the same degree of insularity with regard to friendship formation among legal immigrants who are in a position to actively court and cultivate friends through occupational and social networks. They are legally permitted to assimilate, whereas the illegals are not. The structural constraints imposed by illegality promote insularity in the new Irish community.

Close friends are held in high esteem and can be turned to in times of need. Such relations are governed by a strict norm of reciprocity:

My best friend here is someone I have known for 25 years. He's a cross uncle [through marriage] and a dear friend. He is good to me, and alternately, I do him a good turn. As regards "friends," I don't really know what you mean. I have no peers as such that I would turn to in need.

Trustworthiness is a quality much valued by the undocumented because of the precariousness of their work situation. Stories of immigrants who have been exposed by vindictive employers or co-workers circulate in the community, fueling the already pervasive feeling that only those who are trusted and known should be taken into confidence. If you cannot establish the credentials of an acquaintance (as generally can be done within the immigrant community) you leave yourself open to false leads, disappointment, and the possibility of exposure and/or apprehension. The outsider is perceived as having more leverage when it comes to securing employment, but ultimately he or she is not accountable to his or her client. He or she cannot be challenged because the immigrant cannot trust him or her not to make a report to the authorities. Acquaintanceships may initially be founded on mutual trust and equality. But as soon as complications occur, the subordinate position of the illegal immigrant is revealed, as Barry discovered after a car accident involving himself and an American girl:

She lost control of the car and we nearly went under a truck. I had a whiplash injury and also hurt my leg. She needed stitches in her head. At the hospital I started to get anxious. I didn't have any insurance, and I didn't want to start giving my name and address. Although I wasn't well enough to leave I signed myself out. I spent three or four months out of work. The girl's father was an ex-cop involved in the insurance business. He picked our gear out of the car, and dropped mine around without saying a single word to me. A lot of people told me I should sue. But we were not brought up that way. It just wasn't the way we did things at home. One night several months later, I met the girl in a bar. She came over and said that if I sued, her Dad would have me deported. I was really mad when I heard that. I went to a lawyer then but he told me not to waste my time.

Aware of their vulnerability, immigrants must be extremely circumspect about the kinds of relations they form. They know that in every relationship there is a point of contact beyond which it may be foolhardy to proceed. Confidences are not shared, intimate friendships are not encouraged, and social contact with people outside of the immediate immigrant community is restricted.

Friendships with outsiders may have repercussions, as Brigid found out when she invited a mixed group of workmates back to her apartment for a party:

People were drinking and smoking pot, and things got pretty noisy. My roommate (another Irish immigrant) asked people to leave because things were getting out of hand and someone turned to her and said, "Cool it. I could have you arrested by the INS [Immigration and Naturalization Service] in the morning."

Although Brigid received some sheepish apologies the following week at work, she was not appeased:

I was totally taken aback that someone I considered a friend would make a remark like that, even in jest.

This episode demonstrates the vulnerability of the illegal immigrant and the invidious treatment to which they may be subject even by supposed "friends." An illegal immigrant must learn to be highly selective about the kinds of relationships formed with the people he or she meets. In effect, they must undergo a resocialization process. The inclination to be sociable and trusting must be replaced by heightened circumspectness, a transition which is often painful for the individuals:

I feel ripped off from every angle. I used to be a much more trusting person, but you change from living here. You learn not to trust anybody.

People turn inward—to their own immediate circle—in their quest for personal gratification. But even within the immigrant community, the development of close, gratifying relationships is hampered by the absence of commitment. The immigrants see themselves as a transient community. When times are bad (during the winter months) or when there are fresh reports of restrictions on immigrants, talk turns to "moving on." The men talk about working in the mines in Australia or on the Channel Tunnel in England. Stories circulate about conditions and rates of pay abroad and this information is mulled over in the pubs at night. There is always somewhere else to go. Both men and women have a perfect rationalization for not putting down roots or making commitments within the context of a relationship. Tomorrow they might be disembarking at another port of call.

Guys don't know what they are doing with their lives either. None of us seems to have anything to offer each other—no security. You might be half thinking of going to Australia or England so you don't want to deal with a relationship and potential break-up. There is a conflict there. I would love to be involved, yet I don't want to be too involved.

Future plans? No one knows. People are out here for a while, and they are not interested in relationships. They talk about going on to Australia, England, or London. Most of the men are only out for one thing—a one night stand—no phone numbers exchanged. Even though they are earning money, they lack security, and their lack of commitment stems from insecurity.

In a sense, the period of adolescence that normally precedes the period of settling down is extended indefinitely because of the insecurity of the immigrant situation. Men and women in their late twenties and early thirties are no less likely to be settled in stable relationships than men and women in their early twenties. Thoughts of marriage and children rarely cross their minds. Marriage and children are associated with "home"—they require commitment, stability, and security. As Delia says:

Gaelside is just a passing through area. Nobody would actually live, marry, and have children around here. Only a very strong relationship would last in these circumstances. You can really forgot about getting involved.

Just how long the artificial hiatus in the transition into adulthood will last depends on the immigrants' acclimatization to illegal status, their prospects for legalization and/or the possibility of returning home. These questions can only be answered through further research, which is beyond the scope of this study.

There are only a small number of married couples/settled couples, and they tend to socialize with similarly settled couples. For married couples, the problems associated with illegality are compounded. The financial gain of higher earnings for the illegal breadwinner is soon negated by the costs of having and raising children. Married women tend to stay at home with their children, which reinforces their isolation and considerably reduces the family income. Undocumented parents also have to deal with the ever-present fact that they are no longer solely responsible for themselves, but also for their children. If they have to return to Ireland at any point, it may involve considerable disruption. It is not surprising then that they are the most willing of all the illegals to make a permanent commitment and settle in the United States, given the opportunity to do so. They are much less ambivalent in that regard than the single and unattached.

The majority of new immigrants are single and in their twenties. The conditions under which they live and work reinforce a "single's" culture. The relaxation of ties and controls makes for a liberalization in social behavior. Casual contacts in bars may lead to sexual encounters but are not likely to develop into committed relationships. Women complain constantly about the arrogance of the men they meet and the assumptions that these men make:

You tend not to trust people here. You talk a lot of bullshit for a couple of hours and then they want you in bed before you know it. At home you had a lot of supports—family and friends—here you don't really trust anybody the same way.

Fellas here drink solidly at the weekends and the girls are just as bad. It leaves it very hard for nice girls . . . there are no parents here, no one to control, it makes it very hard to meet a guy. Without the element of control, you find that you cannot really trust a guy. Even the decent fella is full of himself because he knows he can get his way with somebody else.

In New York, many Irish immigrants are exposed for the first time to a sexually explicit culture, which contributes to the widely held belief that American women (of all racial and ethnic groups) are sexually promiscuous. The perceived availability of sex outside the immigrant group increases the pressure on the women within the immigrant group. Irish women see them-selves as having to compete on those terms, or not compete at all. There is also a greater awareness among Irish women immigrants of the consequences of profligate sexual behavior:

A lot of the guys go to the brothel in Queens. It's affectionately known as the Irish Volunteer Club! Butter wouldn't melt in their mouths but they are quick to run off to the Oriental women in the brothels. For them safe sex means being choosy about who they go with. I think they are very naive about sex. They don't think they can get AIDS from going with a nice girl.

The position of women in the "single's" culture closely approximates their position in the work force. Women's work is sex-stereotyped and poorly paid relative to men's work. Similarly, on the social scene, women are not treated as equals, a condition that is by no means exclusive to immigrant populations. Rather, they are treated as either sex objects or as mother figures. As Rita says, "The lads will talk about a girl who is good for a ride for a night. But they want their virgin brides in the end." Immigrant women are caught in a bind. They want the intimacy and warmth of a committed relationship, but in order "to get a man," they must make sexual concessions early on. But if they decide to have sex in the preliminary stage of the relationship, they may become labeled as "an easy ride" and have to face the conse-quences. The only alternative is to be a "nice girl"—and earn the respect of their male counterparts. However, once they establish the ground rules by winning the man's respect, they may find they are turned to for friendship rather than love. Delia and Ailish, for example, have accepted the role of counselor/confidante and rejected the role of lovers. They are women in their late twenties who are very popular among a group of men who socialize in their neighborhood in the Bronx. Their social life is largely centered on the local bars:

Our relationship with the Irish guys is more brother/sister. Most of them did try on something at the start, but when we said no dice, they accepted that and friendship ensued. We are like mother figures to them. They enjoy talking to Irish girls. They need someone close, a friend who will sit and listen. It gives them a sense of security that they wouldn't get from other lads or American girls. We give them advice. You know how it is, lads don't have that sort of friendship with each other, but they still have the same personal problems as the rest of us.

The women in the community are acutely aware of the emotional vulnerabilities and domestic shortcomings of their male counterparts:

The guys here are very lonely. They tend to pour their hearts out. It is harder on the guys. They are not fully versed in domestic duties. Half of them are drinking simply because there is nothing else to do. It is harder on the fellas than the girls.

These women may adopt the "mother-figure" role not only to comfort the men, but also to chastise them and exercise control. In a conversation with two women in their early twenties, one recalled an incident that occurred on a trip to a Catskills resort. After heavy drinking, hostilities mounted. Maura got upset and intervened. She succeeded in defusing the fight:

I just turned to the guy causing the trouble and said just imagine if your mother could see you now. He stopped immediately and left the fight. Tempers cooled all round. It was the only thing that would cop him on.

The small number of female bartenders, like their male counterparts, have to be extremely vigilant and frequently act as peacemakers in difficult situations. At a social gathering one evening, I overheard a drunken man admonishing a female bartender, who was an Irish immigrant, for intervening to extricate him from a fight in the bar where she worked. She was annoyed with his attitude and turned to explain to me:

He is starting with me because I pulled him away from a fight the other night. No one knows what I go through. Last week I pulled a knife off someone. A fight started and someone drew a knife. The police were called. I grabbed the knife, ran out, dropped it, and high-tailed it out of there. When the police came they were told that a woman had dropped the knife but they couldn't find me. I could have lost my liquor license but I didn't even think. I saw the knife and just acted instinctively. And just look at the thanks I get.

In general, however, the informal counseling that women do does not go unacknowledged. Most of the men say that they prefer Irish girls to American girls, although this does not preclude them from dating outside the immigrant group. They find it easier to relate to Irish women because they are "more down to earth," "more *craic*" (Irish colloquialism meaning "fun loving"), "more generous," and "more in tune with reality." There is general agreement that in New York, women and sex are more available than at home. The men tend to draw distinctions between different categories of women though, with Irish girls being held in higher esteem than white American women, who in turn are accorded more respect than women from other racial groups. American women are considered more sexually free, but also more culturally distant, and are described in stereotypical terms:

I think there is a real cultural difference between the American and the Irish. They [the Americans] are into money and not into quality of life. They are fussy, fickle, and spoilt.

As we will see later, many immigrants in their discussion of life in America make this point about cultural distance in a more general sense.

As Rita pointed out, there are several brothels in the Irish neighborhood that cater to Irish immigrants. The women are mainly Hispanic and charge $15 to $20 per client. Prostitutes will also congregate around the pubs in Manhattan that are frequented by the Irish immigrants, who may, after a night's drinking, go into a nearby doorway with one of the women. One informant, a member of a tightly knit construction crew, who himself has visited several brothels, explains the attraction:

The lads may not have had sex at the weekend. Everyone asks on Monday, "Did you get a ride at the weekend?" Most of the lads are not interested in a relationship with a woman. They just want to get laid.

The forms of talk the "lads" engage in usually involves much derogation and diminution of women, a characteristic which is not confined to immigrant men. Some have formal girlfriends or wives but this does not prevent them from spending a night with another woman, or visiting a brothel after work. The availability of free sex coupled with the absence of social constraints heightens the instrumental approach to all social and personal relations in the new Irish community.

Women in the new Irish community engage in emotional work to comfort and control the men with whom they associate. Additionally, they perform domestic and menial work that serves to make life easier for men. Parties are almost always organized and catered by women, unless they are held in the bars. At Thanksgiving and Christmas, women such as Delia and Ailish invite male friends into their home to enjoy the festivities. The latter may contribute cash toward the food and drink, but they do not help in the preparation, cooking, or serving of the meal. The women will prepare meals for boyfriends before or after they finish work, iron shirts, and organize the shopping.

The women in the IIRM more often than not have been accorded a secondary role in decision making, organization, and planning within the movement. Indeed, some of the women complained to me that they had been deliberately excluded from policy discussions and had not been informed of important developments. They are primarily called on to do menial tasks like addressing and sealing envelopes, typing the press releases and speeches prepared by the men, "manning" information tables, answering telephone queries, and getting coffee. In the office, the men tend to assume the role of boss or overseer of the routine work performed by the women. The latter's low visibility and status in the organization is a constant source of frustration. They feel that much of their work goes unacknowledged because it goes on behind the scenes.

SUMMARY

Social relationships within the new Irish community tend to be transitory and precarious, reflecting the insecure lifestyle of illegal immigrants. Acquaintanceship replaces friendship; there is a general absence of commitment and trust; and women in this community are forced into a limited range of sex-stereotyped roles.

The Irish bar plays a central role in the emergence of a community of illegals by providing a central location for immigrants to congregate, a range of services, and a venue for social and community events.

Chapter 6

Identity and Ethnicity

Irish illegals employ a number of strategies in constructing a unique sense of their own identity and ethnicity. There are three primary social realities to which these immigrants are oriented: (1) Ireland (the remote environment), (2) the United States (the proximate environment), and (3) the social world of their own ethnic group (the immediate environment). The new Irish locate themselves in relation to these three realities, which form the boundaries of the immigrant experience. The relations formed within each social context are examined in this chapter.

It is at the point of intersection or boundary between the new Irish community and each of these social contexts that their identity as illegal Irish immigrants is articulated. In addition, the sense of themselves as Irish ethnics is framed within a dialectic, which involves the contradictory influences of Irish-American ethnicity, American culture, and contemporary Irish culture.

Identity is established and maintained through a process of negotiation, which takes place against the backdrop of these three social contexts. Indeed, "identity negotiation, or identity bargaining is a central aspect of the individual's broader task of defining the situation and 'constructing' reality" (Gecas, 1982: 2). In defining their situation as illegal Irish immigrants, class boundaries in the new Irish community recede, while ethnic, cultural, and local boundaries take on a heightened importance. The consciousness of community is encapsulated in the perceptions of these boundaries, boundaries that are ultimately constituted by people in interaction (Cohen, 1985: 13).

IRELAND AND IRISHNESS: DISTANCING AND EMBRACEMENT

Undocumented Irish immigrants in New York have an ambivalent relationship to their country of origin. On the one hand, they are highly critical of Ireland. Their opinions suggest a deep rooted alienation from Irish social, economic, and political institutions. On the other hand, this community celebrates its "Irishness," but it is a sense of "Irishness" that has evolved from the social and economic conditions of this wave of immigration.

Immigrants in any society are outsiders, but those without legal status are particularly marginal. Survival in the interstices of the U.S. economy depends on the ability to manipulate one's ethnic identity. The prevalence of clientelism in the immigrant labor market invariably creates cleavages within the new Irish community. Although the widely used term *new Irish* implies a certain homogeneity, in reality this community is fragmented into webs of regional, county, and local affiliations.

The creation of a "new Irish" identity (the term is used widely in the immigrant community and was probably originated by the IIRM) involves a dual process of *distancing* oneself from Ireland, while at the same time *embracing* one's sense of "Irishness." The distancing/embracement process causes a certain amount of ambivalence about identity—immigrants experience conflicting feelings about who and what they are. While they do not fully belong to the host culture or Irish-American ethnic culture, neither do they fully belong to the home culture.

The distancing process is manifested in a general feeling of disillusionment and disaffection with Ireland. Memories are soured by the stagnation that enveloped the Irish economy in the early 1980s. Irish illegals recall limited job opportunities, low job mobility, and an unjust tax system. In such circumstances, emigration appears as an avenue of escape.

For many of these immigrants, disillusionment is accompanied by a lingering antipathy toward a country that they feel they were forced (directly or indirectly) to leave. This sense of alienation was readily perceived by one prominent Irish bishop who visited the United States in 1987 and declared that Irish immigrants feel "let down by the Church and all organized Irish society" (quoted in *Irish Echo*, November 21, 1987). Antipathy is directed in particular at Ireland's political system. In general, these immigrants do not believe that Irish politicians have either the political will or vision to tackle the country's problems.

Irish immigrants are critical of the state's administration, which is seen as top heavy and elitist:

Politicians don't give you much to be proud of. There are too many T.D.s (political representatives) and they are working for their parties, not for the people. They are protected from the reality most of us experience by virtue of their position.

There is little faith in politicians and in their personal commitment to public service:

I have no interest in politics. In my opinion, they are all watching their own backs and lining their own pockets.

No matter who gets in they are still just out for themselves and nobody else. You can see that by looking at the country and the way it has gone down.

Ironically, members of this generation who might have been a force for change, have forfeited their voting rights by leaving. At the same time, they do not enjoy the rights of citizenship or residency in the country where they now reside.

Those who choose to work in America without legal status or protection take on a challenge for which they are often ill prepared. Much depends on their motivation and desire to succeed. Going to America requires them to relinquish the emotional and physical security of being "at home." In its place, each newly arrived illegal must cultivate a hard edged, street-wise instrumentalism. In distancing themselves from Ireland—the country that they feel held them back—these immigrants seek new experiences and a new identity.

Paradoxically, this distancing process is paralleled by an embracement process. While the immigrants distance themselves from Ireland, they, nevertheless, embrace their sense of Irishness. The embracement process is manifested at two levels: a heightened sense of Irish identity, and the maintenance of close ties with home. Unable to penetrate the host culture, their loyalties to the home culture remain strong. This adherence to the home culture is reinforced by the importance attached to place of origin within the Irish-American ethnic culture. Irish ethnic culture is built on layers of local, county, and regional affiliations. The strategic cultivation of such affiliations is crucial for newly arrived immigrants, since it is within the ethnic culture that primary economic and social relations are formed. Pride in Irish identity is expressed in a strong self-concept and a willingness to identify with the symbolic ethnicity of Irish Americans. In addition, the sense of Irishness is evident in the strong ties maintained with the home culture.

Pride in Irish Identity

Many of the illegal Irish immigrants in New York had previously worked in England and speak critically of their experiences there. The Irish in England, especially the unskilled, face prejudice and discrimination from the dominant group. According to Jackson, the reception of the Irish in Britain is conditioned by the past history of relations between the two islands, a history replete with hostility and antagonism on both sides (1963: 153). One prominent Irish chaplain, Rev. Robert Gilmore who works with Irish immigrants in London, says that anti-Irish racism is never far below the surface, usually emerging into full view at times of crisis in Northern Ireland or when the Northern Ireland troubles spill over into Britain. These attitudes exacerbate feelings of alienation (*Irish Voice*, June 11, 1988: 17). The activities of extremist groups, such as the Irish Republican Army (IRA), have the effect of affirming age-old stereotypes that hold that "all Irish men and women [are] similarly irresponsible, dangerous, and disloyal to British interests" (Jackson, 1963: 153). A study conducted by the Action Group for Irish Youth in London found that half of those surveyed had experienced anti-Irish racism, prejudice, or hostility (Randall, 1991: 44). More recently, a British-wide survey sponsored by the *Irish Post* newspaper found that 68 percent of respondents thought the British saw the Irish as less intelligent than themselves. Twenty-nine percent believed being Irish was a disadvantage in Britain (*Irish Independent*, Jan. 8, 1993). The Irish are frequently portrayed derisively in the British tabloid press, which helps to further stigmatize them in the eyes of the British public. In these circumstances, Irish immigrants in Britain tend to keep a low profile, deflecting attention from themselves. In so far as they celebrate their ethnicity and cultural heritage, it is done in a private rather than a public way.

In contrast, New York is a multicultural society, in which ethnic and cultural diversity is not only tolerated but also celebrated. The new Irish in New York, like their forebears, maintain a strong ethnic profile through symbolic events such as the St. Patrick's Day parade, and through a lively ethnic press, involvement in Gaelic sports, and the musical entertainment in Irish bars. In such an atmosphere, Irishness is an identity of which to be proud. This ethnic pride is reflected in the prevalence of a strong self-concept among the new immigrants, particularly those who had previously worked in Britain. As one immigrant explained:

In England you try to keep a low profile, you hid your identity. Because of the inferiority complex and the hostile environment, you play down your Irishness. Here . . . your Irishness is very much a matter of social pride.

It is not surprising then, that many Irish immigrants who had previously worked in Britain equate their arrival in the United States with the achievement of a higher social status position. The ability to embrace one's Irishness more than compensates for the drawbacks of illegality.

Northern Irish immigrants, in particular, embrace their Irish identity. As members of a minority group in a British-run state, Northern Catholics are stigmatized because of their Irish/nationalist identity. As immigrants in New York, they relate to their Irishness because it has much the same currency as any other ethnic or national identity. As one Catholic nurse, who worked in a predominantly Protestant hospital before leaving Belfast for New York, explains:

Being Irish and being able to acknowledge it is something Southerners take for granted. We were always made to feel different, inferior. Being proud to be Irish is something we really only learned since coming here.

New York's multicultural profile legitimates Irishness as a viable and valuable identity, making it an important counterbalance to the ignominy of illegality.

As part of their strategy for developing a lobby for immigration reform, the IIRM has urged the Irish to embrace their ethnic identity. This has been a consistent theme at their meetings and in their literature. They allude to "Irish identity" as a vague, all-embracing label, which unites several loosely related constituencies, as is evidenced by this exhortation by an IIRM activist:

On March 17th we have the biggest public relations day in the world and we have to make the most of it. You're as Irish as anyone else in this country, so march in the St. Patrick's Day parade with the AOH branches, with your county associations, or the IIRM (IIRM meeting, December 3, 1987).

When questioned about his concept of Irish identity, the author of the previous remark opted for a cultural rather than a national definition:

There is an Irish nation but it is a diaspora. We are like the Jews. Ireland is a home base—like Israel, the promised land. We cannot all live on one small island, we have too much to offer the world. The Irish Americans, the Australian Irish, the Irish in Britain are all equally Irish. We are talking about a global Ireland.

In this and other statements made by the leadership of the IIRM, Irishness is understood as a sort of cultural construct—embracing people of different nationalities who share a common tradition and culture. The claim to Irishness is not impugned by the absence of common nationality. Indeed, by invoking a *transnational* concept of Irishness, national boundaries are called into question. The new Irish are part of a symbolic global community, which is linked to the historical past (the hyphenated Irish) and to contemporary Irish emigrants in other parts of the world. A practical example of the cooperative possibilities within this transnational Irish community is the recently formed Irish Emigrant Vote Campaign (IEVC). The IEVC is a New York-based organization formed by a group of Irish immigrants who feel strongly that voting rights ought to be extended to Irish citizens living abroad. They are affiliated to similar campaign groups in cities such as Chicago and Brussels and in countries such as Australia and the United Kingdom, which call for legislative reform on the voting issue (Irish Emigrant Vote Campaign, 1991: 2).

In the literature they distribute, the IIRM try to promote a positive definition of Irishness by encouraging immigrants not to engage in conduct "which might reinforce false stereotypes or generalizations of the Irish character." Illegals are urged to promote an image that highlights "the Irish work ethic," the "Irish sense of humor,"and the "humanitarianism that is common to the Irish character," (Irish Immigrant Reform Movement, 1987).

The ideology of the IIRM is designed to relieve the Irish illegals of any guilt regarding their presence in the United States. The law that excludes the new Irish is "bad law," as one activist declared:

The law not only wrongs the Irish, but wrongs America itself. But I want you all to remember that today's underdog can be tomorrow's chieftain. The wheel will turn for the undocumented Irish and when it turns it will be in our favor (IIRM meeting, February 3, 1988).

By promoting a strong self-concept, a sense of self-esteem, and pride in ethnic identity, the IIRM seeks to gain the confidence and support of the new Irish community. This support is crucial to the organization's strategy in attempting to regularize the status of all Irish illegal aliens.

Keeping the Home Fires Burning

The embracement of Irishness also involves the maintenance of close ties with those left behind in Ireland. The majority of immigrants in the study keep in close contact with their families. While contact with friends at home tends to be casual and intermittent in nature, contact with immediate family is highly routinized. This is the case for men and women, although the latter communicate more frequently with family and friends than the former. On average, the men in the study telephone home between once and twice a month. They telephone friends at home much less frequently, perhaps once or twice a year. They rarely write letters to either family or friends.

The women in the study telephone on average between twice and three times a month. Their phone calls are also supplemented by letter writing. They are more likely to write and receive letters from family and friends (at home and abroad) than men. Letters from home keep them abreast of local developments that do not necessarily make the provincial newspapers, which are distributed through the Irish bars. One woman described how her father sent her the local paper printed in her hometown of Killeen:

My dad tells me everything that is going on at home in the most hilarious detail. I get a couple of papers every time he writes, and I cherish them, reading them over and over again. It keeps me in touch with events at home—what the musical society is up to, what fundraisers are going on.

Many parents, especially those who never emigrated, have few reference points for dealing with the situation of having a son or daughter living as an illegal immigrant in New York:

I think they miss me more at home, than I miss them. For them, my being in America is an open, vacant thing. They worry about how I survive and the loneliness of being away.

This makes regular communication all the more important, as trips home are generally out of the question. The immigrants, however, are necessarily selective about the information they relay home. They feel they need to protect their families from the vagaries of life as illegal aliens in New York. There is also the question of their own pride, which makes them unwilling to admit or acknowledge the less palatable aspects of their existence. Consequently, much of what is communicated to parents is an edited version of their experiences.

Contact with home is so frequent and such an integral part of the immigrants' lives that they see themselves as "an extension of the community" abroad. Few events happen at home of which they are unaware. Occasionally, a story from a small town at home will circulate around the town's community in New York via the immigrant network before it has been circulated in the town itself. In many respects, the ties with home are stronger than the ties to either the host culture or the ethnic culture in which the immigrants are located. The new Irish occupy an ambivalent status by virtue of their attachment to one culture, while living and working in another. This divided existence may create identity problems when the immigrants return home. Their psychological closeness to home reduces the actual distance between them and their home culture. Yet when they return, they may find they are no longer perceived as insiders, although that is how they have continued to see themselves. The label of "outsider" is one to which they have difficulty relating. One informant, for example, described his identity crisis on returning home after a two-year sojourn in the United States. As a transient, he identified more with home than the host culture, but his family and friends had difficulty seeing it that way:

The strange thing for me was that they treated me as a visitor. I had gone away and that was it. People reacted differently to me—"You're going to be gone again in a few weeks" sort of attitude. I hadn't seen myself as an emigrant up to that point, but they saw me as someone who had left. I was just a visitor now. In a way they had accepted that I was gone, but I hadn't.

Media Consumption

Contact with home is also maintained through high levels of media consumption. Most immigrants purchase a national Irish paper on a weekly basis, as well as provincial papers which contain "parish pump" stories about events and happenings in their own country or region. In addition, the majority of the immigrants read one of the two ethnic newspapers published in New York every week. The *Irish Voice*, launched at the end of 1987, has become the firm favorite among the new Irish primarily because it is oriented specifically toward them. (See chapter 7 for a discussion of the impact of the *Irish Voice* on the illegal Irish community.)

Different publications serve different functions. The national Irish newspapers are primarily informational, providing analysis of Irish and international affairs, as well as regular features on the emigrants abroad. The provincial papers, in contrast, serve a primarily entertainment function. People buy them to see if anyone they know from home is featured and to update themselves on local news. The provincial newspapers give people access to community and family events through descriptive articles, features, and photographs. One immigrant whose brother is a sports star at home kept a scrapbook of all the newspaper coverage that he and his teammates received. She vicariously shared in his success, through a reading and re-reading of these articles. The provincial papers also acknowledge their extended communities abroad by reporting on them and their activities in New York. For example, they will cover Gaelic games that take place in New York between teams fielded from the locale in Ireland. The most avid readers of the papers from home are immigrants who are newly arrived and those whose primary commitments and ties are to the home country. Those who have been in New York four or five years are least likely to immerse themselves in the parish pump politics of the provincial papers, although almost all will still buy an ethnic newspaper. This suggests that at least some of the illegals are assimilating, even if they are not consciously aware of that assimilation process. Their concerns are increasingly directed away from the goings-on at home and toward tackling the problem of legalization, which would allow them to settle in the United States.

As with the ethnic press in general, the Irish papers in New York, particularly the *Irish Voice*, combine entertainment with information. Although the paper focuses on primarily the immigrants and immigrant issues, a significant amount of coverage is given to Ireland and Irish affairs. Since most of the immigrants tend to read several publications on a weekly basis, they are able to keep abreast of developments in their own immigrant community, as well as the communities back home. Indeed, many feel that they are more informed than they were previously. Comments like this were relatively common:

I take a great deal of interest in the affairs of Ireland. You learn more about Ireland here than you would at home. There is every sort of stimulus here which directs you toward Irish things. You become more involved, more aware, and develop a greater appreciation of things Irish.

The newspapers generally arrive in the bars on a Monday night. People stop in on their way home from work in the evenings and often have to stand in line in order to purchase their individual selections. Some make it a night out, with the newspapers as the excuse for a Monday night trip to the bar. A major news story of Irish interest will increase the demand for the national newspapers, which quickly sell out. Music is always provided on Monday nights for entertainment. "Newspaper night" has become one of the few institutionalized reference points in the immigrant community. Reading the newspapers, an activity that is frequently done in the bar, has become ritualized behavior, providing the immigrants with a temporary immersion in the social and community affairs that preoccupy those they have left behind. Through the ritualized reading of the newspapers, another link with home is maintained. As one immigrant activist from the west of Ireland put it:

I guess a lot of people read the *Western People*. But to be honest I don't think that half of them ever bought it at home. They go down to the pub, have a few drinks, and go through the paper to see who got fined, who had their license revoked at home, etc. I think it's just force of habit. When they are sitting in the bar reading the paper, sure they could just as well be at home.

The papers serve to re-create the home environment and offer the illusion that the immigrant has not really left at all.

In sum, while the illegal Irish immigrants keep their distance from Ireland, they embrace their sense of Irishness. This process has a pragmatic or rational basis. They need to put some distance between themselves and the homeland in order to face the challenges in New York. The toughness and savvy required to negotiate the world of illegality leaves little room for sentimentality of the shamrock and shillealagh kind. At the same time, their identity as Irish immigrants is crucial in the heartland of ethnic Irish New York. For those who have had to face the uncertainty of an undocumented existence, the cultivation of Irishness (expressed in nationalist as well as local terms) is an essential part of the survival strategy. Irishness has an intrinsic cultural value embracing all immigrants in the symbolic community abroad. But Irishness also has an economic value—expressed in terms of regional, county, and local affiliations—as the currency that facilitates exchanges in the labor market.

ATTITUDES TOWARD THE HOST COUNTRY

The celebration and idealization of Irishness is reinforced through a general rejection of American culture and values. (Interestingly, though, the marketplace value system that supports an entrepreneurial culture is favorably compared to the state interventionist orientation of the Irish economy. It seems that the Irish prefer the rugged individualism of the marketplace to be confined purely to the economic sphere.) The rejection of American culture and values is at least in part a response to the uncertainty of illegality. Many of these immigrants are transients and are unlikely to settle in the United States even if they become legalized. Hence, there is little incentive to acclimatize to a value system and culture to which they are unlikely to make a long-term commitment. To emphasize their separateness (and to a lesser extent their self-sufficiency) the new Irish tend to focus almost exclusively on what they perceive as the negative aspects of the American way of life. On a practical level, the fear of exposure as illegal aliens means that most people keep their contacts outside of the Irish community to a minimum. In so far as they exist, relations with others outside the ethnic community are generally confined to work. The "inward-lookingness" of the Irish immigrants is explained by their fear of apprehension. As illegal aliens, they must be careful not to reveal themselves to anyone who is not trusted or known. Once an immigrant moves outside the protective ethnic enclave, there is always a possibility of his or her "true identity" being revealed. Consequently, most of the immigrants feel that it is better to socialize only "with your own."

Given the limited interaction with Americans, most of the immigrants construct a picture of the host culture that is derived largely from television and tabloid newspaper accounts. They engage in a process of stereotyping in order to delineate the boundaries between themselves and the host culture. Americans are described frequently as "very self-centered," "individualistic," and "shallow"—qualities that seem more characteristic of many of the illegals. Americans, or more accurately American traits, some of which have already been adapted by the instrumental illegals described in the previous chapter, are contrasted with the Irish who are characterized (idealistically) in more wholesome terms—"earthy," "warm," and "in touch with reality." These stereotypical characterizations have their roots in different underlying philosophies or world views. American society is committed to individualism, whereas the Irish tradition is one of collectivism. American individualism, as it is expressed in everyday interaction, is occasionally reinterpreted as narcissism, as evidenced by one immigrant woman's assessment of the American male: "There is no room for anyone else, once they are done loving themselves."

In reality, the ethos of individualism, self-interest, and self-reliance are central to the successful negotiation of the twilight world of illegality. These immigrants succeed because they have internalized the very values they condemn.

Even though the new Irish are living and working in an environment physically removed from Irish culture and values, they continue to subscribe to the latter's general norms. For example, Irish immigrants in New York reject what they perceive as liberal family values in American culture and endorse the more traditional family values associated with Irish culture.

Coming from a country in which there is only limited legal recognition of marital breakdown, the high divorce rates in America appear overwhelming:

They have no culture, no roots. They don't have a proper family life. Because of divorce you can be part of several different families. I think a person's background is very important.

Several times in the course of this research, America was described as a "disposable society"—wasteful of its energy, resources, products, and people. For example, many Irish immigrants feel that the elderly in America are uncared for and unloved, while in Irish culture, older people, particularly in rural communities, remain highly valued and may still exert considerable power in the extended family:

What sort of a society is it that throws its old folk into a home? My grandmother lived with us in her old age. I think the old folks home is symptomatic of this push button society. Things are disposed of at will.

There is no sense of respect for the elderly. It is not considered a duty to look after people when they reach old age. It's so different from home where the old are respected and loved.

It's not a country to grow old in. Nobody cares about you when you are old and sick.

There is a good deal of idealization of Irish society inherent in statements such as these. The contrast between both societies is no longer so stark, yet the immigrants construct a highly dichotomized sense of both realities. The modern, individualized, narcissistic urban culture of New York is contrasted unfavorably with the respect for the elderly, strict virtue, and small-town values associated with traditional Ireland. Given the recent controversies that have dominated political discourse in Ireland—abortion rights, marital breakdown, celibacy, and the ethical standards in business and government—it appears that in many respects "traditional Ireland" has become an artifact of the past. This predilection for idealizing aspects of Ireland's social and cultural reality is not confined to recent immigrants. Indeed, Irish Americans—as we shall see—are roundly criticized for engaging in similar kinds of mythologizing.

THE NEW IRISH AND THE ETHNIC IRISH COMMUNITY

The new Irish stand in relation to two primary constituencies within the Irish ethnic group, broadly defined: (1) Irish Americans—people born in America who claim Irish ancestry, and (2) first generation Irish immigrants—people born in Ireland who emigrated to the United States. It is the latter group who are the *primary* patrons and brokers (and exploiters) in the ethnic labor market and on whom the new Irish tend to be highly dependent. Relations with the former constituency—the Irish Americans—in contrast, are not dominated by labor market relations. Instead, Irish Americans have been embraced by the New Irish (and in particular by the IIRM) as a potentially powerful political constituency whose extensive resources offered the possibility of a successful campaign for legalization.

Relations with Irish Americans

The attitudes of the new Irish toward Irish Americans are based primarily on the perception of Irish Americans as *symbolic ethnics*—a perception that is almost universal throughout the new Irish community—and the perception of Irish Americans as a potential power block to influence immigration re- form—a view held primarily by immigration reform organizers within the new Irish community.

In so far as Irish Americans are aware of the recent influx of Irish immi- grants, their attitude is described by the recent immigrants as largely pos- itive. They are perceived to be a concerned and caring constituency. However, there is also a strong feeling that Irish Americans are poorly informed about the problems facing contemporary Ireland, particularly, the plight of the illegals. The latter feel that Irish Americans are so removed from Ireland that the country of their ancestors has ceased to have any real meaning for them. According to the immigrants, the Irishness of the Irish- American community is largely symbolic. *Symbolic ethnicity* has been de- fined as "a nostalgic allegiance to the culture of the immigrant generation or that of the old country; a love for and a pride in a tradition that can be felt without having to be incorporated in everyday behavior" (Gans, 1979: 9). According to Gans, symbolic ethnicity can be expressed in a variety of ways, for example, the celebration of significant religious or ethnic holidays, symbolic identification with national or international issues, and the con- sumption of ethnic goods or services. He associates symbolic ethnicity with third- and fourth-generation ethnics.

Irish immigrants recognize this symbolic ethnicity in the cultural behavior of Irish Americans. They contend that Irish Americans are either wholly uninformed or misinformed about Ireland. The latter's perceptions of Ireland are based on stock images and stereotypes (often derived from films, such as *The Quiet Man*, or the pageantry of St. Patrick's Day). Such images and stereotypes bear only spurious relation to the country in which the new Irish immigrants were raised. Most were born after 1960, during a period of unprecedented social and economic progress in Ireland. There is, therefore, a general consensus among the new Irish that the Irish-American perception of the country remains hopelessly out of date. (Although this is true of all immigrant groups, the datedness is exacerbated in the Irish case because the last great wave of emigration to the United States was in the 1950s and early 1960s. Irish immigration to the United States effectively skipped a generation, leaving a larger cultural and social gap between earlier generations and the current immigrants). Recent immigrants are steeped in realism; their Irish-American counterparts indulge in romanticism. Those Irish Americans who visit the country are usually bussed through, on a whistle-stop tour, to places whose primary purpose is to cater to the fantasies of Irish-American tourists. They are frequently presented with a highly stylized version of Irish reality. With little first-hand knowledge of the country, they tend to simplify the complexities of the Irish situation. They hanker after an idealized past. As one informant put it:

They have a fairly tale, idyllic image of Ireland. The lakes of Killarney, the Blarney Stone kind of thing. "Top of the morning to you"—is a phrase I never heard until I came here. They don't stop to think why people are emigrating today, and why they and their forefathers before them emigrated.

Predictably, bartenders and waitresses report that Irish-American customers "like to talk about their roots" and, indeed, they find that their authentic Irish identity is a decided occupational advantage. One waitress explained her attraction to Irish Americans:

The Irish-American customers [in our restaurant] come in and specifically ask for me. They love me. A typical speel goes like this—"You're Irish? I'm Irish too. My great-great-grandfather is from Cork . . . I love your accent."

Another waitress describes the novelty (and remunerative) value of her Irishness on the job:

Since I am the only Irish person in my job, I am a bit of a novelty. People at work thrive on my Irish identity and it affects my tips greatly. I put up with the "come all ya" line just for that purpose. The people who come into the restaurant would rarely have any contact with the Irish. After a night's work, it is a relief to get out of the city and into one of the Irish bars. Irish people know what the real Ireland is. They are like me and it is much more comfortable talking to them.

Some restaurants deliberately capitalize on the symbolism attached to Irish ethnicity, especially around St. Patrick's Day. A waitress who had to participate in one such charade complained about the long shifts she had to work during the days preceding March 17:

The boss was packing the place all week with the Tender Loving Care dinners. Old people from all over Long Island were bussed in, everyone wearing green. We did the serving and had to mouth along to all the Irish songs. The boss made a packet out of it.

Several immigrants blamed what they perceived as a preoccupation with symbolism for the initial reluctance of Irish Americans to concern themselves about the illegal immigration problem. Indeed, it has only been at the urging of the IIRM, which gave a formal voice to the illegal constituency, that leading Irish-American figures and organizations began to mobilize around the issue.

To the IIRM, Irish Americans are seen in collective terms as "a sleeping giant"—a potentially powerful electoral bloc of 16 million or more. According to the leaders, if the giant could be awakened—if Irish Americans could be persuaded to make common cause around the plight of the Irish illegals— they could exert influence over legislators and policy makers. In addition, Irish Americans are perceived to be a relatively well-off constituency and are, therefore, a potential source of funding for organizations such as the IIRM. For these reasons, Irish Americans have been singled out by the IIRM as crucial, politically and financially, to the immigration cause.

An American Irish action group was set up within the IIRM to galvanize Irish-American support for immigration reform. According to the action group leader, "The problem is not that they (Irish Americans) don't care, but that they don't know." This point has been reiterated frequently by other members of the IIRM, who see their job in terms of mobilizing previously untapped support. Indeed, the language of the leadership suggests that the aim is to replace the symbolic ethnicity of the Irish Americans with a pragmatic challenge that goes to the heart of their ethnic identity. If Irish America doesn't respond to that challenge, it is faced with the erosion of its identity:

The St. Patrick's Day parade is almost upon us, and we want to move beyond the Leprechaun, Shillealagh, and green hat image this year. We need to put immigration on the Irish-American agenda. Otherwise, there won't be an Irish-American community in ten years time (IIRM meeting, January 6, 1988).

This theme was taken up at a subsequent meeting of the Ancient Order of Hibernians, the largest organization of Irish Americans in the United States. A motion in support of the IIRM and condemning the 1986 Immigration Reform and Control Act as "'genocidal to the Irish-American community" was passed. (The use of the term *genocidal* is interesting in this context. It recalls the preoccupation with the idea of race suicide, which dominated much of the early twentieth-century discourse on immigration control in the United States.)

Although the IIRM see little merit in the artifactual aspects of Irish-American ethnicity, the organizers recognize the value of symbolic imagery particularly in getting a message across through the media. At one meeting of the IIRM, one of the organizers described the kind of image required in order to galvanize Irish-American support:

We want to focus on the real issue of the undocumented Irish rather than on the shamrocks and the shillealaghs. It would be a focus for creating awareness in the Irish-American community. . . . The image of Irish and Irish-American men and women joining together with the bond of common Irish blood would be very good (IIRM meeting, February 3, 1988).

According to the IIRM organizers, the issue of legalization for undocumented Irish workers has the potential to unite all the constituencies within the Irish ethnic group, broadly defined:

The IIRM should be able to count on the support of all the Irish, both the new Irish and the Irish-American community throughout the United States (IIRM meeting, October 28, 1987).

This view was put even more forcefully by another speaker at a subsequent meeting:

We cannot allow people to call themselves Irish American, to call themselves Irish, without doing something for Irish immigrants. We must work toward the day when there won't be one Irish illegal alien in this country (IIRM meeting, January 6, 1988).

Immigration is seen by the IIRM as an issue that can mobilize Irish America, if it is presented in the right way. In the first few months of the IIRM's existence, a concerted effort was made to have prominent Irish Americans endorse the movement. Endorsers included Cardinal Manning of Southern California, Monsignor James Murray, Catholic Charities, New York, and (the late) William Shannon, historian and former ambassador to Ireland. Such well-known religious and political figures served to lend legitimacy to the emergent organization and to present it as a broad coalition of Irish interests.

Relations with First-Generation Irish Immigrants

While relations with Irish Americans are largely symbolic, those with the older Irish immigrants are highly pragmatic, rooted as they are in the "cut and thrust" of the immigrant labor market. It is primarily the older Irish immigrants who provide the new Irish with jobs, especially in the construction sector.

The immigrants of the 1950s and the early 1960s are those with whom the new Irish come into closest contact. This constituency is predominantly composed of rural emigrants, the majority of whom were poorly educated. Those who had skills were generally tradesmen. In this respect, this generation is of a lower status than the present generation of illegals.

Most started their working lives in America on building sites and in the bar trade. Three decades later, they occupy powerful positions in the immigrant labor market—as construction company owners, subcontractors, and proprietors of bars. They also hold strategic positions in many of the construction unions. They represent the front line of potential employers for newly arrived immigrants. This gives them an inordinate amount of power in the employer-employee relationship, power that is open to abuse.

Given that the supply of labor frequently exceeds demand and that the majority of those seeking work are illegal, it is not surprising that employer/employee relations are characterized by patterns of paternalism and clientelism. As a result, the Irish are frequently perceived as the worst employers. Paradoxically, while help from one of "your own" is often necessary for finding a niche in the ethnic enclave, this dependency makes the illegals even more vulnerable to exploitative Irish landlords and employers. In the competitive atmosphere of the construction site, for example, it is almost always a case of "every man for himself." This militates against the formation of solidaristic occupational or social alliances among Irish illegals and among illegal immigrants in general.

The attitude of first-generation immigrants toward the new arrivals is characterized by ambivalence. On the one hand, they dissociate themselves from the new Irish who are frequently labeled as "rude and arrogant." On the other hand, the arrival of a new generation of Irish immigrants offers the potential for a revitalization of the Irish-American community and, in particular, a regeneration of Irish ethnic neighborhoods. This ambivalence is detected by the new Irish as they come into contact with first-generation immigrants:

They have a strange view of us. On the one hand, they say that the new Irish are loud, obnoxious and unwelcome. On the other hand, they welcome us. I am not sure if they want us at all.

One of the priests in the Irishtown parish identified the problem in terms of educational differences between the two groups:

The new Irish are more educated. They have a secondary school education, and they may also have a skill or some other credential. They think they know it all and are not willing to listen. They look down their noses at the older Irish. They haven't coalesced as the previous generation has.

The old Irish mostly had a national school education. They came out to their uncles and aunts and were taught how to conduct themselves. They were taught what was right and wrong by relatives who served as authority figures. They worked hard, kept the faith, and respected the old ways.

This view was reiterated by the two Irish priests who were sent to New York by the Irish bishops in 1988 to offer pastoral support to the illegal Irish community:

They [the older Irish] admire them [the new immigrants], but at the same time, they think they are too cocky. They think, "We had to start out at ground level and work up. The new Irish want to start at the top." They can't understand them [the new Irish]. They see them as very articulate, confident, and educated—different from themselves.

What emerges within the ethnic enclave is a symbiotic relationship between the new Irish and the first-generation immigrants. The first-generation immigrants provide jobs, which the illegals need and probably could not get elsewhere without documentation. In turn, the new Irish strengthen the white constituency in the older ethnic neighborhoods, which are increasingly populated by blacks and Hispanic and Asian immigrants. Their recolonization of these neighborhoods in transition acts as a bulwark against further racial and ethnic diversification. Their mutual relationship then is primarily based on instrumentalism. As one immigrant summed up, "We're using them, and they're using us."

There is considerable social and cultural distance between the new Irish and their first-generation employers. This causes misunderstanding and misperception on both sides, particularly with regard to lifestyle issues, as one informant explains:

Only for them, the new Irish probably wouldn't be getting any work. They had it tough, but they didn't have to look over their shoulder all the time. They don't understand the younger generation. Maybe it is true that we drink more, but whatever the case is, the older people like to think so.

According to the local priests in the parishes of Gaelside (the Bronx) and Irishtown (Queens), the older immigrants do not understand why the new arrivals do not follow "due process," that is, why they do not get their papers in order and settle down as law abiding, tax-paying citizens. The widespread perception that the new arrivals have not made enough effort to regularize their situation creates a feeling of resentment in the community. However, very few Irish illegals qualified for the Amnesty Program, the highly publicized reform package introduced under the Immigration Reform and Control Act in 1986. In addition, while the Donnelly and Morrison visa lotteries have provided an avenue toward legalization for some in the Irish community, they have by no means addressed the needs of all.

One priest also offered the view that there is a generational gap in values, which is particularly apparent in the older Irish immigrants' labeling of the new Irish as immoral and uncouth:

The older Irish think that the new Irish lack morals because they see couples living together, they see people drinking, being rowdy and disrupting the neighborhood. They don't understand why the new Irish don't come in and actively participate in their civic clubs and county associations.

This cultural and social distance is an indicator of a fragmentation of Irish ethnic culture along age and social status (including legal status) lines:

People don't mix easily outside of their own social group. The older Irish tend to be more family-oriented, better established, and more upwardly mobile. The younger, single people are into a totally different life style. Bars are their cultural center, and they tend to close in on themselves.

The first-generation immigrants have more than just a symbolic interest in their ethnicity. They are steeped in their own Irish traditions, which they celebrate through their ethnic institutions and through their cultural and sporting events. Apart from the annual St. Patrick's Day parade, they participate in a variety of county and civil associations, which host annual dinner dances. The new Irish share in some elements of this ethnic culture. For example, Gaelic sports continue to attract followers from among the old immigrants and the more recent arrivals. Their shared interest in, and love of, the game serves to unite the two constituencies. This was shown to me one Sunday morning in July 1988 when I traveled to the Bronx to watch a live satellite broadcast of a championship hurling game played in Ireland:

I got off the train at 9:30 A.M. and already a trickle of people, fully dressed in team colors, were making their way toward the college. Outside the auditorium, crowds of people—mostly men—were milling around. Approximately half were over 35 years, and half of them were under 35 years. Everybody was neatly turned out (Sunday morning), and there was a buzz in the air. My companions hailed people they knew as we made our way into the hall. Two games were being broadcast simultaneously in two separate rooms. There were several hundred people assembled in our auditorium when the first satellite images started to flicker on the screen. Cheers went up when the teams appeared and the entire audience stood for the playing of the national anthem. The game was on. As one team and then the other scored, the audience shouted, rose to its feet, and clapped and whooped heartily. When the game was over we emerged into the noon sunshine, where a postmortem was already in progress. The scene reminded me of an after-mass crowd in a country parish milling around the church gates, exchanging views, news, and gossip.

Despite their shared enjoyment of Gaelic sports, the new immigrants are in many other respects culturally distinct from the first-generation Irish ethnics. In creating their own cultural identity, the new immigrants draw not only on Irish-American culture, but also on the experience of growing up in Ireland in the post–1960s and on the experience of living and working as illegals in New York City. Hence, while they may attend Gaelic hurling and football matches and occasional county dances, the kind of music they will listen to is distinctly contemporary rather than traditional.

The most popular bands on the new Irish circuit play straight rock and roll or rock variations on traditional or Celtic themes—a hybrid derived from traditional Irish music and American rock and roll. Indeed, there is a burgeoning Irish rock music industry in New York City. Many new bands have been showcased in a trendy East Village bar in Manhattan owned by a member of the new Irish generation. While there continues to be a following for authentic Irish music, the genre that attracts an Irish-American audience—cabaret-style reworking of Irish tunes and immigrant laments—is widely rejected. More and more bars are catering to the tastes of the younger clientele in New York by providing rock bands in their bars at night.

Soccer and skiing are popular leisure time pursuits among the immigrants. Soccer is primarily an urban sport in Ireland, Britain, and Continental Europe, and its popularity among the new Irish in New York represents the penetration of urban values into contemporary Irish culture. Skiing facilities are not available in Ireland, so its attraction to the financially able in the new Irish community represents an identification with an international, high status adventure sport. The celebration of ethnicity in the new Irish community is conflated with a celebration of youth, and this distinguishes them from the first-generation immigrants. Broadly speaking, the new Irish culture is derived in part from Irish-American culture. But it also draws on contemporary Irish culture and international youth culture. As such, it is potentially subversive of the ethnic culture. A recent and highly publicized example of such subversion was the clash between the Irish Lesbian and Gay Organization and the Ancient Order of Hibernians (AOH) (Manhattan Branch) over the former's right to participate in the St. Patrick's Day parade. The idea of Irish gays clearly proved anathema to the more conservative elements of the Irish American community.

In sum, the new Irish interact differently with the two Irish-American groups. Their relations with Irish Americans are largely *symbolic*, although an attempt has been made particularly by the IIRM to translate that symbolism into social and financial support. Relations with first-generation Irish immigrants tend to be characterized by *dependency* because of the powerful positions occupied by many first-generation immigrants in the ethnic enclave. However, both constituencies have something to gain by the arrival of the new Irish, so there is a *symbiotic* aspect underlying both sets of relations. The new Irish have the potential to revitalize an immigrant community, which many thought had disappeared forever into the melting pot. Old Irish neighborhoods have been invigorated by the influx of the new Irish, as have New York-based Gaelic sports. Business is booming in the Irish bars and import stores. Many Irish-American county associations, which were all but defunct, have been re-established. There has been a resurgence of Irish festivals and cultural events. And there is the burgeoning Irish rock music industry that extends beyond the ethnic enclave. But despite this revitalization, it is not at all clear that the new Irish are assimilable to the

Irish-American way of life. And since many will eventually return to Ireland, they may never have to fully acclimatize. Hence, they have tended to remain a distinct group within the ethnic Irish community.

INTERNAL STRATIFICATION: CULTURE VERSUS CLASS IN THE NEW IRISH COMMUNITY

One of the striking features about the new Irish is the absence of class stratification within their community. Class distinctions based on education, occupation, or background are almost totally supplanted by the commonality of the illegal immigrant experience. Almost universally, the immigrants testify to a sense of equality with their peers because "we're all in the same boat"—a reference to their illegal alien status. Immigration acts as a leveler because each individual must survive within the constraints of illegality, regardless of his or her personal credentials or resources. Professionals and the unskilled end up doing the same kind of work:

We're all in the same boat, shoveling shit. There are teachers from home out here washing dishes and waitressing, just like us.

Fellas who were in college at home are laboring at the same jobs as us here, so getting an education at home doesn't seem to be of much use.

Class differentiation is seen as irrelevant, given the structure of the immigrant labor market:

There is no real class distinction on the basis of economics because everyone has the same earning potential regardless of their intelligence.

The value of formal education is consistently downgraded by the immigrants, especially by those who pursued degree programs that have had no application in their working lives as illegal immigrants:

Education makes no difference whatsoever. I basically see my education as a waste, given the job I am in. I could do nothing with it.

I have a Commerce degree and a higher diploma in Education, and I am working in construction in New York along with my brothers. I'm the eldest in the family and they were very proud to send me to university. Now I think I would have been better off if I had spent my time learning a trade like carpentry.

One effect of illegality is to wipe out the stratification system (based on educational attainment) that prevails in Ireland. The collective experience of illegality overrides individual differences between immigrants:

You meet a greenhorn out here and they might have an attitude problem but within six months they mellow out. They get the piss taken out of them and realize it is better to become like everyone else.

The "attitude problem" arises when a recently arrived immigrant behaves in a superior or condescending way to other immigrants. This may take the form of belittling the kind of work people do, snubbing people who are considered of lower class or social status, and/or emphasizing one's own class and family background. Immigrants who, in the initial adjustment period, have difficulty with the equality regime soon learn to acclimatize to the new Irish community.

The absence of stratification in the workplace carries over into immigrant social life. People who work together also socialize together, congregating in the same immigrant bars. An immigrant's social status and family background at home assume less and less importance in the intimate social setting of the ethnic enclaves. The social controls imposed by families are effectively removed. Appearances and status consciousness that divided people at home seem increasingly irrelevant among a community that is bonded primarily through their common illegality. This creates greater openness within and between different social circles:

Out here you meet people that you wouldn't have anything to do with at home, maybe because of their background or family problems they may have had. Out here though, it doesn't bother you who their father was—the fact that they were a Tommy Small at home has no bearing on it. Everyone is equal because of the jobs people do. There are people I hang out with here that I couldn't tell my mother about because of their social background.

Emigration is a great leveler. Out here, the fact that you are Irish is the lowest common denominator. At home, you tend to mix exclusively with the same class of people, whereas here you take people at face value.

Relationships that would have been inconceivable at home, because of disparities in class backgrounds, become possible under the conditions of illegality. People from different backgrounds are thrown together in New York, and inevitably, new associations and affiliations are formed. As one former white collar worker explains:

I never would have met someone like my boyfriend if I had stayed in Ireland. He is a carpenter by trade and I guess I would have categorized him on the basis of that . . . I just wouldn't have got to know him.

The absence of class stratification within the immigrant community is primarily attributed to the commonality of their experience as illegal aliens. However, the immigrants also place their own experiences in the context of their perceptions of the proximate environment. Despite their rejection

of American values and culture, they fully subscribe to the American
dream—endorsing the perceived egalitarianism and upward social mobility
in the American social system. This indicates incipient Americanization
among the community of new Irish despite their illegal status. Discounting
their own disadvantaged position, the immigrants see many advantages in
that system. There is universal admiration for what they describe as the
openness of the social structure, exemplified by the upwardly mobile Americans who cross their paths. Success in America, according to these Irish
immigrants, does not breed snobbery:

There is no real class distinction in America. I worked in houses putting in kitchens
and I found that I was always treated with respect, even by people who were
millionaires. The wealthy people out here are just normal guys, working for what
they are making.

I admire the fact that a Vice President of the Transit Authority will come into my
bar and buy a drink for his buddy who sells watches on the street. It contrasts with
the entrenched Irish traditions—no slap on the back when you achieve something,
valley of the squinting windows, and all that.

According to the immigrants, in America all stand equal before the law:

The President and the illegal immigrant are equally dragged across the coals here.

These kinds of remarks indicate that the immigrants evaluate the American
system from the purview of the Irish-American enclaves in which they are
located. Their perspective is one informed by the upward mobility that they
see among white ethnics, in particular, the Irish Americans. Whether consciously or unconsciously, they shut out the "American nightmare"—pervasive racism, high levels of homelessness, and the growing urban
underclass.

The New York-based Irish community is perceived as much less class
bound than some of the class-ridden towns from which these young people
emigrated. For many immigrants, life in New York represents a welcome
escape from the suffocating conformity of life in a small Irish town. One
immigrant recalled how the system of class differentiation reached down
into the town's classrooms:

In the front row sat the children of the town elite—the businessmen and the bank
managers. In the next row sat the children of the teachers and bank officials. And
in the back you had the children of the lower classes—children of farm laborers, etc.
They were considered the "least bright" of all.

The absence of such a rigid differentiation is frequently commented upon:

Class has more of an effect at home than it does here. Every one is here for the same reason, to make a better life and to make money for yourself. Whether you leave school at 16 or 30 years, you are treated the same. People are people here, first and foremost. The sweetshop attendant and the professor come face to face here. Americans take you for what you are, not what you came from. The class distinction at home is really something in comparison.

Class distinction is rampant in Ireland. The bank official, the teacher is looked up to at home. But here everyone is illegal. We are sharing the same ground. America is not as class conscious. Here your status depends on what kind of person you are— your moral values, your personality. You wouldn't clean houses at home but you are not looked down on for doing it here.

Illegal immigrants, therefore, do not identify themselves in terms of social class origin. Social class differences are of little relevance in a labor market where everyone operates under the same constraint. Rather, their shared identity is based on a coalescence of *common nationality* and *common marginality* arising from their illegal status. Their cohesiveness as a community derives from the interplay of these factors and sets the new Irish apart not only from their home culture, but also from the host culture and from the ethnic culture.

Within the boundaries of the new Irish community, however, there is a marked cultural stratification. People combine by cultural affiliation rather than class position. The stratification occurs along two different dimensions: (1) an urban/rural divide, and (2) a bias toward one's place of origin, manifested as localism. In the informal sector, advancement is based principally on ascriptive characteristics (county or town of origin, the right contacts). Achieved characteristics (good education, job experience) have little or no value because without documentation there is no access to the formal sector. In the informal labor market, the individual's ascribed characteristics or cultural affiliations have greater currency than achieved characteristics, such as high educational attainment and high social class position. It is the structure of job opportunity that heightens the importance of cultural affiliations and lessens the importance of social class position.

Culchies versus Jackeens: The Urban/Rural Divide

The most pronounced cleavage is between immigrants from an urban background, known colloquially as "Dubliners" or "Jackeens," and those from a rural background, frequently called "culchies" or "rednecks." (*Culchie* is a term of disparagement derived from the town of Kiltimagh in Ireland's rural heartland. *Redneck* is much less commonly used in Ireland and may in fact be a U.S. term that has found its way into the immigrant vernacular.) This urban/rural cleavage is in large part carried over from Ireland:

There is a distinction between Dubliners on the one hand and "rednecks" on the other. The majority of people fall into the second category, and each group tends to stick with their own.

When I lived in Dublin, I saw the way Dublin people distinguished themselves from the "rednecks" or "culchies." If there is any difference out here it is between Dublin people and people from the country.

Differences tend to be seen in terms of culture rather than class. Dubliners are seen as forward, sophisticated, and arrogant by their rural counterparts. The latter are seen by Dubliners as shrewd, secretive, and extremely clannish. While Dubliners are frequently singled out for criticism by culchies, they are often bracketed with immigrants from other urban centers, such as Derry and Belfast, who are held to be equally offensive:

I find that people from Derry and Dublin are very cocky. They are grand on their own in a one-to-one situation, but get a group of them together . . . they tend to look down on the "rednecks."

According to the Dubliners, there is a natural affinity between them and their urban counterparts north of the border. There is a common bond derived from their recognition of a shared urban culture:

Dublin and Belfast are both cities. You tend to think the same way, that's why Dubliners and the Northern Irish get along. We tend to think the same and dress the same compared to the others. We have the same kinds of clubs and discos.

In the pubs you notice that the Dublin and Belfast crowds always get on great. Country people may not get along as well.

Dubliners feel that the structure of opportunity in the immigrant labor market tends to militate against them. It is difficult to acquire union membership without a direct union contact. Since most of the important contact people in the construction unions are from the western and southern counties, Dubliners tend to have difficulty getting into the union and difficulty getting regular work:

I do think it is harder for Dublin people to get jobs here. Most of the carpenters are "culchies," and it is a little harder to get work, to get into the union because you need connections. You see the "culchies" have a tradition of coming to the States. The Dubs historically went to Liverpool and Birmingham, so they don't have the connections.

In periods of retrenchment, Dubliners complain that they are the first to be let go:

I worked in a job where I had been hired before all the others. The job was being run by a Galway crowd, and when business was slow, they kept everyone from the country on but let the Dublin guys go.

The same discriminatory practices appear to operate against Dublin people in the bar trade. Again, counties with a long tradition of emigration to the United States tend to dominate ownership and control of the ethnic bars. As pointed out earlier, different bars are associated with different counties, and jobs as bartenders and waitresses are generally secured on a personal contact basis. This makes it more difficult for Dubliners to get access to bar work, as few bars are owned by fellow countymen:

It is rare for a Dublin person to get a bar job. I think that they are considered wily, too cute, and too clever. Country people are trusted more.

Resentment can build up among Dublin immigrants as they realize the limitations on their job opportunities. But the resentment (often manifested as arrogance or nonchalance) may in turn exacerbate their marginal position in the labor market.

Localism

The urban/rural divide is symptomatic of the deeper cleavage of localism in the immigrant community. The larger the county constituency in New York, the greater the pool of possible contacts and the more likely it is that the immigrant will make contact with someone from home—from his or her own town, parish, or village community. This puts immigrants from counties with a long tradition of emigration at a distinct advantage. In order to safe-guard their privileged position in the labor market, they often close ranks against outsiders. The case of Local X—a construction union affiliate in New York—was cited repeatedly by informants. Local X is controlled by Kerry-men. (In Ireland, there is tremendous rivalry between the counties of Kerry and Dublin because they are thought to epitomize the ethos of ruralism and urbanism respectively.) Kerrymen have a reputation for shrewdness; there-fore, it is difficult for non-Kerry immigrants to gain access, as one immigrant from the Midlands explained:

It is very clannish out here. It's always Connemara people having a drink together or working together. It is the same for Kerry people. I worked for Local X and it took me three months to squeeze myself in. If I was a Kerry lad I would have been in straight away.

Local X's business agent—the crucial middleman who places workers in construction jobs—is a Kerryman. According to one disaffected immigrant, the union favors Kerry immigrants over others:

My brother and I paid $360 each to join Local X in 1985. We heard we could get $19 per hour plus benefits if we joined. The union is totally controlled by Kerrymen. There is no guarantee of work, however, though when the work is plentiful, you get whatever comes their way. If you're not from Kerry, you have to go down to the union office every morning between 5:00 and 5:30 to wait around for a job. If you were from Kerry you just sat at home and waited for the phone to ring.

The structure of job opportunity to a great extent determines the degree of localism in the new Irish community. A narrow job market, in which a few individuals play a powerful gatekeeper role, reinforces clannishness and provincialism among the immigrants. The paths to opportunity and the barriers to mobility are already in place before the immigrants arrive. Work is contingent on good contacts, and good contacts are most likely to be fostered within county or regional groupings. There is a built-in incentive to forge contacts and alliances with "your own," which is more and more narrowly defined:

People are pretty clannish but it is to do with the way that they come out. I came over to play Gaelic football. You come out and you play for a team, you train with them, you socialize with them and you become a cohesive group.

Other immigrants also point out that the localism endemic in the workplace—particularly in the construction unions and the GAA network—carries over into the immigrants' social life and to their relations with other immigrants:

People have a contact person with whom they get in touch, that person gets them a job, and they stick with that—socializing as well as working with the same people. So people end up in the clan from Mayo or Meath or whatever. It is not because they can't move out of their immediate circle, but because they won't.

The Kerry crowd drink in bars owned by Kerrymen. I've worked with these guys and they're very sweet and nice. But if you try to get information about jobs they clam up. All they say is something like "there are a lot of guys out of work." That is supposed to shut you up. Yet, you see their friends come over from Ireland, walk into a bar, and be offered three jobs off the bat.

While Kerry has a strong foothold in the New York construction market, it is Connemara (mainly the counties of Galway and Mayo) that control the local laborers' union in Boston:

If you are from Connemara it is easy to get in. Otherwise, you need a contact. The union officials are from Galway, and it's getting harder and harder to get anyone outside of Connemara in. The Connies would be the most clannish group in Boston.

As with immigrant groups in general, localism is pervasive in the patterns of sociability within the new Irish community. People gravitate toward bars in which they are more likely to find people from home or, failing that, people from their own county or region. The connection with home establishes an immediate basis for a trusting relationship, which is of special importance to the illegal immigrant. As one woman from Tralee, County Kerry explains:

When you meet someone from Kerry—or from Tralee—there is an immediate association. People love to talk about it. I guess we are very clannish because I mix exclusively with Kerry people.

An immigrant from the border of Derry and Tyrone, who identifies more with the former than the latter, explains the unspoken animosity in his relationship with other immigrants from the locality:

Local loyalties are translated over here. For example, there are two guys out here who lived 20 miles from me in Tyrone, but there is a great difference between me and them. I see them on the street here but I don't talk to them because we would never had anything to do with each other at home.

From time to time, immigrants from a town or townland in Ireland will organize a reunion party in one of the bars. A room is rented and food, drink, and music are provided. The event is advertised through word of mouth. These occasions serve to reinforce the local loyalties of the immigrants abroad. County dances and football dances, like reunions, serve to cement local loyalties and to insulate the new Irish from their proximate environment. As with the job market, it is the structure of the sociability options that promotes localism, as a group of Donegal immigrants explain:

It isn't a conscious decision that leads us to end up mixing with a Donegal crowd. You get to know other Donegal people through those that you already know and through the various events.

SUMMARY

The cohesiveness created by the absence of class differentiation among the new Irish is continually challenged by the presence of other kinds of the cleavages within the community. In addition, each individual uses whatever advantages he or she has to further his or her position. This has the effect of promoting instrumentalism over communalism, in the formation of economic and social relations and in the negotiation of identity and ethnicity. As Petras points out "self-designation of immigrant ethnicity is downplayed when heightened group visibility may intensify negative responses by the dominant group or groups, and accented when group identification can serve the self-interest of its members" (1981: 52). On the one hand, emigration acts as a leveler equalizing all the immigrants through their common status as illegal aliens. On the other hand, there is no equality of opportunity when they set about negotiating entry into the workplace and in the social market. An immigrant's demographic profile to a great extent determines the kind of jobs that he or she will get and the likely friendships he or she will form.

Chapter 7 _____

The Impact of Illegality: An Assessment

The conditions that oppress migrant workers are not so deterministic that they can never be challenged or contested (Cohen, 1987: 179).

This chapter examines the impact of illegality on Irish immigrants, focusing in particular on their induction into a "deviant career." Officially, illegals are deviants because they infringe U.S. laws by working without permission. The lies, subterfuges, and evasions in which illegals engage are indicative of deviant behavior. Yet Irish illegals see themselves as victims rather than law breakers and blame their anomalous situation on what they consider discriminatory laws. This allows them to shift the burden of guilt for their legal infractions from themselves onto the state.

Through a process of intragroup socialization, each immigrant learns to adapt to the role of deviant, and over time, this unorthodox career path becomes "normalized." Despite the normalization of illegality on a day-to-day basis, these immigrants are acutely aware of the barriers illegality raises that exclude them from mainstream society. The isolation of Irish illegals has improved somewhat in recent years by the emergence of institutional supports within the community. These supports are examined later in this chapter. In addition, the possibility of legalization through additional visa allocations to Irish citizens is likely to be advantageous to at least some of the current illegals.

THE DEVIANT CAREER AND NORMALIZATION PROCESS

> The effects of illegality are more pronounced at the start when you first arrive. But then you get used to certain constraints and ways of doing things and because everyone else does the same, the situation becomes normalized (Illegal Irish immigrant, New York, 1988).

Irish immigrants arriving in New York without proper documentation are, upon entry, inducted into a deviant career. This career begins as they encounter immigration officers at the airport and ends only when the immigrant leaves the country, either voluntarily or involuntarily. The prospective immigrant, facing a battery of questions from an immigration official at the point of entry, begins to spin the yarns that evolve into an intricate web of lies and subterfuges over the course of his or her deviant career. This repertoire is used to negotiate the world of work and as part of a general avoidance strategy to deflect attention from his or her illegal status.

I have already explored the effects of illegality in terms of its impact at work, its effect on social life and formation of community, its impact on personal relationships, and its role in shaping the immigrant's self-concept and identity. I will now examine the ways in which Irish illegals respond to illegality and assess how they come to terms with it. In short, how do they learn to live within the parameters of a deviant career?

According to Hughes, the concept of "career" brings together the objective features of an individual's experiences—the sequence of situations by which he or she is confronted—and his or her interpretation of and adjustment to those situations:

Subjectively career is the moving perspective in which a person sees his life as a whole, and interprets his attributes, actions and the things which happen to him . . . objectively it is a series of statuses and clearly defined offices . . . typical sequences of position, responsibility and even of adventure (1937: 409–10)

This section discusses the illegal immigrant's interpretation of and adjustment to the illegal situation. In effect, the illegal immigrant undergoes a normalization process, whereby the illegal reality comes to be redefined as normal reality. Insofar as is possible, the illegal Irish attempt to normalize their situation.

For many of the immigrants, their initial induction is a harrowing one. Before they enter the United States, they must have a prepared story as to the purpose and duration of their visit. One strategy frequently employed is to have a letter from a sympathetic relative or friend inviting the immigrant over to a social event such as a wedding. In most cases, these social events are fictitious, but the authenticity of a personal letter is unlikely to be checked by an immigration official:

I had taken the precaution of getting an Irish-American friend to write to me in Ireland inviting me to her son's "wedding." I also carried a "gift" for the occasion. After checking in, an immigration official asked me to step aside. I was asked to empty my pockets and I did so, casually letting the letter about the "wedding" slip. They pounced on it and read it, which is what I was hoping for. Still the questions kept coming, but in the end, I got a five-day visa with a warning that they would be watching me.

Generally, visitors to the United States must carry a letter from a purported employer or college administrator stating that he or she will be returning to Ireland to continue work/college after a specified period in the United States. The prospective immigrant must also be able to show that he or she has the necessary funds to provide for themselves during their "holiday" in the United States. Stories of lengthy interrogations and people being turned back are replete in the Irish media, which serves to heighten the tension and fuel the fear of those who are seeking entry. As one informant explains:

The trip over was frightening. The week before I left there had been a story in the *Irish Post* (London) about 20 people turned back at Boston, so I sweated the whole way over on the plane. I had everything covered, but still I was a wreck. I haven't been home since then.

Almost certainly, the immigrants have to tell some lies at the point of entry—regarding their destination, the duration of their stay, and their purported reasons for visiting the country. People who are on a return journey from Ireland tend to be targeted for close questioning by immigration officials. Unlike the Mexicans who make persistent attempts to cross the border even after apprehension, an Irish illegal (or more accurately, prospective illegal) who is uncovered by immigration authorities will have considerable difficulty securing a visa to travel to the United States again. Everything depends on their ability to dupe inquisitive immigration officials at the point of entry. It requires considerable psychological resilience to stand one's ground when questioned:

I came back to New York in January 1988, and I was stopped at immigration. A black woman interrogated me. I looked her straight in the eye and told her I was back for a wedding. Some girls got intimidated and broke down under her questioning, but I got through.

They held me for three-quarters of an hour questioning me about what I had done during my previous period in the States. . . . They treated me like an inferior or a slut. They pulled through all my books, jewelry, nightdresses, etc. They took my money and examined my open return ticket. It was the worst experience I had ever had. I decided that I was never going home again.

Immigrants returning to the United States often mail all their personal effects in advance so that there is nothing to suggest that they overstayed their visa previously. Once entry has been negotiated, the next step is to establish oneself within the immigrant community. This means getting a place to stay, finding a job, becoming acclimatized to a new set of circumstances. In the initial adjustment period, illegality looms large:

At the beginning it was a real handicap—not just being illegal but being in a strange country. It was hard to go for a good job, it was difficult to use the pay phones, even asking for a drink in a bar could pose difficulty. There is a real culture shock.

An important step for prospective employees is to acquire the documents that will smooth the path for employment. This is more important for men than for women because the former are frequently asked for identification to comply with the provisions of the Immigration Reform and Control Act. (The act does not apply to domestic employees in private homes.) The two most popular forms of identification are a social security card and a driver's license. False social security cards in the immigrant's own name can be purchased relatively easily. In addition, authentic social security cards that belong to legal residents or American citizens, either dead or retired, are traded within the immigrant network. In the case of the latter, an immigrant works under an assumed name. Since he must produce at least two pieces of identification to comply with the employment regulations, he must obtain further identification under the assumed name. Thus, many of the immigrants have two identities—their own *and* the assumed or fictionalized one used for work purposes. In the past, a driver's license was relatively easily obtained and this, together with the social security card, generally sufficed as evidence of one's eligibility to work. Since the passage of the new immigration law, however, restrictions have been increasingly imposed on the issuance of driver's licenses, especially in city offices. Applicants have been asked not only to produce a passport, but also evidence of their legal entitlement to work in the United States. This has meant that people have had to travel to small offices out-of-town in order to obtain an identification card. On presenting a passport only, they are issued a driver's license. Forged passports may be acquired within the community for those who require identification under an assumed name. A forged passport may be used by an immigrant to obtain a driver's license in the false name. He or she may also, at another time or in another office, acquire a license in his or her own name. Thus, some immigrants, such as David, maintain two separate identities:

I work under another name and it can be confusing sometimes. At first it was hard to live with the name Peter, and I wouldn't always answer to it, but you get used to it. It is a bit of a problem though because half of my i.d. is in that name, and the other half is in my real name. I can't open a bank account in my own name because the checks are made out to the other name. And I can't use my driver's license as proof of i.d. in the bank, since it is in my own name.

When asked if this dual identity bothered him and if he would prefer to have one identity and work above board, David responded to the contrary:

To be honest, I would use the same system—two names—if I thought it would help me to avoid paying taxes. If you pay taxes you get screwed. I would do the same in Ireland if I got a chance to avoid paying taxes.

Since illegal immigrants are already operating outside of the system, there is an added incentive to evade taxation:

I'm getting on as good as the next man. My sister is legal here, and I guess if I wanted I could start the process of sponsorship through her. But I am doing well as I am, and I don't really want to rock the boat. I don't pay taxes, my job is secure, so I'm not worried.

It's not really in my interest to be legal. If I became legal then I have to pay my taxes, social security, etc. By the end of the day I wouldn't be any better off than I am in Ireland. So what would be the point of being here then? The illegality actually makes it financially advantageous to be here.

Such views tend to be expressed by the immigrants described earlier as holiday-takers—a group that is closer to the sojourner model than to the settler model of migration. They are not interested in making a permanent commitment to the host society, but rather see their future back in Ireland. They prefer to work "off-the-books" rather than earn "dead money" (money paid in taxes, union dues, and social security contributions) even if it means foregoing union and other benefits in the short-term. This attitude is directly related to the transitory nature of their lives.

Those who work for small contractors may pay neither taxes nor social security, and the contractors may choose not to file tax returns at the end of the year. Those who do pay contributions fabricate wives and dependents as a way of augmenting their tax-free allowances. Since they see themselves as working largely outside of the system, they come to accept and to a certain extent expect, an arrangement that will free them of these tax obligations.

Many of the immigrants have already been disaffected by their experience as overburdened taxpayers in Ireland. One of the few perceived "benefits" of illegality is that the immigrant can decide what, if any, contributions he or she wishes to make to the system. Their official "invisibility" means that identities can be borrowed, created, and exchanged. Official data such as place of birth, work histories, numbers of dependents, tax exemptions, can be fictionalized at will.

The interplay between fiction and reality provides a motif for understanding the illegal immigrant experience. The immigrant's position in the social structure is ephemeral—while he or she is connected to it (through the labor market, for example) he or she is not of it (participation in the labor market has no legal basis). The immigrant's connections to the social structure is based on real behavior which is, however, frequently described in fictional terms. Filaments of story fabrications and embellishments serve to reinforce the immigrant's deviant career.

Separate identities are not just maintained for work purposes. In order to prevent the possibility of the INS or any other law enforcement agency apprehending them, immigrants may avoid getting an apartment lease, a cable television subscription, or a telephone bill in their own name:

I rent an apartment with another Irish illegal but it is in a third person's name. Our names are not on the lease, neither are they on the door. We slip the super some money just to cover ourselves.

The thing that struck me when I first came over, for example, was that people didn't have the phone in their own name. People would not respond to a voice they didn't recognize on the phone.

During the initial adjustment period, many of the immigrants are apprehensive and worried about their status. However, as they become assimilated into the new Irish community, this fear subsides. They quickly learn the rules of the game. Stories and subterfuges become part of the immigrant's repertoire and are employed almost defiantly to deflect the inquisitive and to dissuade the suspicious:

Illegality doesn't have a day-to-day effect. It wouldn't affect me socially for example. I'll give a story to anybody who asks.

Storytelling is commonplace. Its rationale is understood and tacitly accepted by the priests who provide pastoral care to the illegal Irish community. One of them privately acknowledged that "the new Irish have to tell lies about themselves—it is a fight for survival on their part."

The officials of the IIRM also give legitimacy to the subterranean existence that these immigrants lead. Through a public acknowledgement of the problems and difficulties illegals face, they identify with their constituency. They offer a forum within which the fears, hopes, and strategies of the illegals can be discussed. It is possible to state their case in an open forum because it has not been the practice of immigration officials to pursue or harass Irish illegals. Law enforcement agents are overwhelmingly deployed along the U.S.-Mexican border. In 1983, less than 2 percent of all apprehensions by the INS were from countries other than Mexico (Passel, 1986: 186). The awareness that the Irish community has not been targeted to any great extent by the INS assuages the immigrant's worse fears. Apprehensions of Irish illegals generally result from spot checks by the INS or from a direct tip-off. Although these are isolated incidents, they are highly publicized in the media both in Ireland and in the ethnic press in New York.

The IIRM offer a rationalization for the (necessarily) deviant behavior of their constituents, by reinforcing the normalization process, as this field note recorded at an IIRM meeting shows:

At the meeting a young man got up and said that all he wanted to do was make a living in a democratic country having come from another "so-called" democratic country. "We have the right to demonstrate in our own cause," he said. This remark was followed by a loud clap from the audience. The meeting was brought to order by a member of the steering committee who said that the only crime people had committed was that they had been born later [than previous generations of immigrants, and thus had less opportunity to emigrate under restrictions imposed by the 1965 Act] (IIRM meeting, February 3, 1988).

On another occasion, the use of false documentation was tacitly endorsed by a member of the steering committee:

Officially, we cannot condone the use of false documents, but I think people would be well advised to observe the Eleventh Commandment "Thou shall not get caught" (IIRM meeting, December 3, 1987).

Normalization is achieved by shifting the burden of guilt from the immigrant and onto the system. It is the law that is deviant, not the immigrant, according to the IIRM activists:

We are the generation who will take over the banner from the current leaders in the Irish-American community. We must prove ourselves worthy of that task by proving that we are responsible. We must turn up for work on time and not drink too much. Remember—it is the law that is wrong, not you (IIRM meeting, October 28, 1987).

Clearly the assumption here is that Irish illegals are potentially settlers— they are presented as a new generation of permanent immigrants willing to place themselves under the mantle of Irish America. This assumption on the part of the IIRM is not supported by my data. For political reasons, the IIRM must present a case for the legalization of *all* the undocumented Irish, in order to justify legislative change to increase visa allocations. The new Irish are eulogized as a hard-working group anxious to become permanent residents and abide by the laws of the United States. In fact, the new Irish constitute a diverse community with a range of contrasting interests. While some illegals are willing to settle, others intend to return home, and a significant proportion remain undecided about the future. It is by no means clear that all would avail of legalization opportunities if they become available.

Nevertheless, the view expressed by the activists has currency within the illegal Irish community, probably because it is bound up with the issue of ethnic pride:

[Illegality] doesn't affect me on a day-to-day basis. All they can do is send me home. One thing I wouldn't like is if someone said to me something like "Fuck off, you illegal Irish" or tried to belittle the Irish in some other way. We are illegal because of a law which was written by two Irishmen in the past—the 1965 Act of De Valera and Kennedy.

The 1965 Hart-Celler Act has passed into immigrant folklore as an act of collusion between U.S. President John F. Kennedy and the then President of Ireland Eamonn De Valera to reduce the hemorrhage of emigration by excluding the Irish from America. In fact, the act was part of a general civil rights initiative begun by Kennedy and passed into law after his death. The 1965 act sought to equalize the numbers of immigrants from the Western and Eastern hemispheres. It is unlikely that the Irish would have received preferential treatment whatever lobbying they might have engaged in. Within the immigrant community, however, the 1965 act serves an ideological function as the act that betrayed a new generation of Irish immigrants, who have been denied an easy passage to America. This historical "act of betrayal" serves to legitimate their own presence in the country today.

The awareness that illegality is a communal rather than an individual experience serves to blunt its impact. The people with whom I spoke were almost unanimous in saying that illegality did not affect them on a day-to-day basis: it is not a constant source of worry or anxiety chiefly because of the commonality of the experience and their response to it:

There are so many people in the same boat as ourselves that we consider our situation to be a normal one at this stage.

The first year I was scared and apprehensive a lot of the time. I did a lot of looking over my shoulder but I got used to being here after a while, and now I really don't think about it at all.

The normalization process begins once an immigrant has secured a job and a place to live. Social life, largely revolving around the ethnic bars, creates a sense of a common culture and affords protection against the vagaries of life as an illegal alien. Among their own, it is possible for the immigrants to suspend the label of illegality because it is of little relevance within the community. The solidaristic basis of that community provides an antidote to the highly individualized relationships that exist at work. The immigrants consciously attempt to live as "normal" a life as possible, given the various constraints and the threat of apprehension:

You can't let yourself think about it all the time. If you did you would end up going nuts. It wouldn't be worth staying if you were making yourself sick with anxiety. It's not a way of living.

Many of the new Irish believe that they are going to go home eventually, so the limbo in which they find themselves in New York is viewed as a temporary rather than a terminal condition. For those who want to stay permanently in New York, however, the illegal issue becomes a problematic one. Even the potential settlers perceive themselves as "transients" rather than immigrants because of their illegal status. There is a degree of fatalism in the immigrants' responses to their situation. They tend to develop a blasé attitude, adapting the view that with so little control over their destiny, they have little choice but to accept whatever happens:

You just have to be philosophical about it—if they are going to deport you they will. It wouldn't be the end of the world. My father always reminds me that I have a home to go to. If the INS wanted us, they know where to find us.

Illegality doesn't bother me in the least. I have always had a forthright attitude. Deport me if you want to, I don't mind as long as you are picking up the tab on my ticket home. I have always tried to maintain my dignity despite being here illegally.

IMMOBILITY AND EXCLUSION

> Loneliness is the number one problem facing the new Irish. They are
> not able to go home and in this sense they are under "house arrest"
> (Immigrant priest, New York, August 1988).

The impact of illegality is felt most keenly through the restrictions imposed on travel. The most pressing problem that the undocumented face is their imposed exile from Ireland. Frequent trips home are out of the question because of the risk of apprehension and the possibility of permanent exclusion from the United States. At some point during their sojourn in the United States, most will risk at least one trip home. Some, particularly those with aging or sick parents, fear the inevitable phone call to summon them home to a funeral. More often the trip home is for a special family event or to celebrate Christmas, which has particular symbolic significance to Irish emigrants all over the world. For the undocumented Irish, the anxieties about getting back into the United States often interfere with the enjoyment of being united once again with family and friends:

I would love to be able to go home whenever I want to. But this is my life here, and I have no job to go home to. On my way back after my first holiday in two years

I spent 15 minutes at immigration and I just couldn't go through that every six months. I also took the precaution of flying back via London.

It wasn't really a holiday going back home. I was worried the whole time about getting back in.

The restrictions on mobility make planning for the future impossible. Legalization is seen as most valuable for the freedom of movement it would afford people:

You could go over and back. You would know you were going home in the summer and that you will get back. You don't have that certainty if you don't have a green card.

The problem of separation prompted a novel response by a group of Irish immigrants in March 1990. A committee drawn from the new Irish community organized a special flight from Ireland, which brought families of immigrants to New York for the first time. The committee members, working in conjunction with an immigrant chaplain and the IIRM, underwrote the visitors' touring and transport facilities with various fundraising activities (*Irish Voice*, March 17, 1990). The fares of the 150 visitors were paid by their sons and daughters in the States.

Apart from restrictions on travel to Ireland, there is a considerable risk attached to other trips that immigrants would normally expect to make within the United States and to Canada and Mexico. Crossing a border once again puts the immigrant at risk of apprehension, but even a trip within the States can be fraught with anxiety:

I was worried the whole time that I was on holiday in Ireland. It was the same thing when my girlfriend and I went on a trip to Florida. We hired a car but we really didn't enjoy ourselves because we were worried if anything happened—like an accident—what would we do. You could never just relax and enjoy yourself in either place.

One immigrant, who after several years as an illegal secured a green card, said it made no significant difference to his life except in one respect: "It made it possible to go home without a heavy heart."

Although people undergo a normalization process, which helps them adjust to their illegal status, their exclusion from the wider system of American institutions remains an ongoing cause for concern. The illegal immigrant works and socializes relatively freely *within* the Irish ethnic enclave. The restrictions imposed by illegality are most keenly felt when the immigrant, for whatever reason, tries to penetrate the boundaries of his or her own closed community. Encounters with systemwide institutions tend to generate fear and frustration. On the one hand, there is the fear of being exposed as an illegal and having to face apprehension. On the other hand, there is the frustration of not being able to make a commitment or investment of even the most rudimentary nature in the host country.

The immigrants fear accidents or injuries. Most of them do not have medical coverage of any kind and so a trip to the hospital can be expensive. Unsure of their entitlements and fearful of apprehension, they generally sign themselves out at the first opportunity:

I went unconscious for a few moments after being knocked off my bicycle. Two police cars and an ambulance came on the scene. I told them I was over on holidays. I was actually suffering from concussion but I didn't want to be admitted to the hospital. Apart from being illegal, I had very little money, and I knew that I couldn't afford a hospital stay. I didn't know my rights, and I didn't know if I could tell the truth. So I refused to be admitted.

The practice is generally to give a false name and address if one is admitted to a hospital. People who work under an assumed name who pay union dues and benefits in that name will use the assumed name at the hospital. Generally, no follow-up treatment is sought, and a convalescence or recuperation period is made possible only through the goodwill of family and friends within the Irish community:

I had a broken leg and the boss said he would help me out but he didn't. I had to make up a social security number at the hospital before I could get treatment. I avoided paying the bill by giving a false address. Afterwards I spent eight months recuperating with friends upstate. A good friend helped me out, and others contributed a few dollars here and there.

Another illegal immigrant who sustained a serious leg injury was hospitalized for several months after the accident:

I was lying on my back for weeks on end and the pain and loneliness were unbearable. I had tried to conceal my accident from the family, but as soon as they found out they were over. I was out of work recuperating for four months after I came out of hospital. Some of the lads threw a benefit for me which raised a couple of thousand dollars. It wasn't much but it helped.

A degree of subsidized medical care for illegals who need help has become available in recent years through Project Irish Outreach, a program run by Catholic Charities and described later in the chapter.

A primary source of frustration is the lack of financial security. A social security number is required to open a bank account, which excludes the majority of the immigrants and presents several problems. Without a social security number, illegals have to negotiate cash payments for jobs or take their checks to a bar to be cashed. Then there is the problem of what to do with the money. Keeping large amounts of cash in an apartment is generally not a viable alternative given the high rate of crime in the city. Nevertheless, cash is sometimes buried under floor coverings and beneath mattresses. Those who are committed to saving send their money home. Without the convenience of an accessible bank account, there is little incentive to save. High earners in construction or the bar/restaurant trade are unable to invest in property because they have no way of establishing credit. Without a bank account, there is no possibility of getting a bank loan, which is often the only way that an immigrant, particularly those working in construction, can set up or expand a business. In addition, credit card companies will generally not extend privileges to a client unless he or she has a good credit rating. But a credit rating cannot be built without access to a bank account. So many immigrants find themselves in a vicious circle:

I think about buying property but I have no credit, and therefore no way of raising a mortgage.

It is really difficult to filter into the system. For example, I can't get a bank loan to buy a truck for my business because I haven't been able to build up a credit rating. If I were able to buy a truck it would be a tax-deductible item because I would be using it for business. When you don't have credit cards, you don't have a credit rating so you can't buy property either. The last three years have been wasted because we are illegal.

Despite their limited resources, some immigrants take the initiative in order to overcome their exclusion from the services of financial institutions:

I bought a car and established a credit rating by convincing the garage to co-sign for the car. Once I had that paid off I applied for a credit card, and once I got that, I applied for a lot of other charge cards.

One couple saw an advertisement in a shopping mall, which offered a credit card recommendation if the client deposited a minimum sum for a specified time period. They lodged the money in the bank in California and were able to obtain credit cards as a result. As with the previous case, they used one credit card to get other credit and charge cards to build up their credit rating.

To a lesser extent, people also feel excluded from educational opportunities. Many of the colleges in the tri-state area require social security cards or other identification, such as an alien registration card (green card) for registration. This is discouraging, particularly for those who are most interested in furthering their education—the women. The nature of their employment is such that they tend to have the least documentation, and this militates against them applying to educational institutions:

I was going to go to college in the evenings but it's difficult to get in without a social security number so I didn't follow it through.

There is also a feeling of exclusion from the political institutions of the country:

This place hasn't been bad to me—you should work for what you get, but you should also put something back in. The country has given me a better life and I would like to be able to vote—it is part of me and I am part of it.

It is not just the insecurity of the job market that affects the immigrants, but also the fact that they can exercise little control over their own destiny. Their exclusion from the system means that effectively they have little or no access to medical, financial, educational, or political institutions.

INSTITUTIONAL SUPPORT SYSTEMS IN THE NEW IRISH COMMUNITY

The Irish Immigration Reform Movement

Until the passage of the Immigration Reform and Control Act in 1986, prospects for Irish illegals in the labor market had been relatively good. The most profound effect of the act on the illegal population was to formalize a sanctions procedure for employers found guilty of hiring illegal aliens. The short-term effect was to make employers wary of hiring foreign workers who could not produce the necessary documentation to authenticate themselves. This greatly reduced access to secure employment, as well as restricting the level of mobility in the illegal Irish job market.

In the case of the Irish illegals, it was the deteriorating conditions in which they found themselves in the post–1987 period that proved to be the crucial catalyst in the establishment of a movement aimed at immigration reform. As the provisions of the act began to take effect, the Irish community mobilized to protest its case at the highest levels of government.

Mobilization and Politicization. Acknowledgment of the Irish illegals began in May 1987, when a group of young people came together to establish an organization to fight for legislative reform that would permit them to regularize their status. They called themselves the Irish Immigration Reform Movement (IIRM). In the manner of its establishment and the way in which it developed, the IIRM closely followed the model outlined by McCarthy and Zald, who define a social movement as "a set of opinions and beliefs in a population which represents preferences for changing some elements of the social structure and/or reward distribution of a society" (1977: 1217–18).

The impetus for the establishment of some kind of organization to address the problem of illegality came when Patrick Hurley and Sean Minihane, two friends from the same town in Ireland, presented a graphic account of the situation of Irish illegals to members of the Cork County Association in New York. The association members—made up of older Irish ethnics, most of whom had long since decamped to the suburbs—were disturbed by what they heard (*Irish Echo*, June 27, 1987). White-collar Irish Americans affiliated to these county associations would have had little first-hand experience of the illegal Irish problem. Those with business interests in the ethnic enclave were already aware of the illegal problem but were not anxious to raise the issue, believing that the less said about the matter the better for all concerned. (In 1986, my concerted attempts to obtain a comment on the illegal Irish problem from a spokesperson for the United Irish Counties Association—the umbrella organization for all the county associations—were futile. He refused to admit that there was a problem.) By bringing the issue up in a public forum, the two young Corkmen forced a response. The association offered its support, providing the premises for the inaugural meeting of the IIRM on May 20, 1987.

Enlisting the help of a New York-based Irish priest (also from County Cork), Hurley and Minihane devised a set of objectives and planned a strategy for the organization. Those objectives were (1) to secure an amnesty for all illegal aliens presently in the United States of America, (2) to establish a large annual nonpreference quota on immigrant visas for Ireland and the other 35 countries adversely affected by the 1965 Immigration Act, and (3) to address the problems of the new Irish aliens, both documented and undocumented. They planned to achieve these objectives by mobilizing the Irish government, the Irish-American community and the new Irish into one united front.

The organizers were careful not to promote the movement purely as a vehicle for obtaining preferential treatment for Irish illegals. By embracing other countries who had also been adversely affected by the 1965 act, they sought to build a broader appeal for the movement. Also by appealing to all sectors of the Irish constituency in America, they sought to maximize their access to resources.

According to McCarthy and Zald (1977), social movement organizations develop not from grievances directly, but *indirectly* through the moves of actors in the political system. There is no doubt that these two Irish men possessed considerable courage and political acumen in getting the movement off the ground. They tapped into a reservoir of grievance, which until that point had no real channel for expression. As a broadly disorganized collectivity, the population of Irish illegals was ripe for mobilization through the leadership provided by these key actors or "energetic entrepreneurs" (Jenkins, 1983: 530). Studies of successful social movements have demonstrated that organizers are both politically experienced and resourceful (Freeman, 1973; Jenkins and Perrow, 1977). Minihane and Hurley had been politically active in Ireland before emigrating, and several other key figures on the original steering committee had been previously active in national politics, trade unions, or student politics.

From its inception, the IIRM followed a centralized, bureaucratic model of organization with a clear division of labor—the type of model most likely to be successful in achieving organizational goals (Gamson, 1975). In the first few months of its existence, the IIRM formalized its initial set of objectives and set about adopting a written constitution. It maintained a formal list of members—individuals could affiliate to the movement for a fee of $10—who received a monthly newsletter and information flyers. Organizationally, the movement had two internal divisions: (1) the national council (a policy-making division) composed of delegates from the steering committees, which meet intermittently, and (2) the steering committees that ran the movement on a day-to-day basis at branch level. In the first year of operation, nine branches were established in New York, Boston, Chicago, San Francisco, Philadelphia, Washington D.C., New Jersey, Hartford, and Phoenix, Arizona. Subsequently, cities as far apart as St. Paul-Minneapolis and St. Louis, Missouri, established branches of the IIRM (*Irish Voice*, March 24, 1990).

The establishment of branches throughout the country created a grass-roots network facilitating the dissemination of information and the coordination of lobbying activities at the local level. These branches also provided an effective participatory structure for activist Irish Americans. The decentralized structure of the national organization helped to counteract the bureaucratic tendencies of the organization center in New York. Furthermore, the emphasis on lobbying activities for immigration reform and the enlistment of the support of prominent Irish Americans gave the organization a publicly acceptable face.

In its first few months of organization, the New York branch set up six different action groups (later called subcommittees) which were to address the objectives of the movement in a practical way. The leaders of the action groups gave progress reports at the IIRM meetings, held on a monthly basis in either the Bronx or Queens. The six action groups were organized around the following areas: Irish government, ethnic contact, new Irish, Irish-Americans, fundraising, and public relations. This division of labor meant that the different constituencies to which the movement addressed itself would be solicited for support and funds on an ongoing basis.

In analyzing the preconditions for a successful social movement organization, Freeman distinguishes between *tangible* assets, such as money, facilities, and means of communication, and *intangible* or human assets, which include specialized resources such as organizing skills and the voluntary labor of supporters (1979: 172–75). The IIRM was quickly able to mobilize tangible and intangible assets through the specialized action groups that it had established.

One of the first priorities of the nascent organization was to raise funds to cover the considerable administrative costs of producing literature, running a hotline, and sending delegations to Capitol Hill. In its first year of operation, the IIRM reported that it had raised $150,000. The money came from donations given by various county associations and divisions of the

AOH, as well as from fundraising activities (*Irish Echo*, May 21, 1988). Musicians who played the Irish circuit gave their services for free. Concerts and music nights also served to attract new members to the organization and spread the word of its existence. Funds were also raised through the membership drive that got underway in December 1987.

As the organization gained in stature, funding became less haphazard. Money was increasingly available through formal rather than informal channels. As the only organization representing the interests of the new Irish, the IIRM came to be seen as the legitimate voice of that constituency. With the help of Irish-American representatives, the organization was able to obtain funding from city and state administrations. For example, in July 1988, the IIRM was awarded a grant of $30,000 by the Borough of Queens to staff a hotline information center. The IIRM was the only new Queens-based group to obtain funding from the borough offices in that fiscal year. This grant was increased to $55,000 the following year, and a further $25,000 was provided by the Bronx and Brooklyn Borough councils (*Irish Voice*, November 25, 1989). Funds of $10,000 were also set aside for the IIRM in the 1989–1990 New York State budget (*Irish Voice*, April 29, 1989). A further $10,000 was donated to the IIRM by the New York St. Patrick's Day Ball committee in April 1990 (*Irish Voice*, April 21, 1990). In the same year, the IIRM received corporate sponsorship from MCI and Guinness. Finally, the Emerald Isle Welfare Center and Project Irish Outreach in New York received substantial funds from a grant of $314,000 set aside by the Irish government for the welfare of Irish immigrants in the United States (*Irish Voice*, May 19, 1990). As the movement developed and became more professional, the sources of funding diversified to the extent that resources outside of the Irish community could be successfully tapped.

In the early days of operation, the IIRM relied heavily on facilities provided by ethnic Irish organizations. The United Irish Counties Association donated an office and telephone line in the summer of 1987, so that a hotline could be established to address the needs of Irish immigrants. Venues for holding meetings (and fundraisers) were donated by prominent members of the Irish-American community. Many Irish Americans became actively involved in the movement, often acting in an advisory capacity and using their contacts in a variety of American institutions, including the media, to highlight the plight of the illegal Irish. Prominent clergymen, county association presidents, and businessmen were asked to join a panel of advisors to the organization. The IIRM quickly developed linkages with influential groups such as the AOH, the Irish American Labor Coalition (IALC), and the Brehon Law Society. The creation of a united front on immigration reform was achieved with the establishment of the Irish Immigration Working Committee under the auspices of the Irish Consulate in New York in October 1987. This committee gave formal status to the informal linkages that had been fostered between the IIRM, the AOH, the IALC, and Catholic Charities of the Archdiocese of New York. The Irish Immigration Working Committee coordinated the lobbying efforts of the Irish community for a series of immigration reform bills which were introduced into the House of Representatives and the Senate between 1987 and 1990. Each time there was a hearing on the bill a deputation from the Irish Immigration Working Committee went to Washington to lobby politicians to vote in favor of the bill. The various Irish organizations backed up the lobbying efforts with mailings to Irish Americans urging them to lobby their congressional representatives to vote for legislative reform.

The most public and important endorsement of the IIRM came on March 17, 1989, when the IIRM was admitted to the St. Patrick's Day parade, taking its place along with scores of other Irish American groups to make the symbolic journey up Fifth Avenue. According to Patrick Hurley, the IIRM leader, this gesture on the part of the parade committee was of huge symbolic importance: "It shows a coming of age for us. It shows that we have earned our laurels, that the Irish American community have now accepted us" (*Irish Voice*, March 18, 1989).

The IIRM was able to draw highly effectively on a preexisting network of Irish-American organizations which offered financial resources, organizational skills, and local political contacts, all crucial to the emergent organization. The Irish-American community (through the work of the IIRM and its Irish-American action group) was appealed to as a "conscience constituency" of relatively affluent middle-class people who could provide necessary resources but did not themselves stand to gain directly from success in the accomplishment of the movement's goals (McCarthy and Zald, 1977). Why did the various organizations in the Irish-American community rally around the IIRM? The answer to this question centers around the thorny issues of identity and ethnicity.

The attenuation of ethnic differences among whites in the United States has seriously weakened traditional Irish ethnicity in terms of social allocation and social solidarity (Alba, 1990: 16–17). According to Alba, however, ethnic identity—a person's subjective identity toward his or her ethnic origins—remains a salient feature in American society (1990: 25). The belated realization among Irish Americans that a new generation of Irish immigrants were clandestinely living and working in the United States activated their sense of ethnic identity. Here was a new generation of Irish immigrants bringing life back into dilapidated Irish neighborhoods, playing their hearts out in Gaelic Park, and providing a new market for ethnic goods and services. For a significant number of Irish Americans, the reactivation of their ethnic identity served as a catalyst for ethnic solidarity expressed through their involvement in the movement for immigration reform.

Following the classic ethnic solidarity model (Alba, 1990: 17), Irish Americans, in conjunction with the new Irish activists, mobilized themselves to bring about a resolution to the Irish illegal problem. It is noteworthy that this problem is a much less contentious one than the issue of the conflict in Northern Ireland. (The latter tends to be politically divisive, which has resulted in a fragmentation of Irish-American opinion.) In opening up Irish immigration to the United States, the Irish-American community stood to strengthen itself numerically, culturally, and politically. The Irish-American community in the late 1980s found itself with a cause that united all its constituent bodies and created the potential for the revitalization of the Irish lobby as a force among other powerful ethnic groups.

To a lesser extent, the IIRM also drew on the resources of groups outside of the Irish community. Through its ethnic contact group, the IIRM sought to make links with other ethnic groups who could be mobilized around the issue of immigration reform. The Polish and Slavic Center, which was established in the early 1970s to provide social services for Eastern European immigrants in the New York area, endorsed the IIRM and offered support and advice (IIRM meeting, February 3, 1988). Attempts were also made to establish a working relationship with Italian immigrant groups (IIRM meeting, January 6, 1988).

News coverage is critical to sustaining any social movement or organization (Molotch, 1979; Gitlin, 1980). The IIRM leadership showed considerable sophistication in their ability to attract and sustain media attention, particularly in the first year of operation. In the first few months of its existence, the IIRM concentrated on getting their message out to the Irish constituencies in the United States and to Ireland. The widespread coverage that the organization received in the national and international media helped to legitimize the organization as the sole voice of the new Irish in America. Significantly, at the inaugural meeting on May 20, 1987, a radio crew from Ireland's national radio station was present and recorded much of the proceedings. Thus, the inauguration of the IIRM was broadcast to Irish audiences the next morning. The story was subsequently covered extensively by the national newspapers in Ireland.

The public relations committee sent press releases and press packages to all Irish newspapers and Irish-American publications, as well as to television and radio stations. They developed close working relationships with popular Irish show hosts on New York local radio and produced a short message using a celebrity Irish singer for broadcast on all Irish-American radio stations. The national media in the United States had by now started to show an interest in the story. By October 1987, the public relations chairperson reported that the movement had reached a point where "we don't have to go to the media, they are coming to us" (IIRM meeting, October 28, 1987). The *New York Times*, for example, ran several stories on the new Irish in 1987, 1988, and 1989. A color story written by Francis X. Clines, a foreign correspondent who has covered Ireland for the *Times*, appeared in the Sunday magazine supplement on November 20, 1988. The story of the new Irish has also appeared in the *New York Post, Daily News, New York Newsday,*

USA Today, Wall Street Journal, Boston Globe, Washington Post, and *International Herald Tribune,* among others. *Newsweek, The Economist,* and *Manhattan Inc.,* have also featured the story of the Irish exodus to New York. In early November 1987, NBC aired a five-minute segment on the issue of undocumented Irish living in the United States as part of the *Nightly News* program. ABC Television News broadcast a segment on the new Irish in March 1988, as did CNN the following month. A three-part series on the new Irish was shown on Fox Channel 5 in May 1988. Local television stations around the country also featured the story.

The "Irish illegals story" was an attractive feature because it offered journalists a new angle on an old story. The Irish confound the stereotype of the "wetback" illegal alien. In addition, the fact that they are English-speaking and located in the major U.S. cities means that the story can be easily fitted into the television news and features schedule. The IIRM spokespersons (and the various "illegals" whom they nominated for interviews) were educated, polite, and highly articulate. The contrast between the blacked-out profiles on screen in New York and the scenic images of the Irish countryside left behind made for great televisual impact. In the wake of such television broadcasts, the IIRM hotlines were inundated with calls from Irish Americans offering to help in whatever way they could.

Welfare and Information. Although the long-term goal of the IIRM was to bring about legislative reform, the short-term purpose of the organization was to provide welfare and information services to the constituency of new Irish immigrants in the United States. The creation of a telephone hotline in the summer of 1987 for immigrants seeking help was the first part of the IIRM's outreach program. Initially, the line was open twice a week in the evening and calls were taken by IIRM volunteers, the majority of whom were illegal immigrants. According to Patrick Hurley, the hotline serves as "a vital link between the undocumented Irish community and the more established agencies, such as the Irish Consulate, Catholic Charities, and the New York Police Department" (*Irish Echo,* June 11, 1988).

Most of the calls to the hotline were queries about sponsorship and legal status, with calls about victimization and loneliness featuring to a lesser degree. Subsequently, many of these calls would have been deflected to Project Irish Outreach, which was set up with its own confidential hotline number at the same time.

From its inception, the IIRM held regular monthly meetings, which were advertised in advance in the ethnic press and in the Irish neighborhood bars. The public meetings served to affirm the illegal Irish constituency by providing that constituency with a forum in which its members could express themselves openly. A sense of solidarity was fostered as month after month hundreds of people crowded into the meeting halls. Although the meetings were primarily oriented toward the illegal Irish, prominent activists in the Irish-American community were always in attendance, lending further legitimacy to the emerging organization. Each month, representatives from the actions groups would give a progress report to those in attendance. These reports generally served to bolster morale among the illegals by emphasizing the lobbying efforts, the extent of mobilization, and the amount of media attention that the movement had received. But the meetings also served as a vehicle for the dissemination of information relevant to the illegal community. Those in attendance were made aware of their rights (when a victim of a crime or when confronted by an immigration official, for example) by a series of speakers which included members of the New York Police Department Immigration Unit, immigration attorneys, tax consultants, consulate officials, and representatives of Catholic Charities. The Koch administration in New York issued an ordinance in October 1985, which welcomed all immigrants to the city, both legal and illegal, and provided assurance that the agencies of the administration would not act as law enforcers for the Immigration Services. While this message was relayed to the Irish community via representatives of the mayor at the IIRM meetings, it may not have been as widely publicized in other immigrant communities. In any event, most Irish illegals in New York City remained wary of all institutions outside of their own community, preferring to avoid the risk of detection at any cost.

Politicians from the Irish-American community were regularly present and used the organization's platform to voice their solidarity with the IIRM. The focus of the meetings was information—providing free legal advice on immigration law and arming people with the appropriate knowledge about their rights and obligations as undocumented citizens of New York. In its first year of operation, the IIRM produced a handbook for the new Irish and a variety of advisory leaflets for Irish immigrants in New York. In addition, the organization distributed information leaflets produced by the Office of Immigrant Affairs (Department of City Planning, New York) and by the New York Police Department (fraud and detective bureaus).

Irish immigrants (largely because of their strong Irish-American connections) have succeeded in obtaining a particularly sympathetic hearing for their case at all levels of city government. In June 1988, the IIRM in conjunction with other immigrant advice groups in the Irish constituency and the NYC Office of Immigrant Affairs produced a guide for Irish immigrants. All of these publications were designed to reassure Irish illegals that their status did not preclude them from the services provided by city agencies and departments. Paradoxically, the agencies of local government in New York City actively affirm undocumented immigrants, even though the policy at federal level is to apprehend and deport them. The policies toward undocumented immigrants at the local level in New York are, in effect, subverting the policies of the federal government.

As the movement became more established and developed links with social and welfare services agencies in New York, the information function became more specialized. In 1988, the IIRM co-sponsored a series of lectures on crime prevention in association with the New York Police Department's New Immigrants Unit and Crime Prevention Unit. In 1989, a tenant information forum was co-sponsored by IIRM and the Commission on Human Rights as part of the city's Neighborhood Stabilization Program. The IIRM has also sponsored educational seminars on the NP–5 visa program, educational opportunities, and payment of taxes. The effect of such activities has been to affirm the new Irish community and create as many openings and opportunities for them as possible, given the constraints of illegality.

The Catholic Church

I don't consider trying to help Irish immigrants as an act of charity. I consider it an act of justice (Cardinal John O'Connor, quoted in the *Irish Times*, March 24, 1990).

As with the IIRM, a series of precipitating events served to galvanize the Catholic Church in New York into a response to the new wave of Irish immigrants.

From the early 1980s, there was ample evidence of the decline of the youth population in rural parishes and dioceses all over Ireland, although the exodus was not fully reflected in the official statistics (see chapter 1). The destruction of rural community life and the break-up of families greatly concerned Ireland's Roman Catholic hierarchy, who became increasingly outspoken on the problem of emigration while successive Irish governments remained silent. As individuals and collectively (through the Episcopal Commission for Emigrants), the church leaders have expressed concern "that emigration seems to be accepted as part of the solution to unemployment" (Dr. Michael Murphy, quoted in the *Irish Echo*, April 23, 1988) and that the exodus would result in the country becoming the "retirement home of Europe" (The Most Rev. Desmond Connell, quoted in the *Irish Echo*, June 18, 1988). Irish emigrants have been described as "no better off than refugees" (Cardinal Tomas O'Fiaich, quoted in the *Irish Voice*, Jan 6, 1990) and have been compared to "Mexican wetbacks . . . spreading across America in search of jobs which are becoming increasingly elusive" (Dr. Michael Murphy, quoted in the *Irish Times*, October 25, 1990). Politicians have been accused of "sanitizing" emigration by redefining it as a voluntary process (Dr. Michael Harty, quoted in the *Sunday Independent*, November 25, 1990) while the media has been charged with demoting emigration "from the front page to the bottom of page five" (Father John Gavin, quoted in the *Sunday Tribune*, July 29, 1990). The latter went on to criticize government indifference and to describe emigration in Ireland as "a form of social control," echoing Lee's historical interpretation of emigration as a stabilizing influence on the social structure (1989: 374–87 and chapter 1). The Irish Catholic hierarchy has consistently criticized government indifference to the problem of emigration and has called for the establishment of a national task force to study ways of tackling unemployment and emigration. The church has also pursued a number of initiatives on its own behalf. Groups such as the Conference of Western Bishops have promoted the cause of Ireland's western seaboard by collating research on emigration and rural decline. In 1992, the western bishops obtained funds from the European Commission to develop an action plan for the development of the Western region.

In addition to action at home, the church has been responsible for several initiatives abroad. The Irish church has had a long tradition of serving emigrant communities through a well-developed chaplaincy network in Britain. More recently, a chaplaincy service has been established for Irish workers in Germany. No such structure—specifically designed to serve the needs of new *Irish* immigrants—existed in the United States. The hierarchy's concern for the Irish illegals culminated in the arrival of a fact-finding mission of clergy in New York City in the summer of 1987.

At the same time, the IIRM was getting off the ground and stating the case for a welfare service that could serve the needs of undocumented immigrants. In particular, the IIRM called for services that would provide counseling and social services for distressed immigrants, similar to services already provided in London. There was also concern at the prohibitive cost of emergency medical care for immigrants who had no medical coverage. The emergence of the IIRM brought increased pressure on the church (as a sympathetic institution with resources) to respond to the needs of immigrants, particularly in relation to legal advice and medical care. In the eyes of the church leaders, Irish immigrants in New York, like their counterparts in Britain and Europe, are displaced members of their congregations. They feel a moral obligation to provide spiritual and pastoral care to those who have gone abroad. In practice, the pastoral obligations are often supplanted by the need to administer more practical assistance in the form of financial, medical, and legal aid. Through the provision of such services, the church can only enhance its standing in the immigrant community. This in turn serves to reduce alienation from the institutional church among disaffected immigrants and, indeed, may even result in the increase of religious practice.

Catholic Charities, a not-for-profit corporation that coordinates and supervises all the charitable activities of the Archdiocese of New York, responded to the illegal Irish problem by establishing a special program in June 1987 to address the needs of the undocumented. Through its parish network (which had operated as legalization centers for those who qualified for amnesty under the 1986 Immigration Reform and Control Act), Catholic Charities became increasingly concerned about the legal, medical, and social problems arising from undocumented status. The special interest paid to the needs of Irish immigrants reflects the personal concerns of two key men, both Irish Americans: Monsignor James Murray, who developed Project

Irish Outreach, and Cardinal John O'Connor, who sanctioned it. Indeed, the inauguration of Project Irish Outreach owes much to the fact that the ruling elite of the American Catholic Church is still predominantly Irish, and resources can be speedily diverted to minister to Irish needs.

Monsignor James Murray, executive director of Catholic Charities and the son of Irish immigrants, was particularly concerned about the plight of newly arrived undocumented Irish immigrants. His personal interest in the Irish provided much of the impetus for the establishment of the support service to address their needs. Acting as Cardinal O'Connor's envoy, he made several trips to Ireland during the first half of 1987. He met with members of the Irish hierarchy, as well as government officials, conveying the concerns of the church in New York. His efforts culminated in the establishment of Project Irish Outreach in June 1987 and the subsequent assignment of four Irish priests to act as special chaplains to the new Irish community in New York. Two of the latter took up their posts at the beginning of 1988 and were joined by two other priests and a nun later that year.

Project Irish Outreach functions as a "caretaker" institution providing a variety of services in the form of medical care, counseling, economic assistance, information, and advice. Aid is offered as an end in itself, rather than as a means to a more important end (Gans, 1982: 142). A toll-free hotline was established to facilitate counseling and referrals either by phone or appointment. The agency directs immigrants to health care and social and legal services. An important aspect of this help is the availability of emergency medical care at a number of hospitals in the New York area. Immigrants, regardless of their status, are referred to general or specialized Catholic hospital services. This care is charged on a sliding fee basis. Effectively, Catholic Charities stepped in as an intermediary between hospitals and the undocumented immigrant, guaranteeing confidentiality and creating an atmosphere of honesty and trust. However, they also encourage people to take responsibility for themselves by taking out medical insurance.

In the early days of its operation, Project Irish Outreach faced the challenge of getting information out to the new Irish community. They embarked on a public service campaign using radio announcements and local newspapers, as well as meetings of the IIRM to publicize their services. According to Patricia O'Callaghan, project co-ordinator, once information about their services reached the established Irish community, it quickly trickled down to the new Irish community through word of mouth. In the first six months of its operation, 1,000 clients received some kind of practical help. Legal problems constituted about 60 percent of those queries. Among those who sought assistance, there was a significant number of people who were re-emigrating, having previously lived in the United States in the 1960s.

The project now receives approximately 2,500 new calls a year, although many of the calls are now deflected into parishes in which there is an Irish chaplain. Project Irish Outreach acts as a clearing house linking people who have job, accommodation, and financial resources to people who need help. While continuing with counseling and welfare services, the outreach program has expanded its operations to embrace information needs of the documented and undocumented communities. In 1989, they presented a series of eight career seminars on subjects ranging from construction to health care to how to start a business. These seminars were attended by over 1,000 participants. A similar series was organized in 1990. According to O'Callaghan, the seminar series puts the new Irish in touch with the Irish-American community. The latter's expertise, skills, contacts, and knowledge can be utilized in order to encourage newcomers, both documented and undocumented. Since most new arrivals do not in general seek assistance, the purpose of the outreach programs are to facilitate an exchange. By bringing together successful Irish-American businessmen and women, positive role models are provided for immigrants. As in other areas, the outreach program plays a mediating role between the two Irish communities, old and new. It creates an important link between the individual immigrant and the institutions from which he or she may feel excluded.

In 1989, Project Irish Outreach also produced a comprehensive guide for Irish immigrants in the United States. The Irish Episcopal Commission for Emigrants has distributed 10,000 copies of the guide to secondary schools in Ireland, to all parishes, and to a network of bookshops throughout the country. The guide provides more information about emigrating, since those working in support services in New York believe that immigrants are not sufficiently prepared for emigration. A further 10,000 copies of the guide were distributed to immigrants in New York via the immigrant chaplains, the IIRM, the consulate, and parishes in Irish neighborhoods.

Gans points out that caretaking is "a reciprocal relationship in which the caretaker gives his services in exchange for a material or nonmaterial return" (1982: 143). The decision to invite Irish priests to come to New York as immigrant chaplains must be seen in the context of the church's concern with the *pastoral care* of immigrants abroad. Apart from concerns about the problems arising from illegality, Catholic Charities was worried about the consequences of acculturation and the possible loss of identity and values that might result. Indeed, the need for pastoral care was clearly prioritized in a proposal submitted to Cardinal O'Connor, "In addition to, and more important than their social service needs, there is a definite pastoral dimension needed to reach out to those needing spiritual guidance and motivation in their new environment" (Catholic Charities, August 29, 1987). The chaplains who came to work in the new Irish parishes perform a caretaking role for which the nonmaterial return is the strengthening and maintenance of a youthful Catholic congregation. The chaplains see their role first and foremost as one of expressing solidarity with the new immigrants and addressing some of their needs at community level: "You try to assure them in their difficulty that the Church cares and that all that is possible will be done" (Father Brendan McCabe, quoted in *Catholic New York*, March 24, 1988). This means providing support and, where necessary, facilities to enhance the social, educational, and religious welfare of the immigrants. The initial foray by these priests into the Irish communities was complicated by the absence of a pre-existing chaplaincy structure for emigrants and by the fear and distrust of the immigrants toward outsiders. However, their acceptance by the new Irish community was made possible because of their obvious Irish credentials, the endorsement they had received from the IIRM, and the high standing of Cardinal O'Connor in the community because of his expressed concern for Irish immigrants. In the absence of any outreach program on the part of the Irish government, and given the general disaffection and antipathy toward Irish politicians, any effort on the part of the church was likely to be received in a positive manner.

The chaplains organized alternative socializing activities to the bars and integrated the immigrants into the existing parish and community structures. One group of immigrants, for example, working with a chaplain in the Bronx, set up a sports and social club for the new Irish, with a formal membership and committee structure. A former chaplain, Father Michael Harrison, saw his role primarily as a facilitator, encouraging a form of self-government among the immigrants. The club organizes sporting activities, educational courses, and religious retreats. Irish priests travel to New York each year to conduct religious retreats, which are seen as a forum for religious renewal. According to Father Harrison, these visits are another vehicle for the immigrants to renew ties with Ireland: "These people may be away from home, but they are still close to home."

The sports and social club has a welfare fund that is entirely administered by the immigrants. Donations that come primarily from the church and the Irish-American community are channeled into the fund, but it is the club members who decide how the money should be spent. Attempts are also made to integrate the new Irish into the parish by getting them involved in a range of parish-based activities, such as participation in civilian patrols, and the provision of services for senior citizens in the vicinity. These kinds of activities are designed to strengthen links between new immigrants and the settled community. (Most of the parishes in the Bronx and Queens have an aging Irish population because of the exodus to the outer suburbs. There is a general consensus that these parishes can only benefit from an influx of younger people.) According to the chaplains, the church gives people an anchor to establish themselves as part of a large ethnic group in a multiethnic society.

Through the Irish Outreach program, the Archdiocese of New York forged a link with the Irish Episcopal Commission for Emigrants—a link that had not existed prior to the highlighting of the illegal immigration problem. Indeed, at a press conference held in New York in November 1987, at which bishops from Haiti, the Dominican Republic, and Ireland were present, the Irish representative spoke of the church in Ireland and Catholic Charities as "partners" in the outreach program (Archbishop Dermot Clifford, quoted in *Catholic New York*, November 19, 1987). This partnership between the two churches made it possible to use the resources of each effectively in offering aid to new immigrants. Catholic Charities provides practical advice, medical aid, and assistance, drawing on its vast resources as one of the largest voluntary social services agencies in the world. The Catholic church in Ireland provides pastoral and spiritual care by sending Irish priests to New York to live and work among the new immigrants. In addition, the church hierarchy has been seen to champion the cause of the immigrants through their regular pronouncements reported in the national newspapers in Ireland, as well as the ethnic press in New York. Through its concern and compassion, the church can only create goodwill for itself in an otherwise disaffected community.

The *Irish Voice*

The formation of the IIRM in 1987 and the establishment of Project Irish Outreach represented the first formal acknowledgement of the existence of a community of Irish illegals in the United States. In December 1987, that community was further affirmed through the establishment of a new ethnic newspaper in New York, the *Irish Voice*.

The *Irish Voice* provided a vital channel of communication for immigrant activists and the new Irish community as a whole. Sensing a gap in the marketplace, the *Irish Voice* was established by a group of Irish immigrants as an alternative to the *Irish Echo*, which has traditionally focused on the older immigrant community. The *Irish Voice* openly courted the new Irish immigrants, especially the illegals who featured in a special survey conducted for the inaugural issue. The front page of that issue carried a report on the illegal Irish, detailing their hopes and experiences. The report appeared under the eye-catching headline "We'll never return—Young illegals" (*Irish Voice*, December 5, 1987). This defiant statement set the agenda for much of what was to follow in the *Irish Voice*. The paper gave voice to a constituency of immigrants who until then had not only been voiceless but also largely invisible.

The editorial of the first issue sought to prioritize the plight of undocumented immigrants, making an emotive link between them and the post-famine Irish immigrants of the nineteenth century:

This newspaper will be forthright in its attempt to win for the . . . Irish illegals their proper place as full members of this society. The Irish in the U.S. contributed too much to stand back now and accept the permanent reality that "No Irish Need Apply" signs are ensconced at the nation's borders (December 5, 1987).

Indeed, the *Irish Voice* went on to challenge the Irish-American community to address the issue of illegality as a matter or urgency: "There is no greater issue confronting the Irish-American community . . . than the one of illegality. . . . We must ensure that this issue is addressed clearly, forthrightly and without equivocation."

Significantly, in its inaugural editorial, the newspaper highlighted the problem of Northern Ireland and committed itself to covering all sides of the debate without prejudice. During its first year of publication, the *Irish Voice* editorials focused primarily on the themes of immigration and Northern Ireland. Irish and Irish-American affairs featured to a much lesser extent. The decision to prioritize coverage of Northern Irish affairs was an astute one for two reasons. First, such coverage would win the paper readers among the large numbers of immigrants from Northern Ireland residing in the United States. Second, coverage of Northern Ireland would also win readers among the Irish-American constituency, particularly those who had become politicized by the troubles over the last 20 years. In this way, the paper could broaden its appeal (and its readership) beyond the new Irish community.

The *Irish Voice* uses senior Belfast-based correspondents (attached to national Irish newspapers) for major reports. The paper has been particularly sympathetic in its coverage of the cases of undocumented immigrants in the United States appealing extradition to Britain. Overall, the newspaper is perceived as providing broader and more objective coverage of Northern Ireland than mainstream print and broadcast media in Ireland. The latter operate under censorship restrictions in covering the conflict in Northern Ireland, as do their British counterparts. For example, the American-based group Noraid (which raises money for the families of prisoners in Northern Ireland) has been banned on several occasions in Ireland and widely condemned because of its alleged links with paramilitary groups in Northern Ireland. Its spokespersons may not appear on either radio or television in the Republic of Ireland. The *Irish Voice* reports on Noraid's activities, functions, and social events and carries the organization's advertisements. While it stops short of endorsing Noraid, its acknowledgment of the organization and coverage of its activities goes considerably further than any Irish newspaper (except the Republican broadsheet *An Phoblacht*) would be prepared to go. The *Irish Voice*'s position is strictly anticensorship, which means giving space to all viewpoints. This openness makes the paper attractive to a broad spectrum of people within the Irish-American and new Irish communities.

From the start, the paper was innovative, using a tabloid format and color photography and graphics on the front page and inside pages. Its blue masthead and sharp layout instantly distinguish it from the rather staid alternatives in the Irish ethnic press. The format of the newspaper is lively, containing a mix of political news about Ireland and Northern Ireland, society gossip, film, theater and music news and reviews, and extensive sports coverage. From its inception, the paper has carried weekly columns by two prominent Irish journalists—one based in rural Ireland, the other in Dublin. In addition, Irish sports coverage was provided by one of Ireland's leading sports journalists who is an award-winning football player. The youthfulness of the new Irish constituency is reflected in the extensive "rock and pop" coverage. Apart from weekly reviews of live musical events, new albums by Irish and international artists are reviewed in the newspaper. Book, theater, and movie reviews are a regular feature. The "What's On" guide to New York showcases musical, theatrical, and artistic events with an Irish angle, which appeals to all elements of New York's Irish community.

Affirmation. The paper strikes a balance between coverage of the Irish in New York and coverage of affairs in Ireland. This is important because the immigrants see themselves as "an extension of community abroad," and the paper facilitates their keeping abreast of pertinent developments at home. At the same time, it affirms their status as immigrants abroad and serves to represent to them the reality of their experiences. Following the tradition of provincial, local and ethnic papers, each issue of the *Irish Voice* contains a centerpiece spread of photographs taken out and about in the new Irish community. Although this is standard fare in local papers, it has particular significance in the context of Irish illegals in the United States. These photographs, featuring young Irish men and women, give symbolic representation to the emerging constituency of new Irish immigrants in New York. (The *Voice*'s photo gallery is in sharp contrast to the *Echo*'s, which tends to feature the aging and predominantly male members of the Irish–American establishment.) The photographs affirm the existence of a generation of young people, many of whom have had to conceal their real identities from employers, officials, customers, and even workmates. In these smiling snapshots, young men and women emerge from the shadowland of illegality, challenging the facelessness (and voicelessness) of their existence. The photo gallery is supplemented by a roving reporter item, which photographs four people each week and prints their views on any one of a range of immigrant and general interest issues. In addition, the letters page of the newspaper has proved to be a debating ground for a variety of individuals who otherwise would not have had a vehicle through which to channel their views and grievances. All of these features help to create a paper that is not only responsive to the immigrant community but is also a symbolic representation of the existence of that community.

Good marketing is a hallmark of the *Irish Voice*. Strategies used to woo the young Irish audience include regular quizzes and competitions. The weekly green card column gives advice on a wide range of immigration matters, often in a question and answer format based on requests for information from readers. The effort to appeal to the new immigrants is not lost on the readership:

I prefer the *Irish Voice* to the *Irish Echo*. It has better news coverage. I think the *Voice* addresses itself to a younger population. The *Echo*, in contrast, has played itself out.

The *Voice* is a far better paper (than the *Echo*) because it caters to young people. The *Echo* caters to people who have been in this country 50 years or more.

I think the *Irish Voice* deals more with what is going on in Ireland, whereas the *Irish Echo* is more of an Irish-American newspaper.

The deliberate outreach to the new immigrant community extends not just to those living and working in New York, but to Irish immigrants elsewhere. The *Voice* embraces the wider community of Irish immigrants in other cities in the United States, in Britain, Australia, and Europe by carrying regular reports on their experiences. For example, a feature such as the "London Letter" raises issues relevant to the Irish in London, which strike a chord with the Irish in big cities elsewhere. In this sense, the newspaper performs a consciousness-raising role, providing a platform for the recounting of shared experiences. One full-page article on the Irish in London, for example, detailed the hostile environment and hard times that many unskilled Irish immigrants face (*Irish Voice*, January 16, 1988). Pertinent issues ranging from the identity crisis of Northern Irish people in Britain (March 18, 1989) to the problem of construction accidents in London (April 1, 1989) have been raised in the "London Letter" series. Stories such as the one on construction accidents serve as a cautionary tale for immigrants in New York and elsewhere, who face the same kind of hazardous working conditions. A letter from "Down Under" occasionally features in the newspaper. The regular feature "Across Irish America" contains columns compiled by correspondents in San Francisco, Chicago, and Boston. Links are also made with past immigrants through periodic features on the life and times of Irish immigrants in the nineteenth and early twentieth centuries. Typical features include reports on the legacy of Irish immigrant musicians and excerpts from novels that tackle the thorny issue of emigration. The *Irish Voice* deftly draws together the strands of different Irish communities. In the process, it celebrates a single global Irish community which transcends the constraints of time and place.

Information. In its extensive coverage of immigration matters, the *Voice* further affirms the existence of the new Irish community, focusing in particular on the problem of illegality. Each new piece of immigration legislation presented in the Senate or House of Representatives has been subjected to detailed analysis, particularly in terms of its implications for Irish illegals. From 1988 through 1990, the newspaper closely followed the fortunes of the Kennedy/Simpson bill in Congress. The bill went through several metamorphoses under the stewardship of Senators Edward Kennedy and Alan Simpson and later Congressmen Peter Rodino and Roman Mazzoli. Subsequently, it was superseded by the Morrison bill, sponsored by Congressman Bruce Morrison, chairman of the House Immigration Subcommittee. Each new development was monitored by *Irish Voice* reporters. The newspaper also covered the development of the IIRM, endorsing its aims and using its spokespersons regularly for information and advice. The *Voice* provided the IIRM with secondary publicity by reporting not only on their meetings, activities, and events, but also on the coverage the organization received (particular in the early stages of its development) from the mainstream print and broadcast media. Thus, the *Irish Voice* helped to legitimate the emerging organization to its own constituency of readers. Many immigrants first heard about the IIRM through the pages of the *Voice*.

In December 1989, the *Irish Voice* systematized its coverage of immigration matters by launching the "Immigration Update," a four-page monthly newsletter distributed as an insert in the newspaper. These updates contain detailed analysis of the legislative initiatives as well as information on career seminars, educational opportunities, IIRM programs, and fundraising.

Apart from stating the case for immigration reform in order to facilitate legalization, the newspaper also highlights the problems faced by individual immigrants. This is achieved in several ways. The *Voice* monitors the Irish newspapers and the ethnic Irish press in Britain for stories of interest to immigrants in the United States. Thus, the paper serves an information function, disseminating information to which this community normally might not have access. For example, the paper publicized a report which first appeared in the *Irish Times* about the dangerous health risks associated with asbestos. Several hundred Irish workers are estimated to be involved in the removal of asbestos insulation from old buildings (*Irish Voice*, November 25, 1989). Another report carried by the *Irish Voice* revealed that premature death is more common among Irish-born immigrants in Britain than any other ethnic group in that country. The report pointed out that the high premature death rate can be explained by sociological factors linked to emigration (May 12, 1990).

The paper also publicizes developments, events, and activities within the new Irish community. This may mean highlighting the particular problems of specific groups within that community. For example, the paper carried two reports on the formation of Irish gay support groups in New York (February 24, 1990; May 12, 1990). In these reports, the founding members of this group outlined the particular problems faced by gay Irish men and women in New York. Groups such as the New Irish Sports and Social Club, the Irish Immigrant Emergency Fund and the Immigrant Women's Support Group in the Bronx, all of which cater to particular needs within the immigrant community, have been featured at one time or another in the newspaper. Contact numbers as well as additional information on the groups are always supplied.

Investigation. The *Voice's* investigative features have tended to highlight the exploitation of Irish illegals by unscrupulous individuals. Indeed, the paper prides itself on playing an active role in exposing injustices perpetrated against a group who generally have no grounds for recourse or recompense. The second edition of the newspaper reported the arrest of a police officer for selling bogus birth certificates to illegals who could use them to procure American passports (*Irish Voice*, December 12, 1987). The officer was subsequently indicted on a charge of conspiracy, possession of false documents, and fraud (*Irish Voice*, February 20, 1988). Another of the early editions of the newspaper ran a front-page story on a confidence trickster selling bogus immigration documents as legitimate work visas to unsuspecting illegals (December 26, 1987). The article warned of the dangers of presenting fraudulent documents (such as the ones on sale) to immigration officials.

A report on the case of an Irish nanny who was accused by her employers of abusing their children highlighted the legal prerogative of the accused to remain silent. Although the charges were eventually dropped at the court hearing, the woman's attorney pointed out to the *Irish Voice* that she had made incriminating statements to the police before she was charged. He stressed that immigrants should remain silent if and when they are apprehended by police officers and that they should be more discerning in choosing whom they work for (July 7, 1990). Indeed, many of the stories carried by the paper issue these types of "health warnings" for Irish illegals—explicit or implicit advice on how to handle difficult situations. Readers are alerted to the dangers of getting involved with confidence tricksters and other people selling bogus documents, and they are warned about exploitative employers. They are educated in the appropriate strategies for avoiding apprehension and possible deportation.

The paper has played an important role in highlighting the cases of those who otherwise would not have their cases heard. For example, a story about an 18-year-old immigrant who was forced to work over 90 hours a week for $65 was first highlighted by the *Irish Voice* (January 9, 1988). Irish consular officers intervened and the immigrant was offered alternative employment elsewhere. The case received extensive publicity in Ireland. (Subsequently, then Irish Prime Minister Mr. Haughey announced that one of his government ministers would visit the United States on a fact-finding mission.) A story about the victimization of three Irish illegal immigrants in Boston led to the immigrants initiating court proceedings against the offender (*Irish Voice*, February 20, 1988). An Irish nanny and two contacts who had helped her to leave her place of employment were subjected to blackmail and extortion threats by her former employer. The three contacted the *Irish Voice* who put them in touch with attorneys and publicized the case in the newspaper.

In the case of a hit-and-run accident in which an Irish immigrant was killed, the newspaper raised questions about the conduct of a police investigation into the incident. As a result of publicizing the case, the driver of the car was eventually indicted for leaving the scene of an accident in which the victim was killed (October 28, 1989).

Advocacy. The *Irish Voice* plays an important role in defending the Irish from perceived racial slurs or criticism. In June 1988, the newspaper reported on the publication of an article offensive to the Irish community in *Golf Digest*, a subsidiary publication of the *New York Times* (*Irish Voice*, June 18, 1988). The article, written by a British journalist, contained several disparaging references to Irish drinking, "breeding," and work practices. It was first brought to the attention of *Irish Voice* readers in the May 28 issue, when a prominent columnist described it as "the most racist anti-Irish bile I have read in an American publication in years." In the aftermath of this publicity, the *Golf Digest* and the *New York Times* received hundreds of protest calls from Irish readers. Subsequently, the *New York Times* and the *Boston Globe* (which had also distributed the *Golf Digest* supplement) apologized to Irish Americans for the article, which they conceded was "ill-conceived and thoughtlessly published." In the same issue, the *Irish Voice* reprinted an article from an Irish current affairs magazine detailing the anti-Irish bias in the British tabloid media's coverage of Irish affairs (June 18, 1988). In the aftermath of Ireland's run in the World Cup, the *Irish Voice* criticized coverage of the Irish national team in the *Daily News*. The latter was accused of publishing "anti-Irish garbage" and *Voice* readers were encouraged to write to the editor of the *Daily News* and register their protest (*Irish Voice*, July 7, 1990). Some months later, the paper's music critic launched an attack on the standard of music reviews (of Irish artists) in the *New York Post*. Playing on the tabloid's lurid headlining, the article was headlined "Penniless Post Slurs Irish National Heroes." The article offered a serious critique of a reviewer who is charged with anti-Irish bias (*Irish Voice*, September 15, 1990).

SUMMARY

The *Irish Voice* is one of the principal resources available to the new Irish community in New York. The newspaper affirms their identity as a separate and distinct constituency of immigrants; it disseminates vital information on immigration and welfare matters; it plays an investigative role in uncovering injustice and exploitative practices; and it advocates a policy of basic civil rights for Irish people not just in New York, but also in Britain and Northern Ireland. It has helped people to come to terms with their illegal status— their official invisibility—by giving them a heightened visibility within the ethnic Irish community.

The Irish Immigration Reform Movement, Project Irish Outreach and the *Irish Voice* are all recently formed legal organizations providing a range of services and supports to the illegal Irish community. In the process, they not only treat the undocumented as if they should be legals, but also as if they almost were. On the one hand, the illegals feel excluded from public sector services such as education, health, and welfare, as well as private sector services such as banks and insurance companies. On the other hand, many of their needs are being met within their own community by the support services that have come into place. Information, welfare, and legal aid is provided in abundance, while free medical care is virtually assured by Catholic Charities. The community is continually affirmed through the recognition its gets from the IIRM and the *Irish Voice*. In a sense, the illegals have almost assumed quasi-legal status. While some important services remain closed to them and their job mobility is highly circumscribed, symbolically they are almost legal within the Irish ethnic community. In terms of the social support system they can draw on, they are increasingly undifferentiated from other legal Irish immigrants.

Chapter 8 _____

Illegal Irish Immigration to the United States: Overview

The development of migration theory must...be predicated on a holism: sending and receiving areas being treated as a unit with causative structural factors operating on both sides (Cohen, 1987: 39).

The purpose of this study has been to provide an account of the lived experience of illegal Irish immigration by drawing primarily on the personal testimonies of immigrants. Every individual migration, however, occurs within a macrostructural context. The decisions about emigrating from Ireland and/or returning home are foreshadowed to a great extent by external factors beyond the individual's control. Individual preferences and motivations can explain why some people chose to be part of a general phenomenon: They cannot explain the phenomenon itself (Cohen, 1987: 40). It is necessary, therefore, to draw attention to the structural factors and particular historical circumstances that underpin this migration process.

THE STRUCTURAL CONTEXT OF ILLEGAL IRISH IMMIGRATION: IRELAND AND THE GLOBAL ECONOMY

To understand contemporary Irish emigration and in particular, illegal Irish immigration to the United States, it is necessary to examine Ireland's position within a global economic framework. I begin with the relationship of *dependence*, which exists between peripheral and core countries within the international global economy. According to Petras, one can identify at the international level "a series of labor-capital exchanges which constitute a world labor market, and [that] this global labor market has been integral to, and a consequence of, the development of the modern world economy" (Petras, 1981: 45).

Following Wallerstein (1974), Petras argues that the global movement of capital and commodities within a core, semiperiphery and periphery framework has been paralleled by a similar movement of labor across the same boundaries. Furthermore, she contends that the ability of a country to import or export labor has direct economic consequences. The availability of surplus labor is a critical factor in the development of inequalities within and between countries. Petras, thus, sees international capital *and* labor movements as processes that are closely related in practice, although they are often treated as separate analytical categories. Labor movements are primarily motivated by the desire for better conditions and higher wages, whereas capital movements are prompted by the drive toward profit accumulation:

Two contradictory forces are responsible for the tendency for labor to move across national boundaries and toward more flourishing centers of capital accumulation. First is labor's basic drive to seek those conditions and locations where its labor power can be exchanged for the most desirable wages and level of well being. Second is capital's perpetual need for ready and appropriate supplies of labor for its expanding process of capital accumulation (Petras, 1981: 48).

Contemporary Ireland occupies semiperipheral status in relation to stronger economic and political cores, such as Britain and the United States (Seers, 1979; Wickham, 1986). But economic dependency on external cores is not a recent phenomenon. Irish emigrants have for generations been part of the world labor market. The nature of Irish economic dependency has changed, however, along with changes in economic conditions and practices.

According to Breathnach and Jackson, Ireland was incorporated into the international capitalist system during the seventeenth century, as a dependent periphery to the British core (1991: 2–3). Ireland's incorporation into the international system was paralleled by political and military subjugation under direct British rule. Economic subservience to a colonial power retarded indigenous industrial development to the extent that in 1922 when Ireland gained her independence only ten percent of the work force was employed in manufacturing. In these circumstances, the core of unskilled Irish workers who could neither be absorbed by industry nor agriculture left the country to work in the construction, manufacturing, and service sectors abroad (see chapter 1). The marginalized sections of the population were systematically removed from the country through endemic emigration.

During the 1950s, the Irish government responded to the growing emigration crisis with a policy designed to "open up the Irish economy" to foreign development. This reorientation of economic policy away from the protectionism of the 1930s had a major impact on the troubled Irish economy (Wickham, 1980: 56, and chapter 1). An attractive incentive package was developed by the newly created Industrial Development Authority (IDA) to entice foreign companies to locate subsidiary manufacturing plants in Ireland. For example, an overseas investor coming to Ireland receives non-repayable cash grants of 30 to 60 percent of fixed assets costs for a manufacturing plant. These grants are supplemented by training grants, loan guarantees, equity participations, depreciation allowances, and interest and rent subsidies (McAleese, 1985: 335). Hundreds of overseas firms responded to the financial incentives provided by the Irish government and the availability of a skilled labor force. In addition, by locating in Ireland (a member state of the European Community), multinational companies, producing for the European market, are exempt from customs restrictions and tariffs (Mitter, 1986: 80). More recently, the IDA has introduced grants for indigenous manufacturing firms, but these grants are difficult to get and are not nearly as extensive as those available to foreign industry.

In 1961, only one percent of the total Irish workforce was employed by foreign firms. By 1983, that figure had risen to 36 percent (Bell and Meehan, 1988: 76). According to the IDA, by 1989 there were over 800 foreign-owned plants in Ireland, accounting for over 40 percent of all those in manufacturing employment (Industrial Development Authority, 1989: 11, 23). Consequently, a form of dependent industrialization has emerged: As the multinational assembly base has grown, the fragile indigenous manufacturing base declined (Bell and Meehan, 1988: 76). Between 1973 and 1980, a period of sustained industrial growth, more jobs were lost in Irish manufacturing companies than were created, with a net loss during those years of over 2,200 jobs (Kirby, 1988: 112). Industrial manufacturing and production in Ireland increasingly have become the preserve of foreign-based multinational firms, and in particular American firms.

By the early 1980s, Americans had already invested more in Irish manufacturing than they had in the manufacturing sector of either Italy or the Netherlands (McAleese, 1985: 330). Apart from the cash incentives, factors that have attracted more investment in Ireland include the common language, lower industrial wage rates, and good infrastructure. Economic dependence on colonial Britain has been replaced by dependence on the multinational corporation (Wickham, 1986).

Electronics, pharmaceuticals/chemicals, data processing, and financial services are the principal overseas projects attracted to Ireland by the IDA. The most recent strategy has been to market Ireland to potential investors as "Europe's Quality Location"—providing quality people, quality products, and quality business infrastructure (Industrial Development Authority, 1989: 23). There has been criticism of the IDA policy, however, notably in a report published in 1982 by the Irish National Economic and Social Council (Telesis Consultancy Group, 1982). The report charged that foreign companies encourage neither research and development nor independent marketing/decision-making practices in their subsidiaries. Key business functions continue to be located close to home or to major markets (1982: 43). As a result, spinoff employment potential was and continues to be limited. The profit outflow from overseas subsidiaries is such that in 1989 over 10 percent of GNP left the country (Breathnach and Jackson, 1991: 5). Without reinvestment of profits in the Irish economy, job creation targets remain unmet and high emigration levels result. Such criticisms have been reiterated in the government-appointed task force report, A Time for Change: Industrial Policy for the 1990s, published in 1992. Between 1981 and 1990, industrial development has cost the Irish Exchequer more than IR £4.58 billion in incentive grants and special tax relief measures. In that time, the total number employed in industry has increased by just 7,000 after job losses in this sector are taken into account.

As Petras has argued, capital movements are driven primarily by the need for profit accumulation. The prospect of high profits attracted many multinational subsidiaries to Ireland throughout the 1970s and 1980s. Corporate rationalization is often at variance with the job creation strategies of agencies like the IDA, however. Subsidiary plants, even when they are making a profit, may be axed or relocated by decisions made at corporate headquarters thousands of miles away. In the context of the international global economy, Ireland's main function is to serve as a low-tax base for multinational corporations who wish to maximize their profits (Breathnach and Jackson, 1991: 5).

In short, an industrial policy founded upon internationally mobile capital has failed to generate enough jobs, either directly or indirectly, to keep the Irish work force at home. This problem became particularly acute in the 1980s when corporate rationalization lead to the closure of many industrial plants. Declining prosperity at the international level has had serious consequences for the vulnerable Irish economy and the Irish labor force (see chapter 1). Given the high proportion of young people under the age of 25, it is unlikely that any industrial policy could have provided enough jobs for all. However, there is growing disquiet about the rate at which international companies have defected from the country. Had more investment been made in fostering indigenous industry and an entrepreneurial culture, the outlook for many Irish young people may not have been so bleak.

THE MOBILITY OF LABOR AND CAPITAL

The increasing flow of capital into Ireland in recent decades has been paralleled by an increasing flow of people out of Ireland during the same period. The general question of how these two apparently contradictory processes can operate simultaneously has been addressed by Saskia Sassen in her 1988 book *The Mobility of Labor and Capital*. Here, I apply her thesis to the Irish context. Like Petras, Sassen argues that the analysis of capital and labor flows have been erroneously constructed into unrelated categories for the purposes of economic analysis (Sassen, 1988: 12). Her task is to articulate the analytical relationship between the processes of international labor migrations *and* the internationalization of production.

According to Sassen, multinational corporate investment in semiperipheral and peripheral countries is of a specific and limited kind. The kinds of jobs created have been in the manufacturing area with little potential for development in related areas such as marketing and research and development. Furthermore, Sassen argues that multinational investors in search of cheap and quiescent workers have targeted the *female* rather than the male industrial labor force in recipient countries. According to Sassen, "Female labor intensive employment is characteristic of both transnational subsidiaries and native firms producing for export" (1988: 114).

Sassen's argument is based on empirical evidence from the peripheries of South America and Asia. In my view, her thesis can also be applied to the Irish experience. Ireland occupies peripheral status in relation to the European continent, and the country is heavily dependent on foreign investment. The manufacturing sector of Irish industry, which is dominated by multinational firms, is characterized by an increasingly feminized work force. In particular, new growth areas in manufacturing (e.g., electronics and health care products) employ mainly working class women workers at a lower average hourly rate than male workers in the manufacturing industry (Barry et al., 1985: 146). A study of the electronics industry in Ireland (one of the biggest growth areas in the manufacturing sector), for example, has demonstrated that most of the workers in the industry are women, even though Irish women as a whole are far less likely to be in paid employment than women in other countries (Wickham and Murray, 1987). Within the industry, women are concentrated in the lowest paid and least skilled occupations, that of assembly worker. It is noteworthy that, in international terms, employment in the electronics factories in Ireland is intermediate between the United States on the one hand and the newly industrialized countries (of Southeast Asia) on the other. There are proportionately more assembly line workers and less technicians in Irish subsidiaries than in the United States. But at the same time, the Irish industry is more skilled than that of a newly industrialized country such as Singapore in which over 90 percent of electronics workers are assembly workers. Relatively speaking, Irish workers in these firms are less well off in terms of pay and opportunity than their American counterparts, while they are better off than comparable Southeast Asian workers.

Irish women entering and remaining in the work force in greater numbers than ever before are the disproportionate beneficiaries of the new employment opportunities created by multinational subsidiaries. (It must be noted that it is primarily working-class women who occupy these assembly jobs. Middle-class women are much more likely to work in white collar jobs, and it is from their ranks that the emigrant nannies are primarily drawn. It is more socially acceptable for a middle-class Irish woman to be a nanny in the United States than a factory worker at home.)

In the metals/engineering sector (which has been the leading sector of foreign investment in Ireland), female employment expanded at almost exactly double the rate for male employment in the period 1971–1981—135.2 percent increase in female employment as against 67.3 percent increase in male employment over the 10-year period (Breathnach, 1990: 6). In the 1980s, there was an overall decrease in manufacturing employment, but while male employment dropped by 10 percent, female employment increased slightly (by 1.4 percent). The policy of opening up the Irish economy to foreign investment most certainly created job opportunities for all, but significantly, women workers gained more than men in the new industrial sectors. Indeed, Breathnach concludes that access to female labor from a rural/small town background has been a locational determinant of considerable significance to foreign firms investing in Ireland (1990: 7). Consequently, foreign companies have had a much less significant impact on unemployment and emigration than would have been predicted. Both unemployment and emigration have risen steadily since the recession of the early 1980s. The profile of those who have emigrated in that period is distinctly male. Research by Professor Gerald Sexton of the Economic and Social Research Institute (Dublin) indicates that males constituted 58 percent of all emigrants in the first half of the decade. (There is no reason to assume that this proportion would be vastly different for the numbers of illegal immigrants to the United States.)

The failure of Irish industrial policy to create jobs with long-term career prospects and an incremental opportunity structure has made emigration, for many, the only viable alternative. As pointed out in chapter 3, limited opportunity translates into a perception of economic deprivation and disaffection, prime motivators in the decision of tens of thousands of Irish young people to take their chances as illegal immigrants in the United States. For these emigrants to return, there would have to be significant changes in Ireland's industrial policy and economic culture. Imaginative politics practiced by imaginative politicians would be a prerequisite for introducing new policy initiatives on the scale required to revitalize the economy. It is not at all clear that the Irish political system, as currently constituted, can deliver these demands. Ironically, the very people who might have been, if not the architects of change, at least a catalyst for change in Ireland, are now living and working elsewhere.

THE INTERNATIONALIZATION OF PRODUCTION:
INFORMALIZATION IN THE METROPOLIS

The upward trend in Irish emigration in the 1980s has seen tens of thousands of people leaving Ireland for the metropolises of core countries not only in Europe but also in the United States. The numbers of Irish in London, Munich, Sydney, New York, Boston, and Chicago have swelled in recent years. The capacity of these cities to absorb hundreds of thousands of new immigrants from peripheral areas of the globe has been linked to the changing needs of advanced capitalism (Sassen-Koob, 1986; Portes and Sassen-Koob 1987; Sassen, 1988; 1991). While manufacturing plants in far-flung peripheries are staffed by indigenous workers, immigrant workers from these peripheries *also* serve the needs of capitalist enterprise through their participation in emergent informal economies in the metropolises. The evolving pattern of international business organization tends to rely on flexible and disposable workers in both locations. According to Mitter, workers in the international division of labor are stratified by color and sex (1986: 6). It is necessary to add legal status to this model as the unregulated economic sector, particularly in U.S. global cities, relies increasingly on illegal immigrant labor. The internationalization of production and the internationalization of the labor force are inextricably linked.

According to Sassen-Koob, the current phase of advanced industrialization contains conditions that induce the formation of an informal sector in cities such as Los Angeles and New York (1986: 2). The recession of the mid–1970s, triggered by the oil crisis, particularly affected developed countries, causing a profit squeeze. Increased labor costs and/or competition from cheaper foreign produced goods have made the decentralization of work arrangements and informalization in the manufacturing and service sectors in global cities considerably more attractive (Portes and Sassen-Koob, 1987: 54). Smaller firms are better placed to produce customized goods and services to meet the increased demand from the expanding high-income and low-income populations of global cities (Sassen, 1991: 87). These firms operate at narrow profit margins in a competitive environment and, thus, must keep labor costs low.

The informal sector, as defined in chapter 4, includes all employment outside the regulatory apparatus governing pay and working conditions, social insurance, and taxation. Sectors experiencing informalization include the construction industry, where an estimated 90 percent of interior work in New York City is done without a legal permit (Portes and Sassen-Koob, 1987: 46). The informal sector also includes the garment and footwear industries and the provision of consumer goods and services. In essence, there is an expansion of the secondary labor market and, in particular, an increase in the kinds of jobs that service the needs of metropolitan corporate workers.

These jobs are increasingly held by immigrants, many of whom are undocumented aliens. Not surprisingly, "many of these jobs fall outside of the major industry counts, not so much because they may involve illegal immigrants, but because they are part of that expanding category usually referred to as 'off-the-books' jobs" (Sassen, 1988: 158). Most of the Irish illegals find employment in the service jobs within the informal economy, where they cater to "the high-income lifestyles of the growing top level professional work force which global cities attract" (1988: 22).

As pointed out in chapter 4, Irish illegals work as skilled artisans and unskilled laborers for construction contractors and subcontractors, as service staff in family-owned restaurants and bars, and as providers of childminding and companion services in private homes. It was also noted that the caregiving work performed by Irish nannies in the home frees middle-class/ professional women to participate in the formal labor market. It is increasingly the case that most of the jobs occupied by undocumented Irish workers fall outside the regulatory apparatus governing tax, health, safety, and minimum wage laws. The Irish remain concentrated in the informal sectors because they lack the documentation that would ease their access to the formal sector. Although better educated than previous generations of Irish immigrants, they have little or no job mobility and even less job opportunity.

Immigrants, particularly those who are located in the informal economy, play a distinctive role in the labor process:

Immigrants, especially in the United States, are often employed in firms where the system of control rests not on techniques of production and elaborate organizational arrangements, but on the powerlessness of the workers. Control is not structural, but immediate and personal (Sassen, 1988: 42).

The kinds of clientelistic controls exercised over Irish illegals in the ethnic enclaves of the labor market and the exploitation to which they are subject have been documented in chapter 4.

Changes in the organization of work in global cities is a direct result of the changing needs of international capitalism. The informalization of global city economies created new job opportunities in the secondary labor market, which are particularly attractive to new immigrants and, in particular, those without documentation. The influx of tens of thousands of Irish illegals into New York and other American cities during the 1980s was possible only because enough jobs (in the informal sector) had been created to absorb them. Structural factors, largely beyond the individual's control, create the conditions that encourage or impede migration.

UNEQUAL ILLEGALS

According to Sassen, immigrants without documentation constitute "a pool of cheap labor which is included through participation in the indigenous work force and excluded through the assignation by national authorities of a criminal status as undocumented or illegal aliens" (1988: 36). But within the illegal immigrant sector, there are important differences in degrees of inclusion and exclusion. As this study has demonstrated, one cannot assume that all illegals, regardless of nationality or ethnic identity, share a commonality of experience in the informal labor market and in the host country. In fact, immigrant labor is stratified on the basis of racial, ethnic, and legal status, as well as economic location.

Irish construction workers, for example, occupy a relatively privileged position in the informal economy and many have succeeded in penetrating the formal sector within the construction industry. This has been possible because of their instrumental use of ethnic connections in the construction unions. Similarly, Irish workers in the restaurant and bar trade occupy the highest paid positions as waiters/waitresses and bartenders. While they deal with the customers, the kitchen and janitorial jobs are almost exclusively reserved for Central and South Americans. Even in domestic work, Irish immigrant women report that an American family enhances their prestige by having a white nanny rather than a black nanny in their service.

Three factors, in particular, help to explain the different experience of Irish illegal immigrants. First, as Irish nationals, they have privileged access to Irish ethnic enclaves and employment networks, principally in the construction and bar/restaurant trades. A tradition of patronage and brokerage within the Irish ethnic community serves newly arrived illegals and eases their passage into employment. This process has been described fully in chapter 4.

Second, the ability to speak English gives Irish illegals greater negotiating power than their Asian, Hispanic, or European counterparts in the workplace. For this reason, it is not uncommon to find different wage rates in operation in the informal sector for people performing the exact same work. Proficiency in English also makes it easier for illegal immigrants not only to state their case publicly, but also to have their story reported in the national media. A white, English-speaking, generally well-educated constituency is more likely to gain media attention than other minority groups. The success of groups like the IIRM in highlighting the plight of Irish illegals (who constitute an insignificant number in comparison to the total illegal population) must largely be attributed to this factor.

Third, the Irish illegal is not likely to face the kind of racial prejudice with which many immigrants (both legal and illegal) from nonwhite peripheries have to cope. As white immigrants from a "seed" country, the Irish illegals are perceived as potentially more assimilable than many legal immigrants arriving in the United States today. From the purview of the older Irish ethnic communities in New York City, the influx of white immigrants— regardless of their legal status—provides them with the opportunity to rebalance the racial composition of their neighborhoods.

Taken together, these factors were crucial in providing an opening for the Irish (both the new immigrants and Irish Americans) to mobilize effectively in order to push for legislative reform that would allow more legal Irish immigration to the United States (see chapter 7).

SUMMARY

Irish illegals occupy an *intermediate position* within the U.S. stratified labor market. On the one hand, they may be perceived as relatively deprived in comparison to legal immigrants. They have little or no access to the kinds of jobs for which they may be qualified. They have little or no job mobility or opportunity. On the other hand, they may be perceived as relatively advantaged in comparison with illegal immigrants from non–English-speaking, nonwhite peripheries. They see that they are better off than many Hispanic and black groups in the United States, both documented and un-documented. Their preferential "context of reception" (Portes and Borocz, 1989: 620) differentiates the Irish illegals from the majority of illegal aliens and allows them to seek and obtain better pay and conditions in the labor market. While they remain largely excluded from the primary labor market, they occupy the upper stratum of the secondary labor market. In addition, the emergence of powerful institutional supports within the Irish community has conferred upon the new Irish a kind of quasi-legal status.

The structural forces that underlie advanced industrialization provide the context for an analysis of contemporary Irish emigration. In particular, we need to understand the political and economic links that contribute to the formation of migratory networks (Portes and Walton, 1981). An individual's decision to emigrate must be understood against the background of these forces, which operate transnationally and which link the international movements of labor and capital. The movement of capital from one country to another is characterized by a high degree of flexibility, which contrasts sharply with the rigorous admission procedures to which migrant workers to the United States are subject. Indeed, it is precisely the control that states exercise over borders that defines international migration as a distinctive social process (Zolberg, 1989: 405). Admission procedures for prospective immigrants are based on the premise that admission ought to be granted on a restricted basis and only to those willing to make a permanent commitment to the country. Current immigration policy leaves little room for *legally* processing a "transnational" or temporary worker who is by choice a so-journer rather than a settler.

Future trends in illegal Irish immigration will continue to be linked to the economic profiles of Ireland and the United States. Unemployment remains high in Ireland—20 percent—and the economic forecasts predict that high rates of emigration will persist, although possibly at a slower rate than in the past decade. Where will Irish emigrants go in the present decade?

Economic recession in the United States has already resulted in a contraction in the traditional employment sectors of the informal economy, such as the restaurant and bar trade and the construction industry. Consequently, there will be a decline in the number of jobs available for undocumented Irish immigrants in cities like New York. The rate of illegal immigration will drop, and Irish emigrants seeking better opportunities will go elsewhere as they did in the postwar years. (Given the impetus toward European integration, it is likely that Irish people will favor European destinations over Britain, whose economy has been performing poorly in recent years.) If, however, the United States economy were to enter a period of sustained prosperity, the demand for labor in the informal sector will rise again. In these circumstances, there is every likelihood that clandestine immigration from Ireland to the United States will flourish as it did in the 1980s.

Epilogue

The lobbying efforts of a coalition of Irish-American, Irish government, and new Irish groups (as well as a variety of other ethnic groups) finally came to fruition with the passage of the Immigration Act of 1990. The new legislation, which was passed in the House of Representatives at the end of October 1990 (after my field work was completed) and signed into law by President George Bush a month later, provides for increased immigration opportunities for Irish people who wish to live and work in the United States. The act established a lottery of 120,000 visas to be allocated to 34 countries over a period of three years, beginning in October 1991. Of the 120,000 visas, applicants from the Republic of Ireland are guaranteed 16,000 visas a year for *three* years—a total of 48,000 in all. These visas will be allocated on a lottery basis. Each candidate selected must submit evidence of a job offer from a U.S. employer and an entry fee. Undocumented Irish immigrants in the United States are eligible to apply.

Under the terms of the act, a diversity program will come into effect on October 1, 1993, for countries who presently have a low number of immigrants coming to the United States (i.e., European seed countries). Fifty-five thousand visas will be provided per annum from 1993, of which the Republic of Ireland will receive an estimated 3,850 visas or 7 percent of each allocation. To qualify for one of these visas, an applicant must have high school equivalent education and at least two years' work experience. Along with these provisions, which will help the Irish, the act introduces programs to ease immigration from Hong Kong, as well as special programs for immigrants from Kuwait, Liberia, and El Salvador. The new law also makes provision for increasing the number of immigrants with desirable employment skills who have permanent job offers from U.S. companies.

It remains to be seen how the act will affect Irish immigration to the United States. While the Morrison visas (named after the chief congressional architect of the legislation, Representative Bruce Morrison) offer a way out of illegality for Irish immigrants in the United States, the act does not specifically address their needs. Illegal Irish immigrants will have to compete with the pool of prospective emigrants in Ireland for the visa allocation of 16,000 per annum over the three-year period. Given recent emigration and unemployment trends in Ireland, all the indications are that there will be a high demand for these visas.

A further factor militating against the skilled, semiskilled, and unskilled worker (as opposed to the professional or college graduate) is the stipulation that each applicant for a visa must have a firm job offer from a U.S. employer. Employers in the informal labor market (where most of the immigrant job opportunities are (especially for skilled and unskilled labor) are unlikely to want to involve themselves in the kind of bureaucratic procedures that will be required by the Immigration Services. Many employers provide jobs which are "off-the-books" and are, therefore, not accountable for tax purposes. They will have no interest in drawing the attention of government agencies to their practices. The most likely outcome in these circumstances is that highly trained Irish graduates with good educational credentials will secure the job offers that must accompany the visa applications. The program will benefit those who have the skills commensurate with the requirements of the primary labor market, while the secondary labor market will continue to recruit from a cheap, pliable pool of undocumented labor. In addition, if the recession in the United States escalates, it is likely that firm job offers (in any sector) will be increasingly difficult to secure. This will effectively close off the opportunities created by the act for prospective immigrants, as employers, in so far that they recruit at all, will seek employees from within rather than outside national boundaries. So while recent changes in U.S. immigration law provide an additional channel for some of those wishing to emigrate to the United States legally, the program falls short of providing a broad-based solution to the problem of illegal immigration. The Morrison visa program is by definition a short-term measure, which will favor those in a position to secure legitimate job offers—a difficult task in these recessionary times. Those who are unsuccessful in the lottery program will continue to take the clandestine route into the United States.

References

Alba, Richard. 1990. *Ethnic Identity: The Transformation of White America*. New Haven, CT: Yale University Press.

"Address of Australian Cardinal Moran to American Fleet." 1908, October 31. *Irish World Newspaper*.

Ang, Ien. 1990. "Culture and Communication: Towards an Ethnographic Critique of Media Consumption in the Transnational Media System." *European Journal of Communications*, 5 (2–3), 239–60.

"Another Bishop Speaks Out on Emigration." 1988, April 23. *Irish Echo*.

"Archbishop Alarmed at Emigration." 1988, June 18. *Irish Echo*.

Baker, T. J., S. Scott, and I. M. Kearney. 1989. *Quarterly Economic Commentary*. Dublin: Economic & Social Research Institute.

Barrett, Sean. 1991, April 4. "More Tax Cuts Please, Not Less." *Business and Finance*, 11–12.

Barry, Frank. 1988, May 28. "Anti-Irish Again." *Irish Voice*.

Barry, Ursula, et al. 1985. *Who Owns Ireland: Who Owns You?* Dublin: Attic Press.

Becker, Howard. 1970. "Practitioners of Vice and Crime." In Robert Habenstein (Ed.), *Pathways to Data*. Chicago, IL: Aldine.

Bell, Desmond, and Niall Meehan. 1988. "International Telecommunications Deregulation and Ireland's Domestic Communications Policy." *Journal of Communications*, 38(1), 70–84.

Blessing, Patrick J. 1980. "The Irish." In *Harvard Encyclopedia of American Ethnic Groups*. Cambridge, MA: Harvard University Press.

———. 1985. "Irish Emigration to the United States 1800–1920: An Overview." In P. J. Drudy (Ed.), *The Irish in America: Emigration, Assimilation and Impact*. Irish Studies 4 (11–37). Cambridge: Cambridge University Press.

Bonacich, Edna. 1973, October. "A Theory of Middlemen Minorities." *American Sociological Review*, 38, 583–94.

Breathnach, Proinnsias. 1990. "Women's Employment and the European Spatial Division of Labour: The Case of Ireland." Paper presented at the Conference on Ireland and 1992 at the Institute of Irish Studies, University of Liverpool, May 1990.

Breathnach, Proinnsias, and John Jackson. 1991. "Ireland, Emigration and the New International Division of Labour." In Russell King (Ed.), *Contemporary Irish Migration* (1–10). Dublin: Geographical Society of Ireland Special Publication Number 6.

Brennock, Mark. 1989, November 28. "Emigration Has Merit—Poll." *Irish Times*.

Brown, Thomas N. 1966. *Irish American Nationalism 1870–1890*. Philadelphia, PA: Lippincott & Co.

Brown, Thomas N. 1976. "The Origins and Character of Irish American Nationalism." In Lawrence McCaffery (Ed.), *Irish Nationalism and the American Contribution*. New York: Arno Press.

Byrne, Gerry. 1992, May 10. "The IDA: Is the Party Over?" *Sunday Tribune*.

Byrne, John A. 1987, November 21. "Irish Bishops Discuss Amnesty." *Irish Echo*.

Byrne, Stephen. 1873. *Irish Emigration to the United States: What It Has Been and What It Is*. New York: The Catholic Publishing Society.

Cafferty, Pastora San Juan, et al. 1983. *The Dilemma of American Immigration: Beyond the Golden Door*. New Brunswick, NJ: Transaction Books.

Cardenas, G. 1976. "Public Data on Mexican Immigrants in the U.S." In W. Boyd Littrell and Gideon Sjoberg (Eds.), *Current Issues in Social Policy*. Beverly Hills, CA: Sage.

Catholic Charities, Archdiocese of New York. August 29, 1987. *A Proposal for Irish Priests to Work Within the Catholic Charities of the Archdiocese of New York*. New York.

Cavan, Sherri. 1966. *Liquor License: An Ethnography of Bar Behavior*. Chicago: Aldine.

Chubb, Basil. 1970. *The Government and Politics of Ireland*. Oxford: Oxford University Press.

Civil and Public Service Union. 1990. *Conference Report*. Dublin.

Cohen, A. P. 1985. *The Symbolic Construction of Community*. London: Tavistock.

Cohen, Robin. 1987. *The New Helots: Migrants in the International Division of Labour*. Hants, England: Gower.

Connor, Tom. 1985. *Irish Youth in London: Research Report*. London: London Irish Centre.

Conway, Linda. 1988, January 16. "Why Most New Irish in London Face Hard Times." *Irish Voice*.

Courtney, Damien. 1989. *Recent Trends in Emigration from Ireland*. Cork, Ireland: Cork Regional Technical College.

Curley, Margaret. 1987, December 26. "Con Man's Visa Scam Exposed." *Irish Voice*.

———. 1989, March 18. "Coming of Age for the IIRM." *Irish Voice*.

———. 1989, November 25. "New York City to Axe Irish Funds." *Irish Voice*.

———. 1990, March 17. "The Flight of the Families." *Irish Voice*.

———. 1990, March 24. "Immigration Update." *Irish Voice Monthly Newsletter*.

———. 1990, April 21. "Immigration Update." *Irish Voice Monthly Newsletter*.

———. 1990, May 19. "Emigrant Funding Up for Grabs." *Irish Voice*.

———. 1990, July 7. "Abuse Charges Against Irish Nanny Dropped." *Irish Voice*.

Curtis, Liz. 1988, June 18. "Nothing But the Same Old Story—The British Newspaper Tabloids and the Irish." *Irish Voice*.

Davis, Fred. 1979. *Yearning for Yesterday: A Sociology of Nostalgia*. New York: The Free Press.

Devlin, Mike. 1987, June 27. "Illegal Lives: Patrick H. Is Off and Running." *Irish Echo*.

Diner, Hasia. 1983. *Erin's Daughters in America: Irish Immigrant Women in the Nineteenth Century*. Baltimore, MD: Johns Hopkins Press.

The Economic and Social Implications of Emigration. 1991. Dublin: National Economic and Social Council (NESC).

Edwards, R. 1979. *Contested Terrain: The Transformation of the Workplace in the Twentieth Century*. New York: Basic Books.

Ehrenberg, Ronald, and Robert S. Smith. 1985. *Modern Labor Economics*. Glenview, IL: Scott, Foresman.

"Emigrants Likened to Refugees." 1990, January 6. *Irish Voice*.

Fallows, Marjorie. 1979. *Irish Americans: Identity and Assimilation*. Englewood Cliffs, NJ: Prentice-Hall.

Farrelly, Patrick. 1988, January 9. "An American Nightmare—The Story of Dolores." *Irish Voice*.

———. 1988, February 20. " 'Blackmail' Threat Against Three Irish." *Irish Voice*.

———. 1988, June 11. "Telling It Like It Is: The Emigrant Experience." *Irish Voice*.

———. 1989, October 28. "The Indictment of Police Officer Michael Carty." *Irish Voice*.

———. 1990, March 17. "Construction Slowdown Hits Irish Workers." *Irish Voice*.

Foster, R. F. 1989. *Modern Ireland 1600–1972*. London: Penguin.

Freeman, Jo. 1973. "The Origins of the Women's Liberation Movement." *American Journal of Sociology*, 78, 792–811.

———. 1979. "Resource Mobilization and Strategy." In Meyer N. Zald and John M. McCarthy (Eds.), *The Dynamics of Social Movements*. Cambridge, MA: Winthrop.

Gamio, M. 1931. *The Life Story of the Mexican Immigrant*. Chicago, IL: University of Chicago Press.

Gamson, William A. 1975. *The Strategy of Social Protest*. Homewood, IL: Dorsey Press.

Gans, Herbert J. 1979, January. "Symbolic Ethnicity: The Future of Ethnic Groups in America." *Ethnic and Racial Studies*, 2(1), 1–20.

———. 1982. *The Urban Villagers*. New York: The Free Press.

"Gathering Pace." 1988, January 16. Editorial in *Irish Voice*.

Gecas, Viktor. 1982. "The Self-Concept." *Annual Review of Sociology*, 8, 1–33.

George, Terry. 1988, June 18. "Revenge for Skibereen." *Irish Voice*.

———. 1990, September 15. "Penniless Post Slurs Irish National Heros." *Irish Voice*.

Gibbon, P., and Michael D. Higgins. 1974. "Patronage, Tradition and Modernisation: The Case of the Irish Gombeenman." *Economic and Social Review*, 6(1), 27–44.

Gillespie, Marie. 1989. "Technology and Tradition: Audiovisual Culture Among South Asian Families in West London." *Cultural Studies*, 3(2), 226–39.

Gitlin, Todd. 1980. *The Whole World Is Watching*. Berkeley, CA: University of California Press.

Glazer, Nathan, and Daniel Moynihan. 1970. *Beyond the Melting Pot*. Cambridge, MA: M.I.T. Press.

Glazer, Nona. 1987. "The Decommodification of Health Care in the United States." Paper presented at the Socialist Scholars Conference, New York, April 1987.

Gordon, Milton. 1964. *Assimilation and American Life*. New York: Oxford University Press.

Government of Ireland. 1958. *Program for Economic Expansion*. Dublin: Stationery Office.

Grasmuck, Sherri. 1984. "Immigration, Ethnic Stratification and Native Working Class Discipline: Comparisons of Documented and Undocumented Dominicans." *International Migration Review*, XVIII (3), 692–713.

Greeley, Andrew. 1973. *That Most Distressful Nation*. Chicago, IL: Quadrangle Books.

———. 1981. *The Irish Americans: The Rise to Money and Power*. New York: Harper and Row.

Gribben, Paul. 1989, March 18. "So Who Really Is Irish?" *Irish Voice*.

———. 1989, April 1. "It's Always Hard Labor." *Irish Voice*.

Gutman, Herbert. 1973, June. "Work, Culture and Society in Industrialized America 1815–1919." *American Historical Review*, 78(3), 531–88.

Handlin, Oscar. 1973. *The Uprooted*. Boston: Little, Brown and Company.

Hammersley, Martyn, and Paul Atkinson. 1983. *Ethnography: Principles in Practice*. London: Tavistock.

Hastings, Donald W., Donald A. Clelland, and Robin L. Danielson. 1982. "Gordon's Assimilation Paradigm Revisited: The Issue of Ethnic Communality, Insularity and Return Migration." In C. Bagley Marrett and C. Leggon (Eds.), *Research in Race and Ethnic Relations Vol. 3*, (189–206). Greenwich, CT: JAI Press.

Hastings, Tim. 1993, January 4. "Emigrants 'Losing Out' on UK Jobs." *Irish Independent*.

Hazelkorn, Ellen. 1986. "Class, Clientelism and the Political Process in the Republic of Ireland." In Patrick Clancy (Ed.), *Ireland: A Sociological Profile* (326–43). Dublin: Institute of Public Administration.

Hershberg, T., et al. 1981. "A Tale of Three Cities: Blacks, Immigrants and Opportunity in Philadelphia, 1830–1880, 1930, 1970." In Theodore Hershberg (Ed.), *Philadelphia: Work, Space, Family and Group Experience in the Nineteenth Century* (461–91). New York: Oxford University Press.

"High Death Rate for Irish Emigrants." 1990, May 12. *Irish Voice*.

Hochschild, Arlie Russell. 1983. *The Managed Heart: Commercialization of Human Feeling*. Berkeley, CA: University of California Press.

Hogan, Dick. 1990, October 25. "Irish Abroad Feel Growing Sense of Isolation—Bishop," *Irish Times*.

Holohan, Renagh, and Nigel Brown. 1986, April 24. "Census Reveals Sharp Increase in Emigration." *Irish Times*, 1.

Honigmann, J. 1973. "Sampling in Ethnographic Fieldwork." In R. Narroll and R. Cohen (Eds.), *A Handbook of Method in Cultural Anthropology* (266–81). New York: National History Press.

Hraba, J. 1979. *American Ethnicity*. Itasea, IL: Peacock Publishers.

Hughes, E. 1937. "Institutional Office and the Person." *American Journal of Sociology*, 43, 409–.

Hunt, Janet G., and Larry L. Hunt. 1985. "The Dualities of Careers and Families: New Integrations or New Polarizations?" In A. S. Skolnick and J. S. Skolnick (Eds.), *Family in Transition* (275–89). Boston: Little, Brown.

"IIRM Gets Funds from State Budget." 1987, April 29. *Irish Voice.*

Immigration and Naturalization Service Statistical Yearbooks, 1980–1986. Washington, DC: United States Department of Justice.

Industrial Development Authority. 1989. *Annual Report.* Dublin.

Irish Emigrant Vote Campaign. 1991. *The Case for Emigrant Voting Rights.* New York.

Irish Immigration Reform Movement. 1987. *Guidelines for the New Irish.* New York.

Jackson, John A. 1963. *The Irish in Britain.* London: Routledge and Kegan Paul.

Jenkins, J. Craig. 1983. "Resource Mobilization Theory and the Study of Social Movements."*Annual Review of Sociology,* 9, 527–53.

Jenkins, J. Craig, and Charles Perrow. 1977, April. "Insurgency of the Powerless: Farm Workers Movements 1946–1972." *American Sociological Review,* 42, 249–68.

Joyce, William J. 1976. *A History of the Irish American Press 1848–1883.* New York: Arno Press.

Keenan, Donal. 1989, May 7. "New York, New York." *Sunday Independent.*

Kirby, Peadar. 1988. *Has Ireland a Future?* Dublin and Cork: The Mercier Press.

Kirkham, Graeme. 1990. "The Origins of Mass Emigration from Ireland." In Richard Kearney (Ed.), *Migrations: The Irish at Home and Abroad* (81–90). Dublin: Wolfhound Press.

Lauria, Joseph H. 1987, November 19. "Underground Existence: Bishops from Three Countries in Plea for Immigrants to New York." *Catholic New York.*

Lee, J. J. 1989. *Ireland 1912–1985: Politics and Society.* Cambridge: Cambridge University Press.

Levine, Daniel B. 1985. *Immigration Statistics: A Story of Neglect.* Panel on Immigration Studies, Washington DC: National Academy Press.

Levy, Frank. 1987. *Dollars and Dreams: The Changing American Income Distribution.* New York: Russell Sage Foundation/Basic Books.

Light, Dale B. 1985. "The Role of Irish-American Organizations in Assimilation and Community Formation." In P. J. Drudy (Ed.), *The Irish in America: Emigration, Assimilation and Impact* (113–42). London: Cambridge University Press.

Lyons, F.S.L. 1973. *Ireland Since the Famine.* Glasgow: Collins/Fontana.

McAleese, Dermot. 1985. "American Investment in Ireland." In P. J. Drudy (Ed.), *The Irish in America: Emigration, Assimilation and Impact* (329–51). Irish Studies 4, Cambridge: Cambridge University Press.

McCaffrey, Lawrence. 1976. *The Irish Diaspora in America.* Bloomington, IN: Indiana University Press.

————. 1982. "The Recent Irish Diaspora in America." In D. L. Cuddy (Ed.), *Contemporary American Immigration.* Boston: G. K. Hall.

McCarthy, John M., and Meyer N. Zald. 1977. "Resource Mobilization and Social Movements." *American Journal of Sociology,* 82(6), 1212–41.

MacCormaic, Mairtin. 1989, November 6. "300,000 Flee in Emigration 'Scandal.' " *Irish Independent.*

McGoldrick, Debbie. 1988, May 21. "Busy First Year for Irish Immigration Reform Movement." *Irish Echo.*

————. 1988, June 11. "IIRM Hotline Provides Link to Undocumented." *Irish Echo.*

McLaughlin, John. 1988, August 2. "Ashes to Ashes: Hurling and the Colonization of the North Bronx." *Village Voice*, 141–42.

McSweeney, Declan. 1987, January 24. "Emigration Causes Drain on Resources." *Irish Times.*

Massey, Douglas. 1987, Summer. "Do Undocumented Migrants Earn Lower Wages than Legal Migrants? New Evidence from Mexico." *International Migration Review*, XXI(2), 236–74.

Massey, Douglas, Rafael Alrcón, Jorge Durand, and Humberto González. 1987. *Return to Atzlan: The Social Process of International Migration from Western Mexico.* Berkeley, CA: University of California Press.

Meagher, Timothy J. (Ed.) 1986. *From Paddy to Studs: Irish American Communities in the Turn of the Century Era 1880–1920.* Westport, CT: Greenwood Press.

Miller, Kerby A. 1985a. "Assimilation and Alienation: Irish Emigrants' Responses to Industrial America, 1871–1921." In P. J. Drudy (Ed.), *The Irish in America: Emigration, Assimilation and Impact* (87–112). London: Cambridge University Press.

———. 1985b. *Emigrants and Exiles: Ireland and the Irish Exodus to North America.* New York: Oxford University Press.

———. 1990. "Emigration, Capitalism and Ideology in Post-Famine Ireland." In Richard Kearney (Ed.), *Migrations: The Irish at Home and Abroad.* Dublin: Irish Wolfhound Press.

Mitchell, Brian. 1986. "They Do Not Differ Greatly: The Pattern of Community Development Among the Irish in Late Nineteenth-Century Lowell, Massachusetts." In T. J. Meagher (Ed.), *From Paddy to Studs: Irish American Communities in the Turn of the Century Era 1880–1920* (53–73). Westport, CT: Greenwood Press.

Mitter, Swasti. 1986. *Common Fate, Common Bond: Women in the Global Economy.* London: Pluto Press.

Modell, John, and Lynn H. Lee. 1981. "The Irish Countryman Urbanized: A Comparative Perspective on the Famine Generation." In Theodore Hershberg (Ed.), *Philadelphia: Work, Space, Family and Group Experience in the Nineteenth Century* (351–67). New York: Oxford University Press.

Molotch, Harvey L. 1979. "Media and Movements." In Meyer N. Zald and John M. McCarthy (Eds.), *The Dynamics of Social Movements.* Cambridge, MA: Winthrop.

Moynihan, Daniel P. 1970. "The Irish." In Nathan Glazer and Daniel P. Moynihan (Eds.), *Beyond the Melting Pot.* Cambridge, MA: M.I.T. Press.

Murray, John. 1990, July 29. "Conference Priest Condemns Media and Politicians Over Emigration." *Sunday Tribune.*

Nelson, E. 1975. *Pablo Cruz and the American Dream.* Salt Lake City, UT: Peregrine Smith.

O'Dowd, Niall. 1989, November 25. "Asbestos Scare for Irish Illegals."*Irish Voice.*

———. 1990, February 24. "Gay Irish Group Formed." *Irish Voice.*

———. 1990, May 12. "Irish Gay Group Is Formed." *Irish Voice.*

O'Murchu, Sean, and Patrick Farrelly. 1987, December 12. "Bronx Bust of Birth Cert Bootleggers." *Irish Voice.*

O'Neill, Paul. 1991. February 7. "7,500 Left Diocese in 5 Years—Bishop." *Irish Times*.

O'Reilly, Liam. 1988, February 20. " 'False Birth Cert' Cop Indicted." *Irish Voice*.

O'Toole, Fintan. 1989, September 28. "Strangers in Their Own Country." *Irish Times*, p. 10.

Park, Robert E., and Herbert A. Miller. 1921. *Old World Traits Transplanted*. New York: Harper.

Passel, Jeffrey. 1986, September. "Undocumented Immigration." *Annals, AAPSS* (487), 181–200.

Perlmann, Joel. 1988. *Ethnic Differences: Schooling and Social Structure among the Irish, Italians, Jews and Blacks in an American City, 1880–1935*. New York: Cambridge University Press.

Pessar, Patricia. 1988, May 6. "Dominican Workers in the U.S. Labor Market." Paper presented at The Center for Immigration and Population Studies Seminar, *New Immigrants and Economic Restructuring*, New York.

Petras, Elizabeth McLean. 1981. "The Global Labor Market in the Modern World Economy." In Mary M. Kritz, Charles B. Keely, and Silvano M. Tomasi (Eds.), *Global Trends in Migration* (44–63). New York: Center for Migration Studies.

Portes, A., and J. Walton. 1981. *Labor, Class and the International System*. New York: Academic Press.

Portes, Alejandro, and Jozsef Borocz. 1989. "Contemporary Immigration: Theoretical Perspectives on Its Determinants and Modes of Incorporation." *International Migration Review*, 23(3), 606–30.

Portes, Alejandro, and Saskia Sassen-Koob. 1987, July. "Making It Underground: Comparative Material on the Informal Sector in Western Market Economies." *American Journal of Sociology*, 93 (1), 30–61.

Power, Joseph. 1990, November 25. "Plea for Forgotten Emigrants." *Sunday Independent*.

"PTA Hit Quarter of Irish in Britain." 1993, January 8. *Irish Independent*.

Randall, Geoffrey. 1991. *Over Here: Young Irish Migrants in London* (London: Action Group for Irish Youth).

Report of the Industrial Policy Review Group. 1992. *A Time for Change: Industrial Policy for the 1990s*. Dublin: Government Stationery Office.

Rohan, Brian. 1990, July 7. "Anti-Irish Garbage." *Irish Voice*.

Ryan, Liam. 1990. "Irish Emigration to Britain Since World War II." In Richard Kearney (Ed.), *Migrations: The Irish at Home and Abroad*. Dublin: Irish Wolfhound Press.

Sassen, Saskia. 1988. *The Mobility of Labor and Capital: A Study in International Investment and Labor Flow*. New York: Cambridge University Press.

———. 1991. "The Informal Economy." In J. H. Mollenkopf and M. Cassells (Eds.), *Dual City: Restructuring New York* (79–101). New York: Russell Sage Foundation.

Sassen-Koob, Saskia. 1984. "The New Labor Demand in Global Cities." In Michael Smith (Ed.), *Cities in Transformation* (139–71). Beverly Hills, CA: Sage.

———. 1986, October. "New York City's Informal Economy." Paper presented at the Second Symposium on the Informal Sector, Johns Hopkins University.

Schlesinger, Arthur M., Jr. 1992. *The Disuniting of America*. New York: W. W. Norton.

Seers, Dudley. 1979. "The Periphery of Europe." In D. Seers, B. Schaffer, and M. L. Kiljunen (Eds.), *Under-Developed Europe: Studies in Core-Periphery Relations* (3–34). Sussex, England: The Harvester Press.

Sexton, J. J. 1987, Autumn. "Recent Trends in the Irish Population and in the Pattern of Emigration." *Irish Banking Review*, 31–44.

Shannon, William. 1973. *The American Irish*. New York: Macmillan.

Smith, Anthony D. 1984, September. "Ethnic Persistence and National Transformation." *The British Journal of Sociology*, 35(3), 452–60.

Steinberg, Stephen. 1981. *The Ethnic Myth*. New York: Atheneum.

Stivers, Richard. 1976. *A Hair of the Dog: Irish Drinking and American Stereotype*. University Park, PA: Pennsylvania State University Press.

Tansey, Paul. 1989, November 19. "Figures Hid Facts of Irish Exodus." *Sunday Tribune*, B8.

———. 1990, October 21. "Many Young Men of Twenty Said Goodbye." *Sunday Tribune*, 28.

Taylor, Cliff. 1989, September 2. "Emigration in Focus." *Irish Times*, 7.

Telesis Consultancy Group. 1982. *A Review of Industrial Policy*, Report No. 64. Dublin: National Economic and Social Council.

"This Week They Said." 1990, March 24. *Irish Times*.

United States Catholic Conference. *Migration and Refugee Services Staff Report*. 1988. "Undocumented Irish in the U.S." Washington, DC.

Vaughan, W. E. 1984. *Landlords and Tenants in Ireland 1848–1904*. Studies in Irish Economic and Social History. Dundalgan Press.

Wallerstein, Immanuel. 1974. *The Modern World System: Capitalist Agriculture and the Origins of the European World Economy in the Sixteenth Century*. New York: Cambridge University Press.

Walsh, Brendan. 1988. *Emigration: An Economist's Perspective*. Policy Paper No. PP88/3. University College, Dublin: Center for Economic Research.

———. 1989. *Ireland's Changing Demographic Structure*. Dublin: Gill and MacMillan.

Walsh, James A. 1991. "The Turn-Around of the Turn-Around in the Population of the Republic of Ireland." *Irish Geography*, 24(2), 116–24.

Walshe, John. 1991. February 6. "Universities Face Teacher Training Cuts." *Irish Times*.

Warner, W., and L. Srole. 1945. *The Social Systems of American Ethnic Groups*. New Haven, CT: Yale University Press.

Waters, John. 1992. May 26. "Why the Voice of Youth Goes Unheard in Ireland?" *Irish Times*, 12.

"We Apologise to Irish—New York Times." 1988, June 18. *Irish Voice*.

"We'll Never Return—Young Illegals." 1987, December 5. *Irish Voice*.

Whyte, William F. 1951. "Observational Field Methods." In M. Jahoda et al. (Eds.), *Research Methods in Social Relations*. New York: Dryden.

Wickham, James. 1980. "The Politics of Dependent Capitalism: International Capital and the Nation State." In A. Morgan and B. Purdie (Eds.), *Ireland: Divided Nation, Divided Class* (53–73). London: Inks Links.

———. 1986. "Industrialisation, Work and Unemployment." In Patrick Clancy (Ed.),

Ireland: A Sociological Profile (70–96). Dublin: Institute of Public Administration.

Wickham, James, and Peter Murray. 1987. *Women in the Irish Electronics Industry.* Dublin: Employment Equality Agency.

"Working Mothers." 1988, June 20. *New York Times.*

Yancey, W., and L. Rainwater. 1970. "Problems in Ethnography of the Urban Underclass." In Robert Habenstein (Ed.), *Pathways to Data.* Chicago: Aldine.

Yancey, William L., Eugene P. Ericksen, and Richard N. Juliani. 1976. "Emergent Ethnicity: A Review and Reformulation." *American Sociological Review,* 41(3), 391–403.

Yancey, William L., Eugene P. Ericksen, and George H. Leon. 1985. "The Structure of Pluralism." In R. Alba (Ed.), *Ethnicity and Race in the USA: Toward the Twenty-First Century* (94–116). Boston: Routledge and Kegan Paul.

Young, Mark. 1988, March 24. "Far from Friends: Priest from Home Are a Presence to Young Irish in New York." *Catholic New York.*

Young, Michael, and Peter Willmott. 1957. *Family and Kinship in East London.* London: Routledge and Kegan Paul.

Zolberg, A. R. 1989. "The New Wave: Migration Theory for a Changing World." *International Migration Review,* 23(3), 403–29.

Zunz, Olivier. 1985. "The Synthesis of Social Change." In O. Zunz (Ed.), *Reliving the Past: The Worlds of Social History.* Chapel Hill, NC: University of North Carolina Press.

Index

About the Author

MARY P. CORCORAN is Lecturer in Sociology at St. Patrick's College, Maynooth, in Ireland. She has made a first-hand study of recent Irish immigrants in the United States.